Harmony

on the

High Seas

When Your Mate Becomes Your Matey

By Virginia Gleser

Published by Harmony Publishing
512 14th Street
Modesto, CA 95354
(209) 613-0374

Copyright 2011

ISBN: 978-0-9647247-2-3

Library of Congress Control Number:2011914058

Printed in the United States of America

The typeface used for the text of this book is in Times New Roman.

To my husband, Robert, who has shared our life long adventure and the cruise aboard Harmony. Your Merlin magic kept the boat going no matter what went awry. Every morning on awakening, your 'I love you's' sustained me through the day. I embrace you, my lover, father of our children and best friend.

This book would not exist had it not been for your support and encouragement. You have made it all worthwhile.

Table of Contents

Acknowledgments

I want to thank the brave, savvy, adventurous women who threw off the dock lines and came out cruising the oceans of the world for inspiring me to write this book. You have been my buddies for a swim to shore on a warm Mexican afternoon, and explored the markets of distant towns for tasty, fresh vegetables and fruit. When we chat away on the VHF on a long or rough passage and walk the beaches of foreign shores looking for shell treasures or colorful birds and iguanas, it makes the adventure complete.

The encouragement and assistance of my supportive family and friends has been invaluable in the creation of *Harmony on the High Seas*. My sister, Letitia Rainey, read the book to my mother, Sophie Crane, who spent many years on and around boats with her avid sailor husband, my father, Paul Crane and is a published author in her own right. When macular degeneration prevented her from reading the words at the venerable age of 91, she enjoyed listening to what I had to say and gave me positive feedback and encouragement. Sophie made a connection with Christine Benagh, a retired editor, at her Park Manor apartments in Nashville, Tennessee. Christine generously offered us her editing expertise, making corrections, and wishing that she could go cruising again. Our son, Saul reviewed the manuscript, supplying insightful advice and his wife Irene and our son-in-law, Ben Platt inspired the title. Our daughter, Olivia edited the manuscript and gave her permission for us to use her letter, photographs, and stories from when she cruised with us to Ecuador aboard *Harmony*. Thanks to cousins, Roslyn Pasternak and Robert Montgomery, and cruising buddy, Kathy Everson who read a rough draft and gave valuable suggestions and corrections. My daughter-in-law, Heather Gleser, read the manuscript and gave me helpful encouragement, while taking care of her new baby, our grandson Onyx. I would be lost without the technical support of our son, Eugene. When my computer crashed, that dreaded empty blue screen, he retrieved my lost documents, putting aside his busy schedule to accommodate me. He was my technical adviser showing me short cuts and giving many tips on how to use the computer programs, each suggestion making my work less stressful. Every writer should be so lucky to have a computer whiz in the family.

The early photos from Korea and The Farm were taken by my father, Paul Crane.

Thanks to Ilanna Mandel who was my midwife in the delivery of this creation. She was my professional editor, proofreader and helpful adviser. She spent many hours bringing my thoughts together and organizing them into readable prose.

Heather Bansmer and Shawn Breeding on the boat, *Om Shanti* and creators of the newest, most beautiful Sea of Cortez and Mexican mainland cruising guides, did the layout and formatting. Thank you for all your hard work and patience preparing this book for print.

Barbara and Jerry Philips live near our hometown of Modesto, California, but oddly enough we met on the docks in Mazatlan, Mexico

Our growing group of over three hundred people pooled their resources and bought the land for $70 an acre. In a few years, we added an adjacent seven hundred and fifty acres. During the 1970s, this land was home to, give or take, fifteen hundred people, the largest community of its kind in the country and still exists in a downsized version today. In this lovely country setting we birthed and reared our children, all of whom were delivered in our own bed by *The Farm* midwives.

When we first settled on our land in Tennessee, we spent the first, cold winter in our school buses, heating them with wood stoves and illuminating them with kerosene lanterns. Over the years we built houses, businesses, and infrastructure. On *The Farm*, we held all things in common with all money going to a central fund to be distributed as needed.

A few years later an international relief organization named *Plenty* was established with projects in Guatemala, the Caribbean, and Belize. We knew that a boat would be useful for carrying supplies and the dream was once again given serious thought. Along with several other families we went so far as to move to Mobile, Alabama to become the boat crew and began to look into what buying a boat entailed.

The carpenters in the group started *The Port City Remodeling Company* and in between sheet rocking and painting Robert found a job at the Alabama Dry Dock and Ship Building Company where he worked the swing shift as an Outside Machinist. Each afternoon, he hiked up and down five flights of stairs into the dark bellies of huge oil tankers and freighters. He turned wrenches on the engines, repaired valves deep in the storage tanks, and took apart drive shafts in *shaft alley*. On weekends we went on interesting excursions to check out small freighters, old moth-balled, World War II Liberty ships, and retired shrimp boats moored in the sultry bayous of the Deep South. It didn't take us long to realize the breadth and scope of this enormous undertaking. Although we pursued the idea of buying a ship for

Robert and Virginia, pregnant with her 2nd child, Eugene on The Farm *in 1973.*

several years, nothing ever became of the boat crew project. Robert and I eventually moved on to manage the Age and Youth Center in downtown Miami, a branch of *Plenty*. This project provided care and support to elderly and physically challenged folks, who were alone.

for the general fund and used by the community to repair roads, and for other public services.

* * *

In 1983 during these changing times and after being with *Plenty* and *The Farm* for twelve years, Robert and I decided it was time to bring our children back to California and allow them the opportunity to receive a higher education at the University of California. There was no golden handshake when we left the old commune so Robert spent several months working with friends in Atlanta, Georgia to earn enough money for the trip. He resurrected an old station wagon and we loaded our six children aboard, strapped luggage and some camping supplies to the roof rack, and set out across country. Eventually we landed in Modesto, California, where we were able to find affordable housing for our large family. We followed in the steps of the Dust Bowl refugees from Oklahoma, who settled this valley many decades ago. Work was lined up even before finding a home, and it was not long before we were back into mainstream society.

Rob's first company, *Robert's Roofing and Remodeling*, was immediately swamped with work. From one of his first pay checks I bought a used washing machine for $85, a couple of dozen T-shirts, and some dyes. Starting up my tie-dye company, *Harmony Enterprises* was born. While the five older children were in school and our youngest baby took her nap, I would fold and tie the shirts. One day a week Robert transformed into Mr. Mom, and I would dye. When he worked in the Bay Area he would take time to peddle the shirts [9] to stores near Haight and Ashbury and we began applying to arts and crafts fairs.

It wasn't long before we purchased our first home, with a generous, low-interest loan for the down payment from my parents. The value of California real estate continued to climb steadily upward, and we refinanced our home five times to buy additional, fixer-upper properties that Robert remodeled. We used one building for our business, and the rest of the houses became rental properties.

Whenever our businesses brought us near the coast, we would spend time walking the docks of marinas, looking at sailboats and weighing the pros and cons of the various models and designs. We talked with cruisers, brokers, weekend sailors, and anyone who had an opinion. Eventually the boat fund grew large enough to start looking in earnest, and on one momentous day we bought a 27' Newport sailboat for $3500, which we christened *Harmony*. Even though Robert had resurrected dilapidated cars and houses for years, fixing up a boat and making it functional was a different challenge. Then the moment arrived when we were one of those white doves flitting around in the glorious winds of San Francisco Bay in our own sailboat! Although the Newport 27' design is a great boat for the bay, with our brood of growing children, we needed more room. Before long, it was time to move up.

We traded in our first *Harmony* for an Islander 36,' another terrific design, and like all our houses and boats, she needed plenty of TLC. Following her restoration, she carried us on some longer runs. The previous owners had journeyed to Hawaii and back so we knew that she was a seaworthy vessel. Voyaging out under the Golden Gate Bridge, we sailed downwind to Half Moon Bay and then bashed and crashed upwind on a rather intense, but memorable trip. Sailing through San Pablo Bay to Vallejo and Benicia, we stayed ahead of a J boat, whose captain could not believe that he wasn't able to catch us. On the trip home, an upwind battle sent showers of saltwater over the cockpit drenching me while I steered *Harmony* into the churned up froth. I kept warm and dry in my foul weather gear, and the crew, cozy in the cabin, continually handed me paper towels to keep my glasses clear of the spray. It was time for a dodger and an autopilot!

physical exertion required to handle a sailboat.

The burgeoning generation of baby boomers, who have had their families and successful careers, make up a large number of active and new cruisers. This is a generation of men and women who are ready for a change in their personal lives. Instead of working, making money, raising children, schedules and obligations, they are doing something for themselves. Their children (if they had any) are grown, some money is saved, and there is equity in a house. Is this finally the time to actualize the dream, to set the plan in motion?

Besides the prospect of sailing the world's oceans, it helps if each sailor has a reason and a purpose, for what he/she is doing. When I asked Robert why he wanted to cruise, he said how he had grown up in the wilds of New York City. Then there had been the twelve years of hard work spent on the spiritual commune, followed by a move to California to raise our children while juggling three businesses. Cruising seemed like a perfect way to unwind, de-stress, to play, and spend more one-on-one time with me.

Likewise, women, need a sense of purpose to cruise. There are plenty of reasons to live the cruising lifestyle. It usually begins with the love of sailing, and the chance to embrace the great outdoors and be at one with Mother Nature. Adventure beckons, and there's time to meet interesting people, and travel to new and fascinating countries. There are numerous opportunities to study the birds and the sea life, dive, fish, surf, run the radio nets, have time for writing, art, music, hobbies, meditating, exercise, learning a new language, and helping local causes, to mention a few.

When Robert asked me why I wanted to cruise, I contemplated the question and replied, 'I grew up sailing, and the chance to take our own boat out on the sea, with its moods and beauty intrigued me.' I had also been having some back problems and swimming in warm water, doing yoga, and living a less stressed out life became my goal. While raising our children, we had precious little time to spend alone with each other so I looked forward to a closer relationship with Robert, and I had a few writing projects I hoped to pursue. We both loved to read, and I wanted to spend time savoring the books on my reading list. In my hurried life on shore, I was lucky if I could read a couple of pages each night before sleep took over and the book fell on the floor. I couldn't wait to have our children come to visit us aboard *Harmony*, and give them the opportunity to experience the beauty of nature and the excitement of cruising in foreign waters. When we sailed out of the Golden Gate and turned left to begin our trip to Mexico, we said we would stop when we found warm water to swim in and then decide what to do next. We laid out a simple, open-ended plan, and it has more than met our expectations.

Cruising is not for everyone but in our travels we have met a variety of couples, single-handed sailors, and families out on the seas. There seems to be a growing number of younger couples that find an inexpensive boat and outfit it on a shoestring budget, setting sail with youthful exuberance. They travel as far as their funds allow and then plan the next phase of their lives. What to do? Return home to quickly refill the cruising kitty and get back out there, or is the biological clock ticking loudly? Is it time for a career that is inevitably required when you settle back on land to start a family? We've met several couples who have had their children while out cruising and are raising them successfully in the ocean environment. One young couple had their baby in Ecuador and then sailed across the South Pacific to their home in Australia. Their one big concern was what they were going to do with all of those disposable diapers?

We've met numerous families, with children on board eager to take a break from work and depart from the conventional path to live life at sea for a year or two or more. The children are home-schooled, quickly completing their lessons so they can explore a new anchorage or get together with kids from neighboring boats. A rough day at sea might mean a holiday from schoolwork. The global experience of traveling to foreign countries, learning a new language, and acquiring the skills used to sail the boat gives the cruising child a leg up when they return to school ashore. Children out at sea gain a new planetary view of the world and its people, and a respect for Mother Earth, and the animal and plant kingdoms, which accompanies them home. These families generally sail back to the dock when the children reach high school age, the teenagers preferring to be with their peers.

The wild and crazy idea to go cruising is usually a man's dream. If he is one of the lucky ones, he has found a partner who loves sailing and is an enthusiastic supporter of his dreams. Odds are, however, that he married long ago with different priorities, and his partner now finds all sorts of excuses and reasons why the idea is distasteful. Perhaps the more practical side of the couple fears that it will be too expensive, and what about their ageing parents, and the grandchildren? There are always a million reasons not to go on an adventure. Most of us are molded from millennium of family patterns to stay safe, work hard, and mind our business. Cruising can be a big step into the unknown. The usual naysayers will surely criticize an outside-the-box idea like sailing the high seas. Robert Pirsig wrote in *Zen and the Art of Motorcycle Maintenance*,[10] about a *Dynamic Quality in the world that is constantly calling for change and a disruption to the status quo*. The dreamer stands firm and pushes the limits, gently but firmly petitioning his partner to allow him his fantasies, to share his ideas, and respect his vision, and imaginative musings. Will his partner listen or run away screaming? Will she manipulate, distract, patronize, put up roadblocks, sabotage, or coddle him? Is she working in a satisfying career that she doesn't want to give up? Is there always something else she needs you to do? Are there additional things to spend money on? What sacrifices does this undertaking require? Are there family and friends yammering in her ear, trying to talk her out of your crazy notions? Is it time to ask her to stop for a moment and consider? And then there is always the possibility that the scenario may be reversed. Is your man holding tight to his security blanket? In either case, it is the same challenge, and by bravely rising to the occasion to enter this adventure together, you will be making the first step to fulfill your wildest imaginings.

What happens if you realize you have made a mistake? You take to the seas and decide this lifestyle is not what you expected? At least, you have learned how to change a reverie into a reality. Taking the steps to go cruising can imbue you with confidence, a surety of purpose, and knowledge that will serve you well in whatever endeavor you think up next. Living your dreams and sharing them with your partner becomes the norm.

For twenty years, we ran our tie-dye business, where we made colorful, intricately designed, handcrafted art wear. While we traveled the long, highway miles to sell our wares at craft fairs, we had time to unravel the mystery of the financial details that would enable us to fulfill our cruising dream. The older children were graduating from college and moving out on their own. We had eight more years, minimum, until our youngest daughter would walk the stage for her college diploma. A faint light glimmered at the end of the sixteen-year tunnel of paying tuition to the University of California regents, but Robert wanted to go cruising sooner than that. Eight years felt like a prison sentence. With the way our finances were, I couldn't see any other way, but he urged me to crunch the numbers again, and we began to look at our options. We could rent our home and move into one of our smaller houses. If we downsized our business we would spend less on inventory, and reducing the number of shows we attended would leave the winter months open for living aboard *Harmony*. Starting our cruise when our youngest daughter left for college could shorten our wait to four years. With our new way of thinking, we started implementing our plan. As if by magic, the fewer shows we did, the more money we made. Our customers, not seeing us as often, eagerly spent when they found our booth. Because we were making fewer items, our overhead decreased. Soon the rental money from our houses began to make up a larger slice of the financial pie, especially after we paid off the mortgages. A change in our perspective and outlook immediately impacted the bottom line. Bigger in our case was not better. During the four years that our youngest daughter was in high school, we streamlined our business to support our new lifestyle. Our older children had grown up and were supporting themselves. We cut down on extras, like cable TV, magazines, and the daily newspaper, and did not eat out as often. Instead we created tasty meals at home, buying fresh produce from the weekly farmers' market that was within walking distance from our home. Each dollar saved was another dollar for cruising. **The secret was not how much we made, but how much we spent.**

Today when we drive through Modesto, Robert will point out a house or building and say, 'We almost bought that.' The real estate market soared while we were out cruising and he notices all the missed opportunities. I remind him that he chose to go cruising instead of leveraging our assets and acquiring a real estate empire. The recent real estate crash has since proven that by going cruising we inadvertently made the right choice. By simplifying our lives we were able to do what we wanted to do, unburdening ourselves of excessive stuff and obligations. Whatever the idea or dream, talking about all the possibilities and expectations with open minds and hearts was essential. Our discussions on how we were going to pull off this adventure came into focus through a unified perspective. Once we had solidified a plan, difficult choices and hard work became the next order of business.

We practiced living small. With accelerated payments, we paid down the mortgages, and when we went cruising, our debt was manageable. We eventually sold our business to our son, Brian, and our suburban home to our son, Saul. With the rentals and the monthly payments for the business and home, we are able to live simply but comfortably.

My growing trust in our shared vision and our ability to make our dreams come true was gratifying. By looking at things from a wider point of view, my outlook changed radically from the worried, narrow perspective of; 'We can't do it, we won't have enough money, to a confident, 'This is going to work!'.

Hey There, Dream Boat

Testing out our boats by sailing across the Bay, under the Golden Gate Bridge and out into the swell of the Pacific Ocean, we became aware of their capabilities and shortcomings. Our first sailboats were good for sailing, but did not have the room needed for an extended trip. When we contemplated sailing further off shore, it became obvious that we needed a bigger boat and we decided on a motor sailor with plenty of freeboard that rode well in the big ocean swells. We wanted two cabins and two heads that would allow us some privacy when we had visitors. The kids or guests could have their own space in the V berth away from the main salon and we could have the aft cabin. From experienced sailors we heard that there are often light wind conditions and adverse currents in Mexico and Central America so we decided we needed a stout engine that could push us 'uphill' when we wanted to buck the prevailing winds and seas. After much research we found our boat, the right size at the right price.

In 1997 we put our second *Harmony* up for sale or trade in *Latitude 38*, a popular sailing magazine based in the San Francisco Bay Area.

Harmony *at anchor in the Sea of Cortez.*

Serendipity stepped in when a gentleman from Washington answered our ad. He was looking for a smaller boat for ease of handling around Puget Sound and he owned a 1973 40' Islander Freeport. Robert and I cruised up Highway 5 on a mini-vacation, past snow-capped Mount Shasta, to Tacoma to check it out, and immediately liked what we saw. A ketch, with two cabins, two heads, a big engine, a center cockpit, lots of space, and large windows enclosing the salon fit our idea of what we wanted. This boat had made a trip to Mexico and back, proving herself a capable coastal cruiser. Our bigger *Harmony* was similar to our previous boats in that she required considerable work, but with an affordable price tag. With the trade-in value and a small loan, we became the proud owners of our dreamboat.

Although we were somewhat experienced sailors, we were not yet ready to brave the notoriously dangerous Washington and Oregon coast in a boat we knew nothing about. So we hired a boat mover to haul our new sailboat down to Alameda, California. After dropping off our boat, the truck turned around and carried the Islander 36' back up to its new home in Washington. Splitting the transport fee made it considerably less expensive for both of us..

Many cruisers opt for a sleek, fast and powerful sailboat design, but we compromised for comfort and space. My favorite selling features on *Harmony* were the large salon windows and open, airy floor plan along with a spacious engine room for Robert. This early model was built with the mechanic in mind. Later models provided more living space and stashed the engine into a small cubbyhole. We do not have to remove the stairs or floorboards to reach the engine. There have been several instances while we were underway that something needed attention in the engine room, and Robert was able to climb below to fix things without tearing the place apart. Three wide stairs, leading into a smaller, but ample, salon, was more to our liking, than a long, steep ladder descending into a cave-like living space. Even in heavy seas, it is relatively easy to move around and do things. In the galley/salon while we are cooking and eating, we have a 270-degree view and can watch the action of the changing weather and scenery just above the waves. *Harmony* has a dodger/bimini that is capable of totally enclosing the central cockpit during cold or wet weather and on rough passages. When some of our buddy boats are taking spray into the cockpit, we are sailing along warm and dry and the ride is comparatively stable in our center cockpit. Our heavy full keel is not a fast racing design, but it does give us a smooth ride and we have enough storage space to travel comfortably for a week with up to eight people on board. When the kids come to visit we live in close proximity, but we find room for their suitcases and backpacks. Even when we are living so close together, it's amazing that there is never a sour note since everyone is having the time of their lives.

Our friends, Daniel and Carmen spent twenty-two years building their steel boat from scratch in their back yard; a real accomplishment, but not what most people have in mind when they visualize the sailing life. There are plenty of expensively equipped yachts and then there are folks who cruise by-the-seat-of-their-pants. When we bought our boat, we had what was considered an average sized cruiser, but in the years that we have been out sailing, larger boats up to 50' plus with the latest electronics and equipment aboard have proliferated. When you inch up towards 50', the marina slips are more expensive, the equipment is more complicated and when things break, it may require a longer wait for parts. We decided on a boat that would fit our needs, be comfortable, but remain relatively simple. *Harmony* is not as minimalist as the boats owned by Larry and Lin Pardey [11] , who describe their travels around the world's oceans without an engine or refrigeration in their book, *Serraffyn*, but then again we are hardly lavishly equipped.

A few cruisers intend to circumnavigate the world, and many more dream of a shorter trip to Mexico or the Caribbean. The average cruise lasts from two to five years, and then the crew is often ready to move on to something new. Each cruiser decides which boat will work best to make their vision into a reality. For an extended, ocean passage, we would look for a better sailing boat, one that can sail well to weather and perform in light airs. For coastal cruising, however, *Harmony* has proven to be a good choice.

Purchasing a well-equipped boat closer to the desired cruising grounds is an option. There are many people who, ready to stop cruising, put their boats up for sale, with all the equipment and expensive electronic gadgets already on board. Marinas and dry storage facilities around the world are filled with boats that would love to go out sailing again. Where do you want to go, the Med, Panama, Mexico, Florida, New Zealand, or Australia?

Boat buying was a process that takes time, and we made it into an adventure of discovery. There were features on some vessels that were not to our liking, but knowing what we didn't want was half of the battle. By eliminating certain designs and models, we narrowed our search until we found the One. When we located a boat that fit our expectations with the inevitable compromises, we knew it. Seeing the potential, the possibilities, and the actualization of our dream taking shape was thrilling, almost like falling in love.

Hey There, Dream Boat

~ Equipping the Boat ~

Our newest *Harmony* was our cruising dreamboat, and Robert immediately began the many tasks of fixing and renovating. Because we worked on the weekends, he was able to allocate every Wednesday for his boat day. If we were serious about cruising, he had to create the time to prepare the boat. *Harmony* was built in 1973 and had a long list of things to be repaired, remodeled, and updated. Robert's dedication and hard work soon began to pay off. Frequenting yacht club swap meets, we bought an assortment of useful treasures, and found gems like 200 feet of 3/8th inch chain for $50 from a retiring cruiser. For another $50 a friend on our dock sold us a hard dinghy. My father donated a two-horse power outboard motor to our cause along with his ancient Avon dinghy. A local metal worker inexpensively fabricated davits out of stainless piping, which we mounted on the aft end of our boat. A block and tackle was purchased at a swap meet, and we soon had the dink safely secured. We were pleasantly surprised at how inexpensive it was to commission our cruising boat. Today with on-line market places, it is even easier to find great deals.

A few major purchases lightened our bank account by a few 'boat units,' a boat unit equaling $1000. Robert sent our Benmar, chain-driven autopilot, which was acting strangely, to the factory for a rebuild. The refrigerator unit was replaced and the Electro-san for the head was repaired, a requirement in the U.S., but not in Mexico. We bought new house and starting batteries, a GPS, and a Fathometer. Our Lofrans electric windlass was an important upgrade that makes anchoring safer and easier. Robert built a sump pump for the shower and installed an emergency bilge pump that pumped out a large volume of water in a fire-hose-sized pipe. Our son, Brian, gave us an EPIRB, (an Emergency Position Indicating Radio Beacon) for Christmas. He wanted us to have this updated signaling device that alerts the Coast Guard to our location in case of an emergency.

With her spruced up appearance and fancy upgraded equipment, *Harmony* strutted her stuff around the bay, while we had a chance to tune into the idiosyncrasies of our diva. When the winds were mild and we needed to tack, letting the jib backfill helped bring our heavy boat around. She thrived on the consistently strong afternoon winds coming through the Golden Gate, which gave us invigorating sails across *the slot*, a windy stretch of San Francisco Bay. Our first experience with using a mooring ball turned out to be pure slapstick. With the kids on board for the weekend, we had a brisk sail to Angel Island in the middle of San Francisco Bay. By the afternoon we were tying up to a mooring ball in the small, protected Ayala Cove. A friendly neighbor on a nearby yacht with her dinghy already launched, volunteered to help us tie off and our daughter went with her to secure the lines. In the middle of the night, I awoke with that uncanny feeling that something was wrong, that intuitive feeling that a mother of six children has when easily awakened by an anxious cry or that urge to go check on a sleeping baby. Answering my gut feeling, I peered out of the hatch and realized that we were not secured to our mooring ball and were slowly drifting towards a luxury motor yacht. I woke Robert up and with adrenaline pumping he started the engine. By this time we had drifted close to the yacht and I jumped aboard their back swim step to push us off, preventing us from smacking into them. While I pushed, Robert put *Harmony* in gear and pulled away before I could jump back aboard. I was left behind on our sleeping neighbor's boat! In the calm of the moon soaked night, Robert made a pass by the yacht again, and I quickly grabbed the lifelines and jumped on deck. We wondered if the owners of the yacht slept through the chaos or were awake wondering what shenanigans were taking place topside. Mooring again, we vowed to learn to tie a secure knot and teach the kids too! We checked out a knot-tying book from the library and practiced until a bowline, clove hitch, and a figure eight became second nature. Even better, for future mooring balls, we secured a snap shackle onto one of our lines, a simple solution for grabbing and holding tight. Through all our practice sails we discovered that *Harmony* performed best in strong, steady winds. Having outgrown the bay, she was hankering for an adventure on the high seas.

After two years, Robert had clicked off enough items on the to-do list to feel ready to leave the dock on a trial cruise. Were we totally ready? Not really, but when the fall season arrived with pleasant sailing weather, we were prepared enough to test the waters and sample a taste of the cruising lifestyle.

If we had been planning to go to the South Pacific or around the world, we would have installed a water maker, solar panels, a wind generator, a self-steering wind vane, and loaded up with charts and flags. But our first leg of the journey was going to be a trip down the

California coast or maybe as far as Mexico, so we knew we could manage without everything crossed off of our long wish list. Our trial run would reveal what we needed to add and what we could live without, and it was a relatively short trip home to bring down more boat bling.

Hey There, Dream Boat

~ Our Trial Run ~

In 1998, our daughter, Olivia, was our only child still living at home (the rest of our large brood were attending or had graduated from various campuses of the University of California). In keeping with the tradition of her older sisters, she chose to spend her junior year abroad as an exchange student. The Quaker organization, American Field Service (AFS) does a wonderful job of placing high school students with compatible host families around the world, promoting peace by having young people experience other cultures while immersed in a foreign language. Her sister, Audrey had lived in the Dominican Republic, Rose spent her junior year in Venezuela, and Caitlin traveled to Costa Rica. Olivia decided on distant Ecuador, and while she was scheduling her departure, we began to plan our trial cruise. Since wintertime was the slow season for our business, we could spare a month off in October/November to go south and then bring *Harmony* back to San Francisco in January.

Would we like our first attempt at an extended cruise? There were plenty of stories of people selling their homes, outfitting their boats with the latest equipment, and taking off, only to find that they became uncomfortably seasick offshore and detested the whole thing. Other first time cruisers found that they missed their work and felt unproductive; they found cruising boring, or they could not tolerate things breaking down. We were nearby when a sailor friend arrived at the dock after a stormy night, vowing never to set foot on another boat as long as she lived! She just hated that unsettled ocean! And then we had met a deflated dreamer who could never get comfortable when the boat was heeling. Living with her partner 24/7 was not to her liking either. She yearned for her old life on shore where she and her hubby lived a more independent existence, coming together for evenings, weekends and vacations. She missed the children and grandchildren, her friends and her career. Our pals on a dock nearby jokingly referred to their trip as his dream and her nightmare. That notion was ironically turned upside down when a series of breakdowns turned his dream into a nightmare. Meanwhile, while waiting for parts in a comfortable marina, she had a grand time meeting new friends and socializing. In any case, we felt cautious and it was logical to start out with a trial run.

Our launch date was set for October 12, Columbus Day, a day with particular significance to us since it was the same time in 1970 that we had left San Francisco on the Caravan to rediscover America. For this modern day odyssey, we were off to experience places that we had never visited before.

In the early quiet of a gray, misty morning, a few salty live-aboard friends from the marina threw us our dock lines, bid us a hardy Bon Voyage, and we motored out the calm Alameda estuary into the bay. A dense fog engulfed us, so thick that we could hardly make out the towers of the Golden Gate Bridge. We passed a large barge ghosting by

Alcatraz Island, grateful that our thirty-year old radar was registering the large blip. Motor/sailing under the South Tower, we turned left at the 'light bucket' (a channel marker used as a waypoint so boats can avoid the surrounding shoals) and steered south. The calm, pea-soupy weather accentuated the pungent sea aromas in the still air. Centuries ago Sir Francis Drake had missed the discovery of San Francisco Bay due to a similar, dense fog across the entrance to the Golden Gate. Lucky for us, our trusty electronics were transmitting their valuable information. These essential tools of the modern mariner transform us amateurs into first-rate navigators. When we arrived at the GPS programmed waypoint, the sea buoy was close by bobbing in the waves. 'Right on course, Sir,' Robert called to me.

By midday we emerged out of the gray, fleece-like fog, and blinked our eyes in the bright sunlight. Romping downwind over the ocean swells in the freshening, afternoon breeze, we were on the way to our first stop, Half Moon Bay. We felt unhurried on our trial run. Wherever we ended up when our vacation time ran out would be the destination. It soon became obvious that we preferred the pace of meandering slowly down the California Coast, harbor hopping, taking time to follow the majestic coastline, and visiting sights on shore.

After following along the sea wall into a slip in the Half Moon Bay marina, we celebrated our first day at sea with a dinner of freshly caught fish beautifully prepared at one of the harbor restaurants. The docks were lined with fishing boats just in with their catch, and we hung around chatting with the rugged fishermen, listening for tidbits of lore about their adventures. Eight years later when we visited the same harbor, the few fishermen that remained would be struggling for their livelihood when quotas tightened the noose around their profits.

Early the next morning we rendezvoused with our crew, Dave, and off we went to Santa Cruz, wing on wing, in a freshening breeze.

We had met Dave at 'the crew list party' sponsored by *Latitude 38*, where skippers searched for competent sailors and crew looked for a boat. After interviewing several applicants, we decided on Dave, who had some offshore experience. He was not only an eager participant, but helped us traverse our steep learning curve, teaching us valuable tips along the way. At the party, as luck would have it, Dave won the raffle for a $75 set of Gerry Cunningham's *Cruising Guide to the Sea of Cortez*, which he generously donated to our cause. The pages have become dog-eared and salt splattered from extensive use over the years.

This leg of our sea trial to Santa Cruz was a riotous, downwind run that Dave said was 'Par for the course.' We were overpowered, however, and were surfing rapidly down the waves at over eight knots, full speed ahead for our full-keeled cruiser. Our autopilot parts had not yet arrived from the factory, and we sailed with a heavy helm from the 25-knot winds and towering 8-10 foot following seas. Hand steering required muscle, stamina, and endurance, and sharing the load between the three of us, and switching off every hour, gave our shoulders a break. When it was my turn on the helm, it was all I could do to keep us pointed straight down wind and to anticipate the gusts that threatened to knock us off course and jibe the main, never a good thing. Robert made a mental note to install a better reefing system on the main to lessen the sail area in the next blow. Up until then, he had dropped the main when things became too rough. Hand steering wore everyone out, and the tired crew was relieved when we ducked around the corner into the calmer waters of Monterey Bay.

Crowded Santa Cruz marina usually has limited space for transient visitors, and the harbormaster directed us to raft up to a friendly boat for a few days. While we were there we met a couple on the sailing vessel, *Dancing Wave*, with a tale to tell. They had sailed the same rough seas, but were further offshore in a smaller boat. One rogue, green-topped wave washed the captain overboard, leaving him dangling by his harness and tether. In the riotous conditions, he struggled unsuccessfully to pull himself back on deck. The numbing, northern California Pacific Ocean chilled him and he tired rapidly. His wife struggled to deploy the ladder and finally with the adrenaline power often attributed to life-endangering situations, grabbed him and yanked him back on board. She had alerted the Coast Guard to their situation, and they steamed out to help. They transferred some of the 'Coasties' aboard to assist her in sailing the boat to the marina while the captain thawed out, bundled up in blankets and sleeping bags in the V berth. Four days later he emerged, warmed enough to take his first stroll in the mid-day sunshine.

Our daughter, Audrey, a student at the local University of California, accompanied us on a delightfully sunny day trip from Santa Cruz across Monterey Bay. A large resident pod of more than fifty dolphins greeted us, playing in our bow wave, accustomed to being friendly ambassadors, welcoming new sailors to their watery realm. Dave's knowledge helped steer us off the beaten track into Stillwater Cove, a small tucked-in anchorage around the corner from Monterey Bay, located off the 18th green of the prestigious Pebble Beach Golf Course. Dodging and tiptoeing our way between large kelp beds and rocky reefs, we had our first lesson in navigating safely and cautiously into a tight spot. Dave also coached us with helpful hints about anchoring, something that a San Francisco Bay sailor often has little experience with, and was definitely new to us.

In picturesque Stillwater Cove we made friends with Molly and Carl on *Sea Quest* who owned a brand new, beautifully varnished wooden tender. After returning from town that night, and rowing slowly to *Harmony* in our hard dinghy, we spotted something floating near a reef in the harbor. When we rowed over for a closer look, it

Harmony *underway with Virginia at the helm.*

turned out to be our neighbors' pristine dinghy on the loose. We hauled it back to their boat, and they insisted that we take two bottles of wine for our trouble. That was a nice gesture but we were just helping out. Some of their crew had dragged the dinghy onto shore and left it on the beach without considering the tides or setting an anchor. The high tide came in and floated the little boat out towards the rocks and open sea. It turned out to be an anchoring story with a happy ending.

The weather report called for stable conditions for the next couple of days, so we left *Harmony* at anchor in Stillwater Cove while we borrowed Audrey's car and returned to Modesto to wrap up some last minute business. Sometimes the ties to land have to be interwoven with the seafaring lifestyle. As much as we wanted to drop everything and go, there were things that called to us even out in the wilds of the ocean.

Continuing our trip down the scenic California coast, we left

Point Sur and its misty landscape to port, hand steering all the way. We would set our sights on a distant blue promontory, pass it by, and chose the next point emerging from the haze. When we were not steering, we cooked, ate, napped, read, talked, and spent hours watching the seas, the horizon, the sky, and the land. The panoramic view of the steep, craggy coastline from the ocean was one we never tired of watching. Noting our progress on the charts we discovered little known names of points and landmarks along this pristine, isolated, *Forgotten Middle* where Central California meets the Pacific Ocean.

On this trial run I had to untangle, what I call my physical-plane dyslexia. I found it difficult to remember which side was port and which side was starboard. People who have this challenge can understand how frustrating it can be. The captain would call out, 'Release the port sheet,' and I would have to think hard for a minute to make sure I was on the correct side. While meandering down the coast a game of association finally did the trick. Left has four letters and so did port and it wasn't long before it became automatic. I had similar troubles with the bowline knot and I had to practice the moves, over, under, sideways, and through over and over again. Since unraveling physical plane conundrums was Robert's forte, he was used to doing the mechanical work around the boat, but with normally just the two of us aboard, I needed to learn about righty-tighty and lefty-loosey. When I started to wrap my mind around these alien ideas, I was then confronted with needing to screw a garden hose to the salt-water spigot at our galley sink to wash down a mud encrusted anchor chain. From my perspective, the whole thing looked upside down and reversed. Challenging my attention to stick with it long enough to figure it out without descending into frustration was my exercise. And when I really couldn't get it, my patient matey would be there to walk me through it again and again. His delight in having me share his dream must have kept his impatience under control.

That evening we rounded Point Piedras Blancas' lighthouse in the pitch dark, feeling our way cautiously towards San Simeon Cove. The circuitous entrance turned out to be a difficult approach on this black, moonless night, and we were exhausted from fourteen hours of hand steering. It is generally unwise to enter an unfamiliar port at night, the main reason being that we have poor spatial perception in the dark. The Hearst Castle was clearly lit up in its dazzling splendor atop the hill above the anchorage, however, the navigational lights and the lights on shore melded into one sparkling, jumbled mess. We spotted a red light that looked like an entrance buoy only to have it turn green. That would have been funny if we weren't so tired. We studied our charts, took GPS readings, and using our radar we inched into the channel, finally differentiating the lights and then suddenly, it all made sense. Our first instrument landing at night was celebrated with warm soup and a renewed trust in our electronic gadgets. Our long day at sea was soon forgotten when we were rocked gently into dreamland.

On the short day sail to Morro Bay, we were entertained by spouting whales and curious, oyster-hugging otters floating leisurely on their backs in the kelp. When we started our approach to the harbor entrance I was reminded of the famous photograph of a Coast Guard boat at a nearly 90-degree angle, charging over huge waves breaking over the bar. It must have been during one of those big winter storms, because this time the occasionally dangerous bar was no problem. Receiving a warm welcome from the yacht club members is customary, where they treat each cruiser like a celebrity, attentively listening to our tales from the sea. They directed us to a mooring, provided us with a place to do laundry and take refreshing showers, and pulled up a weather fax for our next day's journey. Many other cruisers agree in our assessment that the members of the Morro Bay Yacht Club are most gracious and friendly. We felt honored to be the lucky recipients of their hospitality.

New sights and experiences kept us in awe of this watery world. We sailed around Point Buchon with its nuclear reactor perched on the shore's edge, to spend a night rocking and rolling in Port San Luis. When we pulled up our anchor the next morning on our way towards Point Conception, the winds decided to take a vacation, and along the way we motor-sailed past a sailboat moving very slowly practically dead in the water. Hailing them on the radio it turned out to be *Ocean's Child* from Canada on their way to Mexico. The bad news was that their engine wouldn't start. The good news was that the currents, swell, and winds, very light as they were, would carry them south even though they were doing only 1.5 knots. We radioed them that Robert would be happy to look at their motor when we both arrived at our next destination, Santa Barbara.

Point Conception bulges out into the Pacific Ocean on the California map, separating the virtual states of Northern and Southern California. Any major promontory can potentially have strange weather, special winds, currents, and swells that conspire to stir up a brew of swirling, confused havoc. A small craft daring to ride around its menacing protrusion can face treacherous conditions so paying close attention to the weather reports is prudent. Fortunately, the ogre guarding the point had taken off for a day in the sun, and we had a delightfully mild afternoon passage in 15 knots of wind. Ducking around the cape, we set our anchor near the railroad tracks at the Cojo anchorage in thirty feet of calm water.

Surfers know Cojo as Government Point an isolated windswept, wave-packed paradise. The gliding pelicans with their wings spread in syncopated flight, sweep low over the cliffs, soaring on the updrafts following the leader over the railroad tracks. Supply ships servicing the big oilrigs offshore tie up to huge mooring balls among a few sailboats, fishermen, and surfing tour boats. As soon as we rounded Point Conception our compass pointed east-southeast, and the high mountains along the coast cut off the cool, northwest winds and boisterous swells. Following in the tradition of sailors since the days of the earliest voyagers, we threw off our layers of foul weather gear. We had arrived in balmy Southern California!

Much to our surprise, when we docked in Santa Barbara harbor the next day, there bobbing in one of the guest slips was *Ocean's Child*. They had been sailing along all day and night while we stopped to sleep at Cojo. Robert took a look at their engine and within ten minutes, had it purring away. It turned out to be such an easy fix that we agreed that in the future in a similar situation, we would stop and dinghy over even if we were well off shore.

After settling into our Santa Barbara slip we met a friendly family on *Different Drummer*, a black, steel-hulled sailboat from Canada that we recognized from the Half Moon Bay anchorage. Many of the mariners whom we met along the West Coast fly the red and white maple leaf flag from Canada or hail from the Northwest states of Alaska, Washington and Oregon. The cold, rainy winters provide a compelling incentive to head toward warmer, sunnier cruising grounds. Meeting new people was a highlight in our new endeavor, and since each sailor had amusing and often hair-raising tales to tell it was a pleasure to spend time together. While leap-frogging down the coast, we continued to encounter our new friends at anchorages or marinas, and we felt privileged to be members of this community of cruisers; a small, intimate group of people who not only would drop everything to help us out, but are a pleasure to be around. It was the closest thing to community that we had experienced since we left *The Farm* in Tennessee. The camaraderie stems from the deeply shared adventure of sailing small boats on the expansive ocean in all of her fickle moods, a love of nature and travel, and the value we cruisers have in our new family far from home. These remarkable and, occasionally, zany vagabonds carry a zest for life and have the courage to leave their safe land haven and set out towards the horizon to discover what is over the edge. On land it might seem that we have little in common with some of these adventurers, but on the high seas we are soul mates in a very intimate sense and we value our friendships.

After leaving Santa Barbara we sailed to Oxnard in a blustery but warm tail wind and a large following swell. When we looked behind us, looming walls of water rose high above our stern, but the waves lifted us gracefully up and gently set us down again. This invigorating sail became even more exciting when we approached the Channel Islands harbor. Surfers, not to miss the unusually high waves, were out in full force and the menacing ocean swell pounded over the breakwater in explosions of white spray. While Robert and Dave hauled in the sails on the bobbing and tilting fore deck, I steered *Harmony* towards the entrance, wallowing around in the troughs. Realizing safe calm waters lay just ahead I revved up the engine and charged through to nestle in behind the protective breakwater. A diesel engine sure came in handy when we needed it.

Arriving safely at the guest dock we met Rick and Marilyn and their young daughter, Lauren, who have turned out to be lifelong friends. They were once again on their way south having sailed in Mexico since the early 1980's. Rick, a weather savvy cruiser, has extensively studied the meteorological patterns, high and low-pressure systems, swells and currents. When he is cruising in Mexico he shares his knowledge generously as the morning weatherman on the Sonrisa HAM radio net.

From Oxnard, mild sailing conditions carried us across Santa

Monica Bay to Marina Del Rey where during one of our boat inspections we noticed that our sacrificial zinc was missing from the propeller.[12] Robert donned his wet suit and had to jump into the cold, funky L.A. marina water to replace the zinc. With his snorkel, mask, and weight belt, he did this work underwater, surfacing often to breathe. Because holding his breath underwater while changing zincs and cleaning the bottom is difficult, to say the least, it wasn't long before we purchased a hookah-rig with a small compressor that pumps air through a long hose into a mouthpiece. It makes the underwater work easier and we often take turns, staying down for as long as we need to. Due to the vibration of the engine on the shaft, the inadequate, short screws that held the zinc onto the propeller had fallen off. On a pleasant walk to nearby West Marine, Robert found a large, long bolt that would hold the zinc securely. After he finished the job and cleaned up, we strolled around the docks of this sprawling marina. It is said that ten thousand boats populate this village on the water and it looked like that might be the case.

That evening we were startled awake by a loud crackling and popping that sounded like an electrical short somewhere in the bilge. Robert went down below to check on things while I searched the lockers and cabinets and found nothing amiss. The next morning while visiting with new acquaintances on the dock we found out the answer to our midnight mystery noise. In the warmer waters of Southern California there are tiny shrimp, called popcorn shrimp, that thrive off of the flavorful growth on our boat's bottom. There's never a dull moment and always an answer to those baffling questions that arise in the middle of a dark enigmatic night.

We woke up to a Los Angeles rush hour traffic report on the FM radio with accidents, construction zones, and jammed highways, but in the tranquil marina we felt far removed from the urban commotion.

After a day or two of enjoyable walks along the canals of Venice Beach and loading up with fresh produce, we were off on a rollicking spinnaker sail to Newport Beach. We skirted the entrance to the Port of Long Beach where we dodged cargo ships moving in and out of one of the busier ports in the world. Dave taught us how to plot an oncoming freighter's course, and once we understood the drill, our stress level about colliding with one of those huge ships decreased. For starters everyone was traveling at slower speeds near the harbor. By monitoring the freighters, taking a few sightings five minutes apart, we could tell if an oncoming boat would pass to port or starboard or was standing still. When we sight a boat moving down the length of the port side, for instance, it is passing to port. If it is moving up toward the bow it will cross the bow and pass on the starboard side. Today with the new AIS (Automatic Identification System), it is possible to find out about the large ships in your area up to two hundred miles away. All the information pops up on the screen; the name of the ship, what direction they are going and at what speed. But since we do not have this latest system, when we see a boat coming toward us out in the ocean, we move one way or the other to guarantee plenty of clearance. On rare occasions when we felt a little too close, we have hailed a ship on our VHF radio to give them a heads up that we were in their area. We inevitably have had friendly conversations with the radiomen of these freighters and cruise ships out on the midnight sea. On one dark night we were sailing very slowly in barely a puff of wind with a disabled engine. Spotting a large cruise ship coming our way, we alerted the radio operator that we were without power and in his path. They made a sharp turn to port, allowing us ample sea room, and he left us in his wake wishing us a safe journey.

When we arrived at Newport Beach Harbor we rented a mooring ball for the great deal of $5 a day. There was just enough time to go on a romantic walk along Balboa Beach where Robert had proposed to me nearly twenty-eight years earlier. Watching the sun dip below the horizon he asked me again if I would marry him. Unlike the first time when I was young, nervous, and unsure of myself, I felt no hesitation to say yes. We were living our dream together and I was more in love than ever.

Newport Harbor is surrounded by expensive but closely spaced homes. Halloween season found the houses decorated with jack-o-lanterns, goblins and witches swinging in the air. On a stroll along the boardwalk in the warm evening air, we were amazed that most of the elegant homes kept their curtains wide open for all to see, until we realized that our beautiful sailboats in front of their large picture windows were contributing to their spectacular million-dollar view.

The last legs of the trip were to Oceanside and then paralleling Interstate 5 to San Diego, both easy sailing days with modest winds. The congested highway traffic backed up along the coast while we cruised on clear waters. On shore loomed the two round towers of the San Onofre Nuclear Power Plant resembling massive mammary glands pointing to the sky, nourishing our society's appetite for energy. When we passed the Marine Base of Camp Pendleton, helicopters flew out and circled over us. Around Point Loma we sailed in a perfect afternoon breeze into bustling San Diego Harbor, cruising down the waterfront alongside the Star of India, the famous tall ship moored at the dock. Around the bay were numerous sailboats, a few submarines, and destroyers bedecked in their fancy war jewelry. We sailed under the gracefully arching Coronado Bridge and found a berth at Chula Vista Marina, a reasonably priced spot to dock *Harmony* for a month. Dave left us to return to his other life on shore amid thanks and well wishes, and we settled into marina life for a few days.

With our diesel tanks low on fuel, and not wanting to leave them empty, we left the marina early one morning for the nearest fuel dock several miles away. When we purchased *Harmony*, we were not exactly sure how big the tanks were and the gauge was not working. Wouldn't you know, in the middle of San Diego Bay we sputtered to a stop, out of fuel. To make matters a bit more chaotic, a massive aircraft carrier was making its entrance into the harbor escorted by speeding, navy inflatables, with machine guns mounted on their bows charging around like protective bees around a hive. They sloshed up the waters, circling us several times, checking us out. We must have looked threatening with our little pirate ship windows in the aft cabin bedecked with tie-dyed curtains. In actuality what was truly dangerous was that we were slowly drifting closer to a rock-lined park. Usually we take the sail covers off when we leave the dock but this time we figured we were not going far. Another lesson learned in the relentless school of hard knocks, close calls, and adrenaline highs. Quickly stripping the covers off, we hoisted the sails that hesitantly caught the light airs just in time to steer clear of danger. We then slowly tacked up the bay from shore to shore towards the fuel dock while dodging the huge naval vessels. Several hundred yards from our destination, we found ourselves in the lee of the land, stopped dead in the water. It wasn't long before a friendly cruiser in his dinghy came by and we asked for a tow. He grabbed our line and as soon as he started to pull, a puff of wind came up and all of a sudden we were pulling him! This went on back and forth until we finally reached the wharf safely. Sailing up to a dock without an engine on our 40-foot sailboat was an interesting exercise. Fortunately the friendly stranger helped us in using his dinghy like a tugboat, and then waved good-bye, happy to lend a hand.

After a surprisingly graceful landing, we noticed the Canadian flag flying on the boat tied up in front of us and it turned out to be *Different Drummer*! It's always nice to have friends waiting there on shore to catch our lines. After our diesel fill-up, we finally knew exactly how much fuel we carried in our two tanks. That had been more excitement than we had bargained for and we were ready for more benign cruising. While sailing slowing back to Chula Vista we had several hours to discuss our recent adventures. We were impressed with the serendipitous events that brought to mind an old tale about the quirky sailor tradition, the lore of the lucky box. An imaginary treasure chest is implanted in the heart of each boat during its construction. When we go out to sea, life creates situations where we can help others in small and large ways and the lucky box fills up with Lady Luck's intangible treasures of fortune. When it's our turn to need assistance, the lucky box materializes the help we need out of the accumulated stash of good karma. And so it goes, we helped someone start their engine and recovered a missing dinghy, and in return we were helped to the dock when we ran out of fuel. The spirit of generosity and the good will generated by people helping people is a wonderfully intrinsic part of the cruising experience.

Back in Chula Vista our vacation time had run out. Putting *Harmony* to bed, we returned home to work at the holiday craft shows.

* * *

When we first left San Francisco, we could not anticipate how our plans would pan out, how far we would travel, or where we would end up when our time ran out. We discovered a comfortable cruising pace, sailing slowly without expectations or rigid itineraries, and we came to understand the saying, 'It is the journey not the destination.' It wasn't only about making the passages, but also spending time relaxing in port, meeting other cruisers, restocking, and exploring. We were totally enamored with our first attempt at cruising and fortunately neither of us suffered from seasickness. On the contrary, we felt invigorated by our days at sea. Watching the rugged coast from several miles off shore inspired me to paint pictures and take photos of the lighthouses from this unique perspective. We agreed that we liked cruising, and even though we were only half way done with our trial cruise, we started planning the next longer trip south of the border to Mexico.

For the winter holiday season of 1998 the family joined us in San Diego to begin our return sail north. We installed our newly repaired autopilot, and with "Piley," working like a charm, our hands were free to sit back and relax with our children and their friends. We sailed to Catalina Island for New Years, spent time hiking the mountain trails, and the young adults partied well into the next morning at the nightclubs. Our kids who weren't with us called us long distance on our new cell phone to wish us a Happy New Year. Amazingly enough we had children scattered on four continents and five countries that New Year's Eve: Indonesia, Canada, Costa Rica, Ecuador, and Italy. Lucky us, we were out exploring too.

From Catalina we sailed to Newport Harbor, moored bow and stern, and our son, Saul, hopped on the train back to San Diego to pick up the van that we had left at the marina. After driving up the Central Valley to Modesto, we helped our students pack up for another semester at the university. Returning to *Harmony* we spent a harrowing night in Newport harbor weathering a Santa Ana windstorm. The gusts began to howl in the late afternoon and the boat vibrated violently. At one point Robert thought that some motor was on and went below to take a look. It was the power of the 50-knot winds roaring through our rigging that sounded like a diesel engine revving. Everything was humming and rocking, but our snap shackles and extra lines held us tightly to the mooring balls.

After the weather settled down we began our northward climb to San Francisco Bay against the wind, current, and swell. While cruising in Southern California we spent time in the offshore Channel Islands, sailed slowly by the arched rocks of Anacapa Island and anchored for a few days in Fry's Cove on Santa Cruz Island. We were the only boat there, seemingly so isolated, and yet so close to the large population centers of Southern California. Bright red and orange starfish were scattered over the ocean floor, easily seen in the crystal clear water from our deck. Having mailed in our check for the permit to go on shore, we explored this natural area, marred only by some rusty railroad tracks remaining from the past century. Overlooking the bluff we watched a pod of five whales cruising close by, a calf swimming among them, all surfacing and blowing together. From our observation perch at the cliff's edge, we were able to see them dive deep in the glassy blue-green water, while inland the wild boars shrieked and bellowed, their squeals echoing from ridge to ridge.

Leaving the rustic Channel Islands behind, we scooted across the 26-mile strait to Santa Barbara on an exhilarating broad-reach to await a favorable northbound weather window. January 1999 was no exception to the rule of small craft advisories almost every day. The wind howled and the seas sprayed its foamy surf over the protective, rock-lined walls of the marina. While doing the usual boat projects and provisioning, we had time to make the acquaintance of enchanting Santa Barbara. Hiking the flower-lined streets, we toured the Spanish mission atop the hill with its red tiled roofs. This choice real estate has a sweeping view of the beaches, ocean, and islands in the distance and we stopped for a moment to smell the prize-winning roses ringing the mission grounds. Further up the road was the Natural History Museum displaying, among other interesting artifacts, the canoes of the Chumash Indians. These sturdy canoes were made of wood, stuffed with the tarry pitch that often clings to the soles of bare feet when an unsuspecting tourist takes a sunset stroll along the local beaches. The Chumash were known as the Phoenicians of the West

Coast, traveling and trading up and down the shoreline and between the Channel Islands and the mainland. It's a sad commentary that such a long-lived and gallant sea tradition was snuffed out in a short gasp of history. We went on long walks, watched the newly released movie, Shakespeare in Love, and loaded up the pantry with fresh fruits and veggies from the friendly and abundant farmers' market. The fourteen days that a visitor is allowed to stay in the marina without a major price increase was slowly ticking by.

Finally the seas began to settle down around Point Conception, from a riotous 16-20 feet to a slightly more sensible, but still disorderly 9-13 feet. The weather radio predicted reasonable 3-4 foot seas in the Santa Barbara Channel down from the steep-walled 4-6 feet. Chomping at the bit, we decided to make a run for it, even though the red, small craft advisory flag still fluttered above the Harbor Master's office.

Before the January sunrise could warm our bones, we threaded our way past the buoys and out of the harbor. While punching westward near the skeletal oilrigs, we raised our main sail to keep us steady. *Harmony* was the only boat out on the early morning waters as far as we could see. While we were plowing along, an announcement came over our VHF radio that the oilrig nearby was *perforating* and vessels should stay three miles clear. We scooted away from the rig, noticing a large oil slick on top of the water. Although we did not have any idea what perforating meant, it had a menacing ring to it. We later learned that the danger was explosions not oil leaks. Those hull-smudging oil slicks apparently are a natural occurrence in those waters. Further down the channel toward Point Conception, we heard they were test-firing rockets from Vandenberg Air Force Base well away from our position but still out to sea! The small craft advisory for rough seas was not our only concern while we beat our way out of Southern California waters.

The winds picked up as the afternoon progressed but the seas were still manageable. When we passed Cojo we noticed the hulk of a large, steel-gray, navy boat being smashed against the rocks. Apparently it had recently run aground, because it wasn't there on our trip south. We later heard that the crew had been evacuated to safety by helicopter and the ship declared a total loss.

Sailing plans start with a Plan A, but we often settle for Plan B or even Plan C. With one destination in mind, depending on weather, whims or whatever, we may take a detour and end up in a different quiet anchorage or make an overnight run to the next safe harbor. Since Point Conception is one of those fickle, unsettled promontories, where it behooves one to be cautious, we left our plans open-ended. With the sun low in the sky, we made the decision to round Point Conception on our first overnight voyage, with the option of turning tail into Cojo anchorage for the night if the weather deteriorated. At the Point we pitched face first into a spectacular sunset that disappeared below the swells and then reappeared, sun up, sun down, sun up, sun down. The lighthouse beam came on, and turned around and around while we hobby-horsed north. The heaving swell calmed down once we rounded the corner and we proceeded into the night with the waxing crescent moon setting to the west shortly after dark.

The weather report proved to be correct, a good night to travel, and we proceeded on to Morro Bay. In the inky black, moonless night, we followed the car headlights, which beamed out from shore, winding their way around the curves and switchbacks along California's coastal Highway 1. The moderating swells reflected the lights, imbuing us with a comfortable feeling that everything was all right. The only problem to mar our successful midnight get-away was that the belt powering the alternator snapped and all of a sudden the radar went fuzzy and the autopilot would not hold its course. Robert quickly started the generator to charge up our batteries, replaced the belt, and soon the power was back, his mechanical wizardry rescuing the night.

Waiting in the early dawn outside of the Morro Bay entrance, we radioed the Coast Guard to find out how the entrance over the bar looked that morning. A friendly Coastie responded saying he would check on it and soon called back with the go ahead. We had a mild surf ride across the sand bar, tucking in behind the breakwater. Soon the red carpet welcoming committee again greeted us at the yacht club dock. After showers and refreshments we were chatting with the club members when another sailboat motored up to the dock. Apparently they had been following us all night. While we were slogging up the West Santa Barbara Channel, they had come from the Channel Islands, registering steady 35-knot winds on their anemometer. During one particularly violent gust, the jib sail was yanked out of the roller furling gear. Water had steadily sloshed over their aft cockpit and occasionally splashed down into the cabin. With an experienced six-person crew, they were able to take 30-minute shifts easing the strain and fatigue. Even so, it had been a rough night with no way to dry out. They all showered, dried their wet clothes, and set out again on their journey north to Oregon. We decided to spend the night and rest up from our first ever, overnight passage.

The next morning we received the yacht club's weather fax that called for clear skies with a weather front advancing into Central California in twenty-four hours. By our novice calculations we had a twelve to sixteen-hour, overnight trip to Monterrey and would make it in before the gale. We set out on a lovely afternoon sail across Morro Bay, leaving Punta Piedras Blancas in our wake. The sun disappeared behind a large, dark cloud front reflecting its warm, orange rays. The witching hour, midnight, approached with menacing clouds that marched across the star-studded heavens, hiding the moon and stars as the front came in hours earlier than expected. The seas became confused like a washing machine with the prevailing swell from the north and storm waves from the south kicking up a turbulent brew. Squalls with strong winds started to march over us. The approaching storm cells made white, fuzzy blobs on the radar, and the building waves sprinkled the screen with white blips. I watched the radar and warned Robert of the incoming, gusty rainstorms, while he manned the wheel to help the autopilot stay quartering to the waves. We were approaching the lighthouse of Point Sur with its powerful, rotating, beam piercing through the storm. Point Sur is a northern cousin to the notorious Point Conception, and in a gale there is little mercy from this high, steep-walled promontory. To escape the point effect we would have had to go many miles out to sea, which we tried, only to prolong our agony. I noticed a large blip on the radar and called Robert over to take a look. We had sailed close to the shipping lanes and when we looked out of our windows we saw a huge freighter moving swiftly past us less than a mile to port. The freighter was lit up like a small town in the middle of a dark, menacing sea.

The longest, roughest, stormiest night that we had ever experienced was a test of our stamina, nerves, and resilience. The illuminating light from Point Sur stayed with us hour after fitful hour, mocking us as we inched slowly, steadily northward. Blustery winds blew from all points. The white-capped, churning waves were huge twenty-footers, and what we call our tilt-o-meter registered 30 to 40 degrees down one side of a wave to 30 to 40 degrees down into the next trough. It seemed that the dawn would never break through the wintry darkness, while we clawed our way up the coast. We continued on, knowing that there would be no stopping short of Monterey Bay, since Stillwater Cove would be anything but still water in the southerly swell. A call to the Coast Guard on the VHF confirmed that idea.

"Are you all right out there?" the friendly voice asked.

"Yes, everything is fine," I said. "Well, not fine exactly, but yes everything is working on the boat. We're looking forward to tying up in port." The radioman then gave us the VHF channel monitored by the Monterey Harbor to arrange for a berth. Finally, as the dawn began to silhouette the coastline, we could see what we had only imagined in the inky blackness. The monster waves were white-bearded and menacing. Approaching the outlying rocks of Cypress Point, a spectacular, giant, vertical plume of water shot into the air with each crashing surge. We had barely had anything to eat or drink during the tempest, and my half-eaten apple lay in a cockpit drain where it lodged itself in the middle of the night. Riding that storm, we felt like little ants in a walnut shell, so tiny in the scheme of the vast, agitated ocean. Despite fatigue and fear, we had stayed up, keeping each other company, living each tilt and plunge together. In reality the boat was tougher than we were. *Harmony* plowed through the rough seas, strong and sure, bringing us safely through each hour of the exhausting, unsettled voyage.

When we came abreast of Monterey Bay, we turned in toward the harbor, blasting down the big following seas. What an exhilarating feeling, surfing on our 40-foot long-board on large swells, riding a wave for a 100 yards before being let down gently into the trough, and then scooped up by the next roller. We eventually landed gracefully by a large, red buoy where we stopped to regroup and prepare the lines and fenders for a dock landing. One of those dreaded squalls came over the Monterey hills, but we felt only gentle rain and calm waters in the lee of the land. A troupe of harbor seals performed a circus act around the harbor marker. Like blubbery clowns they scrambled awkwardly onto the buoy, displacing their buddies who, barking loudly splashed into the water. Even though we were exhausted, we were able to laugh at what nature dished up; first the wild storm and then the acrobatic jumps and twirls by the seals of Monterey Bay.

Carefully we motored through the narrow entrance to the marina and tied up at our assigned dock. A local fisherman caught our lines while we pulled into our slip. He was amazed that we had been out in that mess, and welcomed us warmly into the safe harbor. As soon as we were securely tied up, Robert jumped ashore and kissed the dock. We'd made it!

After showering and devouring a soothing hot, bowl of clam chowder at a pier restaurant, we went to sleep for twelve straight hours. Awakened refreshed from a full night's sleep, we jumped back on our horse and galloped across the bay to Santa Cruz, a short afternoon romp, on calmer seas. Although the swell was still large it was nicely rounded, and not a problem.

As we sailed along with our thoughts and 20/20, Monday morning quarterback vision, we reflected on what had occurred. In some distorted way we actually welcomed the storm in all of its discomfort. It had challenged us beyond our limits, and proved to us that *Harmony* could perform like a champ, even in rough conditions. We would be more cautious in the future, and would avoid playing roulette with incoming storms. The Oregonian boat that we had met in Morro Bay must have known something that we did not. Despite their exhaustion, they had pushed on, avoiding the rough, stormy night. We now knew that we could handle a tough situation and our confidence grew. Hopefully, we were also a bit wiser.

In Santa Cruz our daughter, Audrey came aboard and traveled with us for the last big push to our homeport. She was surprised at how big the seas were after we turned the corner out of Monterey Bay powering north. To appease her stomach's queasiness, she watched the horizon, and soon her sea legs steadied her. After a comfortable night anchored at Half Moon Bay, a friendly tide and mellow winds pushed us under the majestic, red-orange Golden Gate Bridge. Even though the afternoon breeze was howling across *the slot*, it was the calmest waters we had seen on our entire trip home. The energized crew on *Harmony* flew before the wind, down the estuary to our welcoming Alameda Marina berth.

Even after an uproarious ride north, we still came away feeling that we enjoyed sailing the open ocean. This initial sea trial was what we needed to confirm our plans for the next cruise. The storm had given us a confidence that we had not known before. We had dealt with our fears and survived a dangerous situation. *Harmony* had proven herself seaworthy and a good companion for our boating adventures. She turned out to be a solid boat that we now had tested, if not to her limits, certainly to ours. Like a faithful steed she had dazzled us with her performance.

Hey There, Dreamboat

~ Designing the Master Plan ~

A typical cruising plan is *'written in the sand at low tide.'* On land we are accustomed to having logically thought out agendas, itineraries, schedules, and appointments, but on the sea, these can become mere suggestions. The weather conditions and the ocean's temperaments are too variable and capricious to be captured and locked up in the cage of time. Like a bird, a sailor is free to roam, but only on the time line of the rhythms of the sea, the changing seasons, and the heartbeat of the earth. While creating tentative plans, we try not to find ourselves in the classic dilemma of having to sail into rough weather to meet a schedule. When we lock in plans by inviting family or friends, or to catch a plane flight home, we make sure to leave plenty of time and not compromise our safety and comfort.

We have known several couples who set a departure date to begin their cruising adventure, only to find that they were not ready. They postpone their trip for a week, a month, and sometimes, due to extenuating circumstances, wait until the beginning of the following cruising season. Weather is always a paramount determiner of plans and every year the weather gods throw in a few surprises. Is it El Niño or La Niña or a heavy storm or hurricane season, or is it a year when strange low-pressure systems bring rainy weather to an otherwise dry season?

On our trial run to San Diego and back to San Francisco, we decided to take a two-month vacation from our business. We originally thought we might make it to Cabo San Lucas in Mexico, but early on it became obvious that San Diego was a more realistic destination. A thousand miles in a sailboat translated differently than the same distance by car. We had a relatively easy harbor-hopping trip south to San Diego with time to recoup, celebrate the winter holidays, and tend to the fix-it list, before we had to bring the boat home. On the trip north, we allotted only a month for the voyage back to the Bay Area and that month was January, a notoriously stormy month. With two weeks waiting out the weather in Santa Barbara, we had less than two weeks to bash north. If we had allowed more time for the return trip there would have been enough pleasant sailing days with the added bonus of having plenty of time to explore towns along the way when the blustery weather kept us in port. For our next trip, we would factor all that into the equation.

With a saltier perspective, we began to make plans for our first cruising season to Mexico. Rearranging our fair schedule enabled us to squeeze out a generous four months for our excursion south of the border. We planned to sail down the Baja coast and eventually put our boat on the hard in San Carlos, near Guaymas across from the Baja Peninsula in the Sea of Cortez. Our business commitments required us to be home by the first of March.

When we created our master cruising plan, we had a general

idea of where and when we would be traveling, and then allotted some elbow room for unexpected circumstances along the way. A long-range itinerary will be in constant flux as life pitches its curve balls into the plans. One of Robert's dreams is to sail under the Verrazano Bridge into New York Harbor, alongside the Statue of Liberty and Ellis Island, where his four grandparents immigrated in the early 1900's. Our initial plans were to sail out the Golden Gate Bridge, and take the proverbial left on our way south to Mexico. We would proceed along to Central America through the Panama Canal, experience the Caribbean islands, and motor up the Inter-Coastal Waterway and on to New York City. After all if you look on a map, it's only a few inches to here and a few inches to there.

At the college orientation for one of our daughters, we were informed that half of the students enter with an undecided major, and if they did choose a subject to major in, many change it before they graduate. The university experience alters a student's perspective when they leave home and discover what their interests truly are, unencumbered by their parent's expectations. Like freshman entering college, many first time cruisers reach the cruising grounds only to find that their plans change drastically. U.S. and Canadian West Coasters have to decide whether to sail further south or west, or return home, bashing north. Slowing down and spending time in Mexico is usually an attractive option. Central America and the Panama Canal sound intriguing, but it can be an ambitious goal for one season. For the long distance mariners, a fleet of boats is gearing up to go on the three thousand mile voyage to the South Pacific and are busily preparing for the *Puddle Jump.*

If you want to sail many miles in a relatively short time, it is possible to reach Ecuador, the Caribbean, and the South Pacific from the West Coast in a season or two. The Mediterranean and the Indian

79

Ocean are more comfortably taken in two or more years. Of course for those hardy sailors with a competitive spirit, a circumnavigation can be accomplished in one to three years and the record to date is now 48 days [13] ,but that isn't a 'stop and smell the roses' kind of trip. Circumnavigating at a mellower pace is more often accomplished in a seven, ten or even a fifteen-year excursion. With determination, time, and money, a small, adventuresome group of cruisers sails further from home. There are marathoners, and there are those just out for a stroll, so the crew designs the trip that fits their idea of a good time. The cruising dream is a grandiose plan, sailing off into the sunset. Keeping an open mind cushions us from surprises when plans go awry. By allowing the experience to take the lead, we rest assured that when it is time to decide what the next move will be, it will become obvious. Once we left home and were out on the high seas we did what made us happy and traveled at our own comfortable pace. We go where we want to go and do what we want to do, truly living the *light fantastic*. When we are ready to stop cruising and move on to new endeavors, we will have memories to last a lifetime.

Hey There, Dreamboat

~ Throwing Off the Dock Lines ~

For the next year and a half following our trial run down the California coast, Robert worked on *Harmony* every Wednesday and on occasional weekends. Olivia was a senior in high school, and for the school year we hosted an AFS exchange student, Blanca Lopez-Rodriguez, from Seville, Spain. I enrolled in Spanish 101 at the local junior college, and with Olivia and Blanca's tutoring, I started to understand the fundamentals of the language. Robert studied for his HAM radio license, spending hours practicing test questions on the Internet. More time was devoted to deciphering the Morse code tapes, unraveling their hidden messages over and over again. When he was able to pass the on-line test with a high percentage, he took his technician license exam followed by his general exam with code. He passed them both, which enabled us to broadcast on the HAM radio bands and sign up for the Winlink e-mail service, free for HAM radio operators. (Fortunately for anyone wanting a HAM license today, the challenging Morse code requirement was eliminated several years ago.)

With the fall season approaching, a discernible chill in the air beckoned us snowbirds to sail to warmer climates. Olivia had graduated from high school and we hauled a vanload of her things to the University of California, Santa Barbara campus. We then wrapped up our business for the year and finished some last minute boat projects. Robert had several friends and gurus for mechanical, electrical, and computer advice and they helped him install our 12-volt generator. These hardy sailors encouraged us to go, with a consensus that we were ready and had enough equipment to cruise safely. They had seen too many wanna-be cruisers stay roped to the dock, waiting to install every gadget while running low on money or time and eventually placing their dreams on hold. Someday we hoped to be able to install solar panels, but installing the Ample Power Genset, a 12-volt, 200 Amp, diesel generator to charge our batteries turned out to be the right choice. A HAM/SSB radio was purchased and our friend, Sparky, the computer whiz, helped us set up the system, and showed us how to install the copper foil ground-plane. A Pactor modem, hooked up between the radio and our lap top computer, was tested allowing us to send and receive e-mail at sea. Our son, Eugene, rode up in the bosun's chair to install the antenna on the backstay. As a special gift for *Harmony*, we ordered a new dodger with removable sides that totally enclosed the cockpit. Scotty, our canvas man toiled late into the last light of the evening, securing the Sunbrella covering and isinglass windows over the aluminum supports. Once again we set Columbus Day for our blast off date, but this time instead of the coast of California we were off to explore Mexico.

October 12, 2000 was a sparkly, sun-drenched day, filled with fresh, sweet smelling air that followed a stretch of inclement weather. Since a blustery storm had lambasted the Bay Area for a week, there were other sailboats geared up, like racehorses anxiously waiting in their starting gates for the gun to go off, to charge out the Golden Gate. In the early morning, our friends from the marina again helped us cast off our lines, and the curtain opened up on our dream of a lifetime. We sailed down the estuary in the shadow of the high-tech company, Wind River where our daughter, Rose was employed at the time. Calling her on our cell phone, she and her colleagues came out to give us a rousing farewell and we waved to each other until we were out of sight around the bend at Jack London Square.

Under the Bay Bridge we motored on calm, gray seas, skirting the romantic San Francisco waterfront. Coit Tower loomed over us, and brought back memories of long walks through Little Italy when I lived on the edge of Chinatown. The cable cars were revving up for a day of carrying tourists up the steep hills 'halfway to the stars.'[14] We were living our dream, leaving San Francisco Bay after working hard, raising our children, and putting them through college. Everything felt so good and to see the city from the water reminded me of the delightful times spent there. I thought about where we had met thirty years before and our marriage license, the symbol of our commitment that created all of this, filed away safe and secure in the halls of the domed City Hall. Sailing in between the Embarcadero piers and Alcatraz Island, we set our sights towards the Golden Gate Bridge. The warming sun had scattered the morning mist and we could see four yachts in front of us and five more behind, with two large freighters steaming into the Bay. It was invigorating to actually be underway on our great adventure! Several of the boats in our small fleet sailed with us to Half Moon Bay and the rest glided over the waves, pushing on further south to Monterey and destinations beyond. Perfect fifteen-knot winds from the NW blew us to our first harbor, where we anchored amid other yachts. While the sun disappeared amidst pastel rays illuminating the lighthouse overlooking Pillar Point, we felt the incredible elation that comes from having taken our first step towards Mexico.

While Robert went below to take a shower, I began to prepare our celebratory dinner. Suddenly I was overcome with the acrid smell of an electrical fire and saw smoke rising from the panel. I yelled, "Fire!" and Robert immediately jumped out of the shower, naked and dripping wet. Frantically we searched for the source of the smoke. On a boat there is nothing scarier than a fire, with us sitting on two full tanks of diesel, not to mention three bottles of propane for the galley stove and gasoline for the dinghy. The smoke cleared almost as fast as it had appeared, and we discovered the source of the problem. A wire from a newly installed fixture had shorted out and the insulation had burned. Fortunately the breaker had tripped before anything else was damaged. With the adrenaline easing out of our systems, we tried to settle down by cleaning up the mess and eventually sat down to enjoy our meal. How lucky we were that it was an easy fix with no harm done. It was only our first day out, and we had experienced earth, water, wind and fire. What a complicated tango we were dancing with the elements!

In a repeat performance of our trial run we barreled down the California coast to Santa Cruz with a strong wind behind us, accompanied by the usual boisterous swell. Instead of being overpowered like we had been two years earlier, Robert had his systems in order and with a reefed main we bounded south at a comfortable seven knots. Our shoulder muscles were relieved since the autopilot was operating perfectly, and the many other improvements on *Harmony* made life easier on board. Having some open ocean miles under our keel instilled in us a splash of self-assurance.

While approaching Santa Cruz, someone on the tawny hills overlooking the ocean hailed us on the VHF radio. He wondered if we had seen his friends, a boat named *Jasmine Isle*. We mentioned that it might be the boat a few miles in front of us that we had been following all day. When we pulled into the Santa Cruz marina, the harbormaster gave us the usual instructions to raft up alongside another boat. As coincidence would have it we rafted up with *Jasmine Isle*. They welcomed us by throwing out extra fenders and catching our dock lines. Once we were settled we couldn't help but notice that our new neighbors had several piles of large black plastic bags stacked on their deck. When we asked what was going on, they told us their sad tale. They too were leaving for the southland. When they were under the Golden Gate Bridge near the south tower, a large container ship entering the bay from the opposite direction created such turbulence around the bridge stanchion that they watched to their horror while the bow nose-dived into a whirlpool. The day was warm, with light airs so they had their hatch and back portholes open to the cooling breezes. When their boat plunged into the hole, gallons of salty water came pouring down their front hatch drenching their newly covered cushions and bedding. More water came swirling down the decks and around into the aft portholes saturating everything with briny water. The big chore of the day was to wash all the covers and bedding to remove the salt. They were usually vigilant about closing their hatches when sailing out the Gate, however this beautiful, calm day had lulled them into complacency. The person hailing us on the radio as we approached Santa Cruz was their friend who was driving down to help them with their mountain of laundry. The unfortunate opening act to their cruising adventure didn't leave them discouraged, and over several years we followed our new friends' progress all the way to Florida.

On the short afternoon passage from Santa Cruz to Monterey our adult children, Audrey and Saul, came along for the ride. We had an invigorating romp across the bay while Saul, our avid fisherman, unwittingly caught a monster piece of kelp on his trolling line. The customary welcoming committee of dolphins zigzagged around us for miles and played in our bow wave. When the afternoon winds picked up and the white caps spread across the bay, they kept us company, bidding us adieu when we neared the seal encrusted breakwater. Saul had no luck with the fishing line so he fed his squid bait to a passing seal. To our chagrin, the insistent seal barked what sounded like, 'Saul, Saul,' next to our boat all night long begging for another handout.

After waving good-bye to Saul and Audrey at the dock the next morning we rounded the point of Monterey Bay, watching it fade into the morning haze, and pointed our bow south. Sailing gently by the sleeping giant, we paid our due respects to Point Sur, marveling at its changeable moods. Journeying through the night, we arrived at the entrance to Morro Bay, shrouded in a dense, pink blanket of fog, so thick we could barely see the bow of our boat. In the early dawn we made our way around the breakwater in the company of another sailboat that emerged behind us out of the gloaming. When we both docked at the yacht club we noticed that our fellow traveler did not have radar, and when we asked him how he managed to navigate through the impenetrable haze and dodge the numerous fishing boats outside the bay, he answered, 'What fishing boats?'

After a pleasant stopover to shower, do laundry and explore the quaint fishing town of Morro Bay we continued on to Point Conception. Motor-sailing under a thick, gray marine layer on calm seas, the otters and seals entertained us while they fed in the abundant kelp beds. That night we traveled cocooned in a deep, black shroud of fog, spotting nothing on the radar except for a few oilrig service boats. When we rounded Point Arguello the lighthouse beam streamed out, piercing the dense fog, and the wispy white remnants of mist scattered while we crept close by. To change the mood our autopilot suddenly stopped working. Robert tried to fix it, but since it was a mere ten miles before we reached the Cojo anchorage, I volunteered to hand steer the rest of the way. A lopsided, waning, orange moon rose magically over the coastal range, while dolphins jumped in the moon glow over glass-like seas. Cheers were the order of the night when we approached The Point in a flat calm. The memory of us pounding our way north through high, turbulent seas two short years before was still fresh, but this time we were able to glide past the fickle cape in tranquil splendor. The Conception Point lighthouse was broadcasting its bright beam across the water, and with things under control, Robert went below for a nap. I was motoring along enjoying the nighttime beauty when I realized the lighthouse was no longer shining its comforting glow. I thought maybe I was off course and for a minute I looked around trying not to panic. After I plotted our bearing on the charts and took a radar and compass reading, I knew that we were right where we should be. We have an agreement that if anything weird happens at night to wake up the off watch and Robert came sleepy eyed into the cockpit to have a look. The fog had not returned but the Point Conception light was dark. While motoring by, the outline of the white lighthouse showed up against the barren hills in the moonlight and there was definitely no rotating beacon. The light on a major California promontory was out! Cautiously making our way around the point leaving plenty of sea room, we dropped anchor at rustic, weather-beaten Cojo. The dense fog then rolled in from the shore to greet us under the lee of this majestic cape.

After catching up on our sleep and repairing the autopilot, we rowed our dinghy over to say hi to the folks on the only other cruising boat in the anchorage. That evening while the sun was setting we shared some wine with Will and Lucinda of *Sweet Water*. They were also going to Santa Barbara the next day and became our first buddy boat. *Sweet Water* accompanied us on our trek along the warmer, oil rig-dotted coast and from time to time we would chat with them on the VHF.

We sailed within hollering distance of Olivia's dormitory at the University of Santa Barbara, across the oil slicked waters off of Coal Point. Once we were settled in the marina, Olivia lent us her car and we used her dorm's laundry facilities, happily reversing the child/parent roles. On a pleasant Southern California evening, seven of her dorm mates boarded *Harmony* for a sunset cruise outside the Santa Barbara Harbor. Olivia's new friend, Allison was starry eyed and said that now she had a reason to finish college and get a job, so she could afford a boat and join the next generation of cruisers.

Our daughters, Olivia and Rose accompanied us on the next leg to Oxnard, with *Harmony* weaving its way through a sailboat race returning from Anacapa Island, their billowing spinnakers flying. To have had our adult children take different segments of the journey and share our dream always added a special dimension. They were a hardy, enthusiastic, and supportive crew and we had a wonderful sail watching our travels unfold through their eyes.

In the early morning we dropped the girls off in Oxnard to catch the train back to Santa Barbara, and left the harbor with a light breeze and all sails set. A kayaker, a big freighter, and *Harmony* were the only boats out on the water when about an hour out of port, a Santa Ana wind suddenly started blowing 40-knots plus, instantly heeling our boat over to the rail. We rushed to release the sheets, drop sail, and mull over what to do next. When we checked the continuously updated NOAA weather report on the VHF, they predicted that the Santa Ana would blow itself out and calmer weather would return by the afternoon. It was an easy choice to hoist the reefed sails and continue south to Marina Del Rey on the north shore of Los Angeles. The wind let up as soon as we sailed under the lee of Mugu Point where the steep mountains drop into the sea and the wind doesn't funnel so violently down the canyon chutes. Several hours later and for the rest of that day the Coast Guard sent out a bulletin on Channel 16 for any word of a kayaker out of Oxnard who had not returned. We wondered if that was the same paddler who had left with us that morning. It was a violent windblast in our 40-foot boat, and we hoped that he returned home safely.

In Marina Del Rey we picked up our friend and fellow artist, Lee Risler [15], to crew with us to San Diego. Lee is the founder of Kiwi Sandals and has been a leather craftsman for many years as well as a sailor and a surfer. Early one morning on his way to an arts and crafts show in Southern California, a vehicle sideswiped his van and sent him careening off the highway over a steep embankment. He landed in a dense thicket of trees that trapped him in his truck. He yelled for help and honked his horn until the batteries ran low, but to no avail. Who could hear him in the noisy rush down the Los Angeles freeway? In trying to cut himself free, Lee chopped off his thumb and first three fingers with his knife then used his little finger as a 'handle' to pull his hand from the first trap only to discover that he was also pinned at the elbow by another branch. When he pulled his hand free, the branches clicked shut with a loud crack. He was so happy that he still had a free hand, but his other arm was still ensnared. Later he attempted to cut off his trapped arm, but that was too much and he blacked out. He spent three days entangled in his vehicle until a highway worker noticed the wreckage and called for help just hours before it would have been too late. When he regained consciousness, his rescuers were cutting him away from the van and he remembered being rushed to the hospital. His wife could hardly recognize him and he was unable to swallow due to dehydration. His arm, unfortunately, had to be amputated above the elbow. Lee became a celebrity overnight, featured on the *Today Show* as a hero and a man who had beaten the odds. He made appearances on the *Oprah Winfrey Show* and was all over the news. His bravery, strength, not to mention his wonderful sense of humor, and strong supportive family sustained him through his healing process.

The following year when we were set up next to Lee at one of our big craft shows we filled him in on our cruising plans and showed him pictures from our trial run. Lee had an open invitation to come on whichever leg he would like, and in Los Angeles, he took us up on the offer. What a thrill and honor for us to have him in our midst, aboard *Harmony* alive and well. We spent hours listening to the story of his ordeal and it was both amazing and horrible. There were times when we had to take breaks to integrate the pain-filled story before he could continue.

Newport Beach was the usual, comfy stopover where we hooked up to the five-dollar mooring balls. The warm welcome from the harbormaster, and a refreshing hot shower was a perfect ending to a long but pleasant day cruising down the Southern California coast.

Much to Lee's chagrin we motor-sailed in the customary light Southern California airs. He was ready to fly the spinnaker all the way to Oceanside, but no wind meant turning on the Iron Genny. Oceanside, a sweet overnight stop, has guest docks that are easy to negotiate. Soon after we landed, a sport fisherman came in hauling a huge fish tied to his aft step that turned out to be a thresher shark. The thresher has a long broad tail that is used as a bludgeon to hit and stun his prey when he swims through a school of fish. The shark then turns around and swims back through the school feeding off of the injured fish. These fishermen had caught it by the tail, which resulted in a four-hour fight. When they finally brought it in close to the boat, they finished it off with a few pistol shots to the head. They asked if we could lend them a hand and Lee, always the joker, cheerfully held up the stump of his arm and said, "I already gave at the office." Lee and Robert then helped the fishermen wrestle the shark onto a cart where it was taken to the scales. Local spectators crowded around and a spontaneous pool was started to guess the shark's weight and length.

The monster fish turned out to be 11 1/2 feet long and weighed a hefty 254 lbs. Our reward was several thick shark steaks that we cooked on the grill. What a delicious feast it was! Eating from the sea's fresh bounty, we were evolving from a long tradition of being vegetarians to *pescatarians* (pez being the Spanish root word for fish). Our diet now included seafood with our grains, legumes, fruits, and vegetables.

On the last day of our California sail into San Diego the perfect wind that we had been promising Lee materialized. *Harmony* cautiously meandered through the kelp beds off of Point Loma and we were glad to be sailing, because our motoring prop would have become fouled with clumps of seaweed. After dropping Lee off on Coronado Island, where his wife met him, we continued on down the bay to our Chula Vista berth. Friends who we had met two years earlier caught our dock lines; a sweet homecoming.

While waiting for Jim Pederson who would crew with us down the Baja Coast, we did our final U.S. provisioning. Deciding to have a third person to share the watches was a wise choice since we had little experience with such a long passage that included three overnight legs. Also our insurance company encouraged us to have extra crew for safety's sake. Finally on a late October afternoon with hurricane season almost over, we pointed our bow towards Mexico.

Under drizzly afternoon skies we gave Jim a turn at the wheel while we navigated through busy shipping traffic, under La Loma Point and between the numbered buoys that mark the San Diego bay entrance. The grayness could not dampen our high spirits when we cruised passed the Coronado Islands and entered Mexican waters. What an exhilarating feeling to cross the international border at sunset, then sail by the twinkling lights of Ensenada on our way toward Turtle Bay. The prevailing northwest winds and swell continued to push us south. Robert experimented with his HAM radio flipping through the channels until he found some *good old boys* chatting away. When he joined the conversation and told them he was sailing in Mexico, the tone turned serious and they admonished him in no uncertain words to turn right around and head back to safe U.S. waters. They wondered if we were carrying a gun because we were going to need it! Robert tried to humor them while explaining that it was illegal to bring firearms into Mexico. Too bad that this kind of xenophobia discourages would be vacationers from exploring the colorful and accommodating world of our closest neighbor to the south. At sunrise the next morning we were south of Ensenada gliding along at a pleasant pace. The lack of potable water, unpaved roads, and long distances from towns preserves this isolated paradise. Harbor hopping down this coast is an option but we decided to sail the conventional way; three overnighters and rest stops at Turtle Bay, Bahia Santa Maria, and then on to the tip of the Baja Peninsula, Cabo San Lucas.

Each year in early November, the Baja Ha Ha cruiser's race and rally follows the same course. More than one hundred and fifty sail boats with an occasional trawler, depart from San Diego bound for a lively party in Cabo San Lucas, land's end. Many cruisers use the Baja Ha Ha as an alarm clock to signal their departure from U.S. waters. The deadline not only motivates them with a specific time line but there is a feeling of safety in numbers not to mention all the fun parties. They meet new people interested in the same lifestyle while learning from the more experienced sailors. The group stays in contact by VHF and SSB, (the short wave radio that most of us have on board) and a morning radio net that includes weather reports and check-ins from the fleet. Some cruisers complain that the pace is too fast and opt for a slower trip, but many appreciate this rally which sets a date to cut the ties to shore and head south to Mexico. Since we still had our seasonal tie-dye business, we were limited to a four-month window for our first foray into Mexico. The plan was to reach La Paz and put *Harmony* in the marina so we could return stateside to be with our family for Thanksgiving. In order to ensure a coveted spot in the usually crowded marinas we made sure that we were out in front of the rally. (Since 2000, several more marinas have been built in the La Paz area creating more space for cruisers even during the busiest season.) As the indented coastline of Baja faded away, we found ourselves fifty-miles off shore with the sun rising over the Pacific to the east. West coast sailors rarely see a sunrise over the ocean unless they are far out to sea. We gathered on deck in the morning calm to snap pictures to celebrate our first day in Mexico and the realization that we were further off shore than we had ever been before.

After breakfast we freshened up with warm showers, and then experienced the scare of our lives. Hearing something unusual, Robert looked below to check on the engine and found salt water filling the bilge, spraying around the engine room. He immediately hit the emergency bilge pump that sucked the water out in no time, but much to everyone's consternation, water continued to flow in. All three of us frantically looked around to see if we could locate the source of the incoming water. Eventually we discovered the culprit, a hose siphoning water from the bilge pump. When we were sailing hard, the aft end of *Harmony* settled down into the sea and the bilge pump thru-hull would be below the water line. There is a slow, normal drip from the shaft packing gland and when the bilge pump went off it created a siphon for seawater to flow back in. When we slowed the boat down, the stern lifted out of the water and the siphon was broken. From then on we kept a close eye on things and we had no more trouble. When we assessed the damage, besides everything in the engine room coated with salt, our starter for the engine and the fresh water pump were the only casualties. (When we reached La Paz we moved the thru-hull to a higher place on the hull and permanently fixed the problem.) We continued to sort things out while we approached Cedros Island north of Turtle Bay, and began to experience the rough seas often associated with this 4000-foot high island. The winds barrel down the mountainsides, creating their own Santa Ana like conditions. The seas were awash in white and *Harmony* was sailing hard. Instead of pushing on to Turtle Bay and landing there in the pitch dark of a moonless night, we found a sweet anchorage on the east side of Cedros called La Palmita. The legendary Manila galleons of old supposedly stopped here at a fresh water spring to refill their barrels. Our old guidebook noted that early mariners planted palm trees around the spring to make it easier to spy from off shore. Sure enough, our GPS brought us close enough to spot the green palms and we made our way through the kicked up seas to find a calm anchorage in fifteen feet of water, our first anchorage in Mexico. We had arrived safely after an adrenaline packed day.

After a moment to take in the new majestic scenery, Robert went to work replacing the fresh water pump with, lucky for us, a spare. He also dried out and did a temporary fix on the starter motor. Thankfully, we were up and running again. Cedros Island turned out to be a welcomed stop. Seawater pouring into the boat had been disconcerting to say the least, but it turned out that everything was okay, and we tried to ease back into the rhythms of cruising. Our first mate went off on an exploratory swim to shore while Robert made the repairs. Jim discovered the spring populated with frogs and brought home a lobster for dinner.

After a peaceful night's rest at our Cedros Island paradise, our nerves relaxed, and our engine purring in the morning calm, we ventured across the Dewey Channel on our way to Turtle Bay. This was our first stop ashore on Mexican soil. We followed *Charlie's Charts* [16] for our cruising guide and also liked the 1972 *Baja Sea Guide, Volume*

II [17], from my father's library. It is filled with knowledge of the local conditions and hazards, along with interesting stories, and historical accounts of the early explorers. We learned that this area was famous for Scammons Lagoon, a large breeding ground for the California gray whales. The whalers of yore would herd the large mammals in towards the shoal waters for the slaughter that eventually decimated them. In recent years, from December through March, the protected whales have returned in increasingly large numbers. A small plane flew overhead and landed at an airfield on one of the nearby islands. Our guidebook mentioned that these small planes fly in with provisions, and carry adventurers searching for a distant get-away. When approaching the peninsula we spotted machinery for harvesting salt, a major product of the Baja.

While making for the entrance to Turtle Bay, a panga, a Mexican open fishing boat, approached and hailed us making it clear using universal sign language that they wanted to trade some lobster for beer, sodas, or candy. The fishermen's bucket was full of live lobsters, their antennae reaching over the rim, searching for a way back to the sea. Having lost track of the days, the fact that it was Halloween never crossed our minds, and yet trick-or-treaters had found us out in the wilds of the Pacific Ocean. Since our larder was empty of candy and sodas, we gave them coffee, beer and trail mix, which seemed to satisfy them. When we entered Turtle Bay and pulled up to the fuel dock, losing track of what day it was became more apparent, for queued up on the high pier waiting to greet us, the children were chanting, 'Halloween, Halloween.' We handed out fresh fruit, raisins, and nuts, but we were no match for the late model powerboat that pulled up beside us. They had prepared little plastic zip-lock bags of treats for each of the children, who were patiently waiting for any arriving yacht.

To top off our diesel tanks for the long trip to Cabo San Lucas, we were told to Med-tie to the rugged pier that rose twenty-feet above our heads. Our first attempt at dropping the anchor and then backing up to a pier turned out to be a stressful exercise, compounded by the Fathometer reading of shallow water. Apparently it is a spectator sport as well as a test for how well we worked as a team. We didn't disappoint the fans, making several attempts before we had it right. A large fishing boat was in front of us filling up with 2500 liters of diesel piped in through what looked like a garden hose strung from the pier to the small ship. It appeared to be a several hours wait so Jim and I took the opportunity to go ashore, and left Robert to watch *Harmony*. Rowing our hard dinghy to the pier, we climbed up the steep, rusty ladder and were welcomed by several boys offering to watch our skiff and take us shopping. Giving one polite and eager boy the dinghy-watching job, we hired another as our guide and off we went up a hill to the village. Ricardo was accommodating and steered us around to one aunt or cousin after another who had little shops in front of their homes. It was an interesting exercise to find everything we needed from four or five sparsely stocked *tiendas*. In our halting, newly acquired Spanish, we talked to Ricardo about his dreams. He said he was saving up his money to go to the university to become a doctor; expansive dreams about the future from a dusty, isolated town. Wishing him the best, we paid him for his services, gave some coins to our dinghy guard, and shared a large bag of cookies with him and his fellow trick-or-treaters.

After a restful stop at Turtle Bay we aimed south on our second leg of the Baja run. The elongated Baja Peninsula has two huge bites taken out of its shoreline. On our rhumb line south, we navigated from point to point, fifty miles offshore. Jim, a meteorologist from Sacramento spent time with pad and pencil explaining the intricate interactions of pressure systems that cause the winds and weather. The winds from a high-pressure system flow into the low-pressure system. The prevailing winds in the northern latitudes flow west to east. The combination of these pressures with temperature and humidity creates our weather. Words like convection, Coriolis Effect, and catabatic winds were added to our vocabulary. When the southwest winds blow on the west coast they signal the approach of a low-pressure storm system and a strong, northwest wind following the storm means the system has moved on to the east. A land mass jutting out into the water can create different weather patterns than far out at sea. We tried to grasp his illustrations and pick up some valuable knowledge from an expert. Jim was also old school and suggested that we look out of the portholes and trust our own observations. The high, wispy *mare's tails* racing across the sky was a sign to the clipper ship captains of old that there was plenty of wind to set the numerous, square sails, and put some nautical miles behind them. Happy or popcorn clouds scatter across the sky on a mild, pleasant day. Frontal systems have a distinct line separating the heavy, rain-weighted, dark, cloudbank from the clear, blue sky. There was no doubt about what a front looked like after our harrowing trip up the California coast. We were beginning to piece together an understanding of how significant the weather was to this cruising endeavor. In exchange for Jim's help, we stopped for an afternoon, anchoring off of Hipolito, so he could surf the well-known but rarely visited, isolated break. Our crewman enjoyed several hours of solo surfing fun before we were off on our second overnight trip, wandering south. During our long watches, wee hour conversations turned to the personal, our histories, relationships, and the infinite.

Late the following day the cliffs of Santa Maria Bay glistened a fiery orange, reflecting the setting sun, and whales spouted their greetings, while we carefully glided by the entrance reefs into the sheltered anchorage. Bahia Santa Maria's isolated beauty and untouched miles of white, sandy beaches, embraced us in its primordial stillness and peace. It lies beneath Punta Lazaro, a dangerous promontory where many a ship (one cruising boat as recently as 2010) has been washed ashore by the currents that often confused navigators before GPS. The early mariners thought they were giving the point a wide berth, when in actuality the swift currents were driving them towards shore. An old rusty hulk still looms menacingly on the beach, a warning to all. If we had it to do over again, we would pencil in more than a couple of days to explore this gorgeous bay.

Santa Maria to Cabo San Lucas is the last big jump down the Baja coast. Magdalena Bay soon appeared, a good stop if the weather turned sour, or if we had needed diesel or supplies. Setting our GPS waypoints *Harmony* sailed out for our third and final overnighter. When Robert came on his watch later in the afternoon and did his usual lat/long reading, he noticed that we were further off shore than we should have been. After double-checking the waypoints, he realized that we had punched in longitude 110 instead of 109. The magical GPS has taken the mystery and uncertainty out of navigation, guiding us to within yards of our destination every time, unless we humans punch in the wrong coordinates or disregard a protruding promontory. The skipper caught the mistake soon enough and we were only fifteen miles off course. On the other hand, since we were further off shore, we had to battle waves banging amid ship while beam reaching to Cabo instead of having the wind behind us. The seas also began to build. It seems that whenever we make a mistake in navigation, we have to pay with some extra uncomfortable hours of heaving and pitching. We hailed a sailboat closer into shore, and the captain aboard *Ornery* (meaning Eagle's Aerie in Swedish) confirmed that it was no picnic where he was either. He was going out on the foredeck to change to a smaller jib. *Ornery's* crew which was aboard an old wooden Swedish built boat was traveling back to their homeland. Over the next several years we followed their progress while they traversed the Panama Canal into the Caribbean and crossed the Atlantic to Europe.

Sailing hard around Cabo Falso, *Harmony* bounced and bumped into the choppy waters at the far tip of the Baja Peninsula. As soon as we were behind the famous picturesque rocks at Land's End, the Arches and Neptune's Finger, the wind and seas moderated. Anchoring off the beach in twenty feet of water in front of the opulent hotels, we celebrated our arrival elated that we had reached this major milestone on an awesome journey. After a pleasant sleep and a delicious Mexican meal at a nice restaurant, we bid farewell to Jim and thanked him for being such a great crewman. He continued his vacation by spending a week surfing the Pacific Coast of Baja before flying home to California.

It wasn't too long ago that Cabo San Lucas was only a small fishing village with nothing but a cannery. Our old guidebook wrote of a single light on in the town. Boat after boat, entering the harbor at night, reported no lights at all. Now the shoreline sparkles with numerous luxury hotels lining the beach, and the marina is filled with boats paying an exorbitant amount for a berth. The tourist fishing fleet charges out in rush hour fashion in the early dawn, and by mid-afternoon the fishermen are racing back to the docks displaying their different colored flags announcing their catch, Dorado (mahi, mahi) and bill fish. When we motored into shore in our small dinghy, the churned up waters of the bay made for a roller coaster ride. If it was not the stampeding herd of sport fishing boats, it was the speeding jet skiers and banana boats lined with squealing children. The cruise ship tenders charge to the dock, dumping their loads of tourists out for an afternoon of sipping the local quaffs, Cabo Wabos, and tequila shots, and shopping for an assortment of tropical clothing, trinkets, and colorful crafts.

Since Cabo San Lucas was our first port of entry into Mexico, it was necessary to check into the country with the Port Captain, Immigration, and Customs. This turned out to be a rollicking two-day adventure in red tape, interspersed with a grocery and laundry run, and local sightseeing. Fellow cruisers explained the dance steps; our first stop would be the Immigration office at one end of town. After filling out the forms, we were directed across the street to pay our fees at the bank. We took a number and a seat in the air conditioned waiting area, watching for our number to appear in red lights above the tellers. The professionally dressed clerk behind the window stamp, stamp, stamped the papers with a flare, and we returned to Immigration for several more approval stamps. Our next stop was to the copy shop to photocopy eight different papers. Each step took place at a different location in offices across town, so we shared taxi rides with a fellow cruising couple also doing the check-in cha-cha. After stopping for a great meal of tacos and tortillas cooked over an open wood fire, we visited the customs agent who wanted to see our boat before he would grant us our ten-year, vessel import permit. Arranging for him to come aboard that afternoon, we agreed to pick him up on the beach in our dinghy and bring him out for a look. By the afternoon, the wind had come up and the waves made a dinghy ride more adventurous than he had anticipated. The official requested that we pull up to the fuel dock for an inspection and the next day after paying our fee, he issued our certificate.

Finally with all of our ducks in a row, we visited the Port Captain with the official paperwork in hand. After a cursory look at our stamped documents, he noticed that an important paper was a copy instead of the original. We must have given the original to the customs agent. Oye! Quickly volunteering to hike the ten blocks back up the hill in the blazing, afternoon sun to exchange them was met with a stern gaze. He stood and looked at us saying 'uno momento,' shuffled the papers one way, and then shuffled them again while we stood patiently waiting. Perhaps this wait, stop, and shuffle routine had royally peeved some antsy, irritated mariner and the official was waiting to see if we would provide them with an afternoon of soap opera drama. Continuing to wait quietly and respectfully, at last he stamped the documents, and we were free to go. The anticipated ruckus would have to wait for a more impatient customer.

In the last few years things have changed. The crew still checks in and out of Mexico and receives their visas and a ten-year import permit for the boat. However, once we check in there is no need to do this same song and dance at every port like we did for the first five years of our Mexican cruising. The local port captains now have their own preferences. A few officials prefer that we come into their office to fill out some paperwork, but without the run to the bank to pay the fee. When we are docked at a marina, the marina office takes care of the check-in/check-out procedure. Mexico has become a cruiser friendly country and we feel honored to partake of their warm hospitality.

We had officially arrived in Mexico! The Mexican people were friendly, and forgiving of our broken Spanish. They graciously welcomed us to their country. Everything was new, exciting, and sometimes a bit confusing and daunting. Despite the turbulent seas, mechanical breakdowns, and miscellaneous scares, we were still enjoying our cruise. The positives far outweighed the negatives and we were ready for some of the quiet Mexican anchorages that we had heard so much about.

Having finished up the required paperwork, we were ready to travel north to La Paz, venturing into the Gulfo de California, also known as the Sea of Cortez. The weather report called for winds on the nose in the range of ten to twenty knots. Sounding like perfect San

Francisco Bay Area sailing conditions, we left Cabo on a beautiful clear day. We rounded the first point, Cabo San Jose, following the eastern coast of Baja. When we sailed out from under the protective cape where we were enjoying five to ten knot winds, the situation changed drastically. Instantly we found ourselves pounding into choppy, refrigerator-sized waves. We had been pleasantly motor-sailing at five to six knots when all of a sudden we were crawling along at one to two knots. When we hit a wave it stopped us cold. The boat would shutter, the motor would grind us back up to four or five knots, and then with a bang we were back to one knot with seawater spraying over the decks. We tried cracking off to starboard but found the beam seas even more uncomfortable and we were going the wrong way. A passing sailboat on his way south assured us on the VHF that it was rough, but that we could make it since conditions were supposed to improve. For him they did for sure, since he was sailing with the wind and the waves, and he soon ducked under the lee of the cape. For us the screaming winds from the East Cape effect built to thirty-five knots, and spray was blown off the tops of the waves, occasionally creating surface whirlpools around us. The water was coming over the bow and dodger as if fifty-five gallon drums were being dumped on us, making it impossible for the scuppers to keep up. Four to six inches of water in the gunwales added more weight to the boat, slowing us down. The wind and pounding waves forced seawater through the zippers of the dodger into our enclosed cockpit. With our 100-horsepower engine and twenty-four inch, three-blade prop, we eventually, after eight hours of battle, pulled into the protected Los Frailes anchorage. An experienced sailor, well versed in local conditions, would never have left Cabo in the first place knowing that a norther was blowing. If they had attempted it they would have quickly turned tail back to the comfortable anchorage. Being rookies at the game, we crashed and banged for a day to learn our lesson. Never again became our refrain after that passage.

The next day with the winds calm and the skies a beautiful blue, we set sail, but soon turned back to wait for another day. The sea-state was still rough and confused and not suitable for comfortable travel. These seasonal blows easily build the seas up to eight feet and higher in some shallower areas. The swells, which are steep and close together in this narrow sea, have a long way to go before lying down. Apparently it takes a day or preferably two for the white bearded buffaloes to stop charging south. Every year a new class of sailors takes the turn around Cabo San Lucas aiming north to La Paz or east across the 200 miles of sea to Mazatlan. Unless they listen closely to the weathermen or ask for information, they risk bashing and crashing into a norther. When I hear on the radio nets of some new arrivals in Mexico rounding the Cape into these conditions, I sometimes have grabbed the mike and suggested that they wait for another day or two. After all, ladies and gentlemen don't need to go to weather when it's like that!

By mid-November we had landed in La Paz, put the boat to sleep in the marina and flew back to the U.S. to spend Thanksgiving with our family. Returning to Mexico for the winter holidays we hosted our crew on the *Harmony Hotel* at the islands north of La Paz. We had ten people on board enjoying the warm beauty of the Sea, swimming with the seals, snorkeling, fishing, not to mention holiday parties and festivities. Our adult children were in their twenties, were not married and there were no grandchildren in sight. We knew that this was a special time when all were free to come join us in Mexico for extended stays and we loved having them aboard.

When their vacation time was over and the last person departed on the bus to the airport, we still had two winter months left to cruise. While anchored off the tranquil town of La Paz, cuddled up together in our gently rocking bunk, I said, 'I really like this. Let's figure out how we can do it some more.' At that moment, all of our preparations and experience had culminated in a successful first venture into cruising. With a strong commitment, making our next plan was easy. We knew that we had more to learn and more challenges to face, but we had become comfortable with our partnership. We loved each other, we loved our shared adventure, and we would keep cruising for as long as it was fun. Our children had refilled our empty nest to overflowing with laughter and activity and now we had each other in our cozy love boat.

Ellie and Jack, cruisers who we had recently met at the marina in La Paz, suggested that we sail to Mazatlan. They were sure that we would love the town, and it would be a warm, pleasant place to spend the month of January. Following their advice, we spent three fun-filled weeks exploring this colorful city with all of its history, architecture and local culture. That left us a month for our trip north to explore the Baja and store our boat away for the summer above the hurricane zone. A month was actually plenty of time, but we often found ourselves pounding through rough, steep, upwind seas, bashing north into an unsettled ocean. During this trip we learned to relax about schedules and watch the weather with respect and patience. Since the winds often died down after sunset, night passages became a viable alternative. Sometimes leaving an anchorage at two in the morning, we arrived at the next stop before the afternoon blow, making the uphill trip bearable.

After a delightful few weeks of gunk holing in pristine, secluded anchorages, we finally reached San Carlos and started checking off the long list to decommission *Harmony* and put her safely on her stands in the Sonoran desert in Marina Seca (Dry Marina). The salt-encrusted sails and lines were taken down, washed clean with fresh water and fabric softener, and neatly put away in our V-berth garage. Messenger lines replaced the halyards so it would be easy to put them back up again in the fall. The dodger, dinghy and in later years, solar collectors were taken apart and the decks were cleared. The engine and outboard were put to sleep and the thru hulls plugged with green pieces of Brillo to keep bugs from making their nests. It's a three-day to a week job depending on the heat and our eagerness to be done with this arduous task. After checking off the last items on our list, we hopped on a comfortable bus, back across the U.S./Mexican border at Nogales, on to Tucson and then caught a flight home. Settling back into our other lives, we opened up our business again for the spring season's craft shows. Our friends and family welcomed us back home treating us like we were adventurers returning from some far corner of the earth. Even though we had only made it as far as Mexico, in a certain sense we had traveled to a distant shore. Everyone looked on our lifestyle as incredibly exotic, and envied our freedom. We entertained them with plenty of tales to titillate their imaginations.

Hey There, Dreamboat

~ Culture Shock ~

Traveling aboard *Harmony* for several months, she had begun to feel like home. Finally embarked on our dream-come-true adventure, we began to relax in the pleasant, new surroundings. During the first stage of our journey our eyes were filled with awe and excitement at all the new experiences, people, and places. After a few weeks in Mexico, culture shock began to sneak up on us and I began to feel somewhat overwhelmed by the whole endeavor. I missed family, friends, and the familiarity of home, and felt like a stranger in alien territory. Inevitably when traveling to new countries, sailors run up against language and cultural barriers and an economic disparity. A new reality sets in accompanied by annoyances that seemed to come from nowhere. Even though we had read every book we could lay our hands on, unsettling situations came up that could never have been anticipated. We had a difficult time finding a part that we needed. Our newly acquired Spanish was not always understood. The unhurried lifestyle was not what we fast-paced Americans were accustomed to. Our bodies occasionally rebelled with the appropriately named Montezuma's revenge. The inflatable dinghy sprang a leak and the outboard wouldn't start. Symptoms can range from feelings of loneliness, homesickness and even depression. It's not uncommon to find tears flowing and a sense of frustration.

When we first met, Robert had traveled for two years in Europe, the Middle East, and on to Afghanistan and Pakistan. Part of our initial attraction to each other was that we could relate when we spoke about our worldwide travels. Our two experiences nearly encircled the globe. When we went cruising we were accustomed to this culture shock phenomenon and were not totally taken by surprise.

When our Thoreau-like existence spent in nature on the outskirts of civilization became a difficult transition, relating with friendly cruisers was our key to sanity. One of the most empowering steps was to make new connections in the cruising community. When we made the effort to meet other cruisers who were also trying to flow with the unfamiliar routine of this different world, it wasn't long before our sea going lifestyle evolved into an easy going comfort zone. The opportunities to talk, laugh, and unwind with our valued friends helped relieve various stresses and strains. Most cruisers have gone through culture shock in one way or another and it was surprisingly easy to open up about our inner feelings with people who were recently strangers. We were soon laughing together about our faux pauxs and strange predicaments, humor being the best medicine to ease the pain.

Although at times I missed home and the grandkids, Robert had to deal with the dilemma of how to fix the boat without a West Marine or Home Depot around the corner. The added challenge was doing repairs without the convenience of jumping into his car to run quickly around town. In contrast to our hometown, there were no mega hardware stores that cater to our every need, however, in the last ten years Home Depots and Walmarts have proliferated in the larger towns. Typically there was a separate small, family-operated store for plumbing, electrical, motor parts, etc. The items were often behind the counter and the salesman could find what we needed if we knew the correct words. The book, *Spanish for Cruisers: Boat Repairs and Maintenance Phrase Book* [18] with all the boat and mechanical parts translated into Spanish helped us immensely when we had to scale the technical language barrier. There have been plenty of times when the shopkeepers would allow Robert to go back into rows of shelves to try to find that elusive widget. Requiring stainless steel components made the quest even more exciting. If one store didn't have a needed item, we were given directions to another shop that might or might not have what we wanted. Having equipment repaired, shipped from the U.S., or possibly fabricated from scratch, could be as stressful as the original break down.

On a pleasant afternoon at a Mexican marina, a group of men can usually be found drinking cervezas and discussing their boats' mysteries and idiosyncrasies, their adventures and fiascoes. They compare notes, and give each other advice, a pleasant replacement to the conversations around the old water cooler at the office. When we hear that other folks have been in the same or even worse predicaments than we have, it somehow takes the sting out of our own troubles. There is an incredible amount of expertise in the fleet and we can usually put our heads together to solve a boat problem. The bonding that goes on over a stalled engine creates a strong connection between new friends.

For those of us who are part-time cruisers, there is something that happens when we return home, a lingering regret that we have left our sailing paradise. Another side of culture shock emerges. Everything at home has mostly remained the same, but we arrive with a distinct feeling that we have changed. We have to make a shift back into our land life just like we did during our sailing life. With our home in two locations, we attempt to readjust into our new space and try to remember where we put things. We have solved some of this dilemma by owning two sets of the basics to minimize the inevitable situation of leaving something behind in our other life. Keeping updated lists helps me to keep our act together; a boat list, grocery list, and things to do lists. Now if I could just stop misplacing those slips of paper, everything would be fine!

When we bring back our tales from the sea, most everyone we meet is enchanted and it sparks wanderlust in their eyes. Occasionally they delve into the deep place within where they have stashed their dreams of adventure. Of course, there's a certain number of folks whose eyes glaze over and probably think we are weird.

Returning home can also result in climate shock. When Ron and Diane left La Paz, Mexico to return to Montana for the winter holidays they made sure that their relatives met them at the airport with their heavy coats and boots. Shorts, tank tops and sandals were unthinkable in 15-degree F weather.

On a return trip north through the Mexican border, we had our own taste of climate shock when we drove into a rare snowstorm. The border guards huddled in their thick coats, blowing on their freezing fingers. When we drove through the mountains of Southern California the following day everything was blanketed with several feet of snow and hordes of children were out riding their sleds, and throwing snowballs. The palm trees and hot temperatures of the tropics vanished like some distant, fairy tale realm, as we cranked up the heat and layered on the sweaters, long pants, and socks. On our return trips to California, we often traveled through various climate zones. When we left *Harmony* in temperate coastal Bahia de Caraquez, Ecuador, we boarded a relatively nice bus that snaked its way up the foothills of the chilly Andes Mountains to the 10,000 foot level capital, Quito. The next morning we were on a flight north with a stopover in tropically sizzling Costa Rica, and then on home to cold country again. It might take from seven hours to four days to reach the U.S. or Canada from the boat, traveling by taxi, bus, plane, and car.

Zooming into the United States, the land of overabundance and hyper-consumption, we faced a jangling cacophony of 'buy, buy, buy.' In the stores, amid a setting of sparkling merchandise, we were inundated with a myriad of choices of soap, toilet paper, and cereal. Freezing temperatures in our grocery stores made me wish I had worn a jacket. And the prices were shockingly higher than we were used to. One hundred dollars' worth of groceries filled half of a cart, where in Mexico or Ecuador our two carts would be overflowing.

The pace quickened and people hurried by with heads down, rushing on to their next chore, leery of a friendly stranger. We lost contact with which phase of the moon we were in and rarely had a dark enough sky to see the stars. Speed, sticker shock, traffic, cold temperatures, road rage, and folks who avoided a "good morning," were just the beginning of a shift into the fast U.S. culture. Things that seemed so important here were not our priority any more. It wasn't easy to hold on to the *no problemo* or *mañana* culture that helped us relax into the easy-going environment of Latin America.

When we eventually immersed ourselves in our land life, the boat seemed light-years away. It wasn't long before our family, the conveniences, the cleanliness, the choices, and the opportunities enveloped us. The boat, the sea, and that *other life* faded out like a dream, a sweet memory of another existence. But those beautiful sunsets, the swimming, the friendly people, and warm sailing breezes beckoned us to return.[19]

Finances

The boating community uncannily resembles the present day Farm in that each of us has our own boat and takes care of our individual finances. Beyond that, the community is a floating cooperative, living together and helping each other when needed. A Farm friend who visited us, remarked, 'This boat feels kind of like the old school buses, same size and shape, only on the water.'

Each cruiser decides which vessel to purchase or build, finding a boat that fits into their budget. Many of the really expensive yachts seem to spend an inordinate amount of time tied up in pricey marinas. The majority of boats that are doing most of the actual cruising for longer periods of time are older, affordable models that are paid for. A cruiser's biggest investment is the boat and equipping it with the essentials. After that, the cost of living can be surprisingly affordable.

There are numerous ways to make your cruising life possible. If you have valuable skills like mending sails or fixing engines, electronics and computers, you can find work in the cruising community. Several of our friends write for the sailing magazines or sell their artwork along the way. The Internet has opened up a whole new way to earn money while living far from home. To support the cost of sailing, cruisers occasionally dip into their retirement funds, social security, pensions, or investment portfolios. Most of us work in the off-season to fund our cruising habit. There are infinite ways for mariners to finance their lifestyle, the question being how much are you willing to invest in the fulfillment of your dream?

The debate continues on whether to sell your home or not. If you can afford it, leaving your home vacant, with a trustworthy house sitter, or short-term renter might be a good choice for your first foray out to sea. All options are still available once you have experienced cruising for a season. If it turns out that you want to return home after a year or two, there will be a house waiting for you. Most of the cruisers we know, who sold their homes, had some regrets. They had no place to call home when they wanted to take a break from cruising during the hot, humid, stormy off-season. Home prices were so exorbitant that they could not afford to buy back in their old area. Then the housing market collapsed and maybe they were the smart ones!

Selling your home creates options that might work out to your best advantage. You are free to go for a long, extended cruise with nothing holding you back and with money in your pocket. There is always the possibility that the place of your dreams may appear on the horizon at a most affordable price and you will have the funds to buy a home when you are ready to settle down. We know ex-cruisers who have bought or built their dream homes in Mexico, Ecuador, Panama, El Salvador, Costa Rica, New Zealand, Croatia, and Australia.

Downsizing worked for us. We rented out our four-bedroom home for three years and then sold it to capitalize on the tax break that comes from selling the home that we had lived in for two of the last five years. After three years we knew that we did not need such a large home with two living rooms, a game room and all the other amenities it came with. It was perfect when we were raising six children, but it was time to let a big family live in it again. We moved into our smallest rental property, which still had a great deal more square footage than our boat, and we loved having a place to hang our hat when we returned to the U.S. Our six-month on/six-month off cruising style required a land-based home where we could be with our children and grandchildren and still allow them their family space. During the summer months we worked on our houses and renewed the one-year leases with our renters or fixed up an empty house for a new tenant. The off season was filled with painting the rental properties, gutter work, building fences, along with the usual to-do repair lists that come with rentals, (not too dissimilar from a boat list). Over the years, we have honed our telepathic radar, our intuition, and gut feeling to be able to better weed out those renters who will be nothing but trouble. It is an inexact science and we still err occasionally. If you plan to rent your home, acquiring the skill of choosing good renters becomes the most important aspect of the business. You can hire a property manager, with the understanding that they will take a percentage of the profits. Choosing a righteous manager will relieve you of the headache of being overcharged when repairs are required.

If you live in an area where the real estate prices are high, for every mile that you move away from that epicenter, the homes become more affordable. Since you are downsizing, you might buy a smaller home or condo leaving you with enough money to cruise. For those of us with children, finding a home close to them becomes a goal. The only problem with that was a lucrative job or a new relationship might entice them to move away. You know how kids are. Another concern is the need to have a place near aging parents, where you can come home from time to time to check in. For those who decide to keep their home, renting it out in order to pay the mortgage or fill the cruising purse is the obvious option. It is a sacrifice to store your personal things and make the house presentable for someone else. While crunching the numbers and making some definitive choices the right plan will emerge.

Insurance is always a lively financial topic when we step out beyond U.S. and Canadian borders. Before we left the marina in Alameda we purchased yacht insurance for Mexico for about $1500 a year. Several years after we left the U.S. a major hurricane caused tremendous chaos in Baja, Mexico. Many boats were lost or sustained serious damage and after that, the insurance companies pulled out, drastically reduced their coverage, or increased their prices exorbitantly. Each year we dutifully signed the renewal notice to our insurance policy, not paying attention to the fine print. Several years later when we were making plans to sail further south to Central America, we called for a rider to cover us when we ventured past the Mexican border. The underwriter told us that they hadn't covered us in Mexico for years. Oh, My Goodness! When she asked if there was anything more she could do to help us, I said, 'Yes, please cancel the policy!' We asked around and found a company offering liability insurance, which costs us around $230 a year and covers us if we should hit a boat or injure someone while in Mexican waters. A certain number of cruisers pay thousands of dollars for yacht insurance especially when they are still paying for the boat, but liability seemed like the way to go for us. It is required at most marinas in Mexico and if we take good care to be safe, we will be okay. (Knock on wood.)

For medical coverage we started out with a policy from Multi-National Underwriters, which covered those of us who lived outside of the U.S. for six months or more out of every year. The price tag for this was $3500 a year for the two of us and seemed reasonable. Their prices rose quickly with each year that we aged, so we canceled that policy when we found that Blue Cross was less expensive. We now have a Blue Cross catastrophic plan for the two of us with a $2500 deductible per person. The deductible is high but when we are out of the country, we've found medical treatment to be inexpensive and comprehensive. We pay out of pocket to get regular check-ups by competent physicians in Mexico.

While we were out cruising there were financial choices to be made. A price tag came with a slip in a marina, dining out at restaurants, and taking inland trips. On the other hand, living on the hook at anchorages was a far less costly experience, with few places to spend money, except for an occasional beer at a palm frond-thatched palapa on the beach, or inexpensive groceries from a small town.

Finances

~ What Does It Really Cost? ~

Once we purchased our boat and equipped it with the necessary systems and gadgets, the cruising lifestyle turned out to be an economical way to live. The idea that cruising is the way to retire from the work-a-day world and have your pension, social security, savings, and investments stretch to meet your needs is true when you are in Mexico, or Central and South America. We have heard that the Caribbean, South Pacific, and the Mediterranean can be more expensive. Our boat is off the grid when we stay out of pricey marinas and we are somewhat self-sufficient. When boats have problems, parts can often be fixed or fabricated quite cheaply in the countries where the local people make things work for years beyond their planned obsolescence.

When our youngest child finished college, our sixteen-year tithe to the University regents ended. Although we sold our businesses, we were still as busy as ever (we just worked for free). We visit the children and babysit the grandchildren, participate at numerous family functions, travel, do all sorts of odd jobs around our houses, and help our children with their fix-it lists. Sometimes it makes us wonder how we had time for work.

Money or the lack of it can be a factor in determining how long you cruise. If repairs take their toll and marina costs run high, you may have to alter your plans to replenish the bank account. Cruisers have lived on incomes ranging from next to nothing to several thousand dollars a month. Factoring in travel back to the U.S., insurance, diesel, food, marina costs, haul out time, and holidays with our children, we have averaged over the years from between $1000.00 and $1200.00 per month while we are actively cruising. Many months when we are out at anchor, we have a hard time spending over $300 or $5 a day each. Travel costs back to the U.S., especially from distant ports such as New Zealand or Australia, can skew the average. Depending on your needs and plans, you will be able to adjust and estimate an appropriate budget.

It is common for yachties to cruise seasonally. They travel on their boats during the favorable seasons and then return home to work, travel, or visit with family. When cruisers want to head out for an extended time, their savings or investment income covers them. Many a mariner has found work in route far from home. Our friendly neighbor to the south, Mexico, does not want people doing any job that would jeopardize a local person's employment. However, many cruisers have skills that are welcomed wherever they travel. We have friends who are doctors, teachers, translators, yacht mechanics, boat electricians, surveyors, riggers, computer experts, editors, refrigeration and radio repairmen, writers, and artists who have been able to finance their trips as they go. A young cruising couple started a sail making and repair business, and musician friends have been able to pad their cruising funds playing at nightspots in ports around the world. But like many seasonal immigrant workers who head to the U.S. or Canada from Mexico, most cruisers return home to replenish their cruising kitty. The off-season is a perfect time to make money, and part-time jobs are available if you cannot or do not want to return to your old job. Of course the cost of living in the U.S. or Canada is high, and you have to work to pay your living expenses, the car, the house, the trappings of the old rat race.

Our friend, Karen, who lived in Colorado, had a flexible arrangement. She managed her office for six months of the year and her partner ran it when she was on her winter cruise. Karen's partner appreciated having the summer months off to vacation with her family. Some jobs are difficult to fill with qualified employees and your old boss may be thrilled to have you for whatever time you will give, welcoming you back with open arms. We know cruisers who work in the off-season as a nurse, anesthesiologist, tax-preparer, x-ray technician, artist, veterinarian, fisherman, firefighter, musician, and dental assistant. They all return to their former place of employment whenever they are home, filling in for co-workers eager to take their vacations. During the summer months, cruisers also work as park rangers, at music and racehorse venues, boat yards, non-profits, summer schools, or that old standby, the local West Marine store. There is surely a niche where you can feel valued and earn money at the same time. Sailors who have long-range plans for traveling to distant shores have found that they can consult, teach on-line classes, or edit manuals or legal briefs while living aboard.

In academia and in the corporate workplace, it is common to take sabbaticals. People go cruising and return to their job refreshed and inspired without losing their place on the career ladder. When companies and governments downsize, a would-be cruiser, nearing retirement, can take a buy out or early retirement and have some extra cash in their pocket. Everyone wins with compromises like these.

A certain number of sailors are disappointed when they run out of funds sooner than expected and have to alter course and return to work. There is a continuum from the young person who can sail around the world on an average of a few dollars a day to those who need a 200-foot mega-yacht to cruise comfortably. The general consensus is that an average budget of $1000 to $2000 a month for two people will leave you in good shape, depending on how far you roam and how many trips back home you make. It also depends on whether you live on your boat year round, frequent marinas, or have major boat repairs or equipment failures. There are many variables, but over the years we discovered what it costs to live within our means.

When we returned to the United States after living inexpensively on our boat we were surprised to discover that our bank account was in better shape than when we left. The monthly rents were deposited into our account while we were in distant anchorages far from civilization and our only expenses were groceries and an occasional fuel up. When we returned to California, the outflow of money stepped up with a car, repairs on our houses, boat parts on our need-it-list, and on and on. It became a simple math equation, that if we wanted to spend less, it was a good idea to stay out cruising.

Taking inland trips to explore new places is part of the fun and adventure of cruising that you don't want to miss. When traveling inland the boat is usually docked in a marina that can be more expensive than a berth in the U. S. The average price for a marina slip in Mexico is from $500 to $700 per month with discounted rates during the summer months. In certain locations the prices can be as high as $800 or more. To store our 40' sailboat on the hard during the off-season the cost is around $160 per month. Some marinas offer lower rates for docks with only water and no electricity and some are no more than a place to tie up. In El Salvador we were able to anchor in the river for free. Friendly neighbors kept an eye on our boat, while we went on an inland trip to Guatemala. A mooring ball up the tidal Chone River in Ecuador was $270. In other words there is something for every budget.

Travel, whether by *chicken bus*, the crowded, local transportation that stops at every town, or an express bus with elegant, plush seats, usually comes with a reasonable price tag. Spending nights in local hotels makes travel a bargain in the countries of Latin America. The rooms may be small, the beds hard and we were lucky if there was hot water, but after a day of touring, we can sleep anywhere. Long distance buses are economical while airline travel within each country tends to be surprisingly expensive. There are plenty of bargains at the pensiones or guesthouses, but if stateside amenities are what you are accustomed to, you will pay U.S. prices. All travel expenses especially airline tickets are factored into our sailing budget. Living cheaply will depend on you and your partner's preferences. Are you a rough and tumble traveler, who will continue your inexpensive lifestyle wherever you go, or do you like traveling in style? In Ecuador, several cruisers bought reasonably priced Chinese made motorbikes and on a minimalist budget, climbed into the Andes, exploring the amazing sights all the way to Peru and Bolivia.

One of the satisfying aspects of sailing a boat is that we are using free wind power when we sail, and free electrical power from our solar panels. When the tendency in the United States is towards over-consumption, to live cheaply on free, environmentally friendly energy, and walk lightly on the earth is a worthwhile and admirable purpose unto itself.

Finances

~ Just Do It? ~

The time was right for us to make the trip to Mexico, but there we were standing together on the shore ready but still hesitating to jump in. We cautiously tested the waters with our big toes. The immense ocean was a little too cold, too deep, too rough, too scary, too, too.... And then in a singular moment we dove in. The water felt exhilarating, transporting us to that place where our souls thrived. Setting off aboard *Harmony* was taking one of life's big plunges. The experience was all so new. Had we prepared ourselves? Were we ready?

When we left Alameda, California, we were not what you would call totally prepared. Rarely can anyone be completely equipped, but it soon became obvious that we brought stuff we didn't need and, of course, there were things that we forgot. There are a few captains who think that they must have it entirely together before leaving the safe and well-stocked U.S. Inevitably the boat remains comfortably tied to the dock until every gadget is in place.

There is definitely some equipment that is best purchased in the U.S. or Canada before voyaging south, like electronics and computer systems. Before we took off for Mexico, our HAM radio and e-mail was wired up and working. A Genset for energy, a small refrigerator, GPS, autopilot, radar, VHF radio and dinghy with an outboard, were our essentials. We bought a power windless with 200 feet of 3/8"chain and a 45-pound Bruce anchor and also carry two other anchors and spare chain. A water maker, solar panels, and a wind generator remained on our wish list. In the ten years that we have been cruising, we have added solar panels, taking us off the grid, and leaving our Genset generator as a back-up energy source. After years out at sea we installed a new set of batteries and found a second-hand radar from another cruiser in Mexico when our thirty year old radar finally gave up the ghost. When the patched dinghy was taking on too much water we ordered one from the Internet at a reasonable price. A Yamaha 8 horsepower outboard replaced our ancient reliable, but inadequate 2-horse motor. If you are planning to go far from home and not returning for many years, then install all the systems that you will need, but if you will be going back and forth, choose your priorities, purchase the basics and go. Much of the work that we have had done in Mexico and South America saved us big bucks, and we were out cruising.

We knew, however, that it would be imprudent to leave without having competent sailing skills or knowing the basics of how our boat worked. If you are new to the game, sailing classes are a good way to acquire the basics. There is knowledge to be gleaned from reading books, but nothing beats practicing sailing, docking, and anchoring your boat in various conditions. An inexperienced sailor may be out cruising, but he could become a hazard to himself or to others if he leaves before he is adequately prepared. We have watched while a sailor dropped fifty feet of chain in thirty feet of water and considered his boat well anchored. It was no surprise that when the wind came up, there he went, dragging down on other boats. A cruiser who knows the basics about sailing, about the systems on their boat, and how to fix them, with an adequate selection of spare parts packed on board (Is there such a thing?) is ready.

Just do it, but do it intelligently. New cruisers often go on sailing rallies like the Baja Ha-Ha to feel their way carefully into the new world. This 750-mile voyage to Mexico with three overnight passages has a departure date set, and a big impetus to meet the deadline. The large group of boaters, including many experienced sailors, can help the new voyager ease into the scene. Although the organizers say they are not a hand holding service, you can feel safer with many eyes on the weather and aid nearby. Other cruisers prefer a slower, less scheduled pace, and sail out on their own, staying as long as they wish at pristine stops along the way. They soon meet other yachties in transit who are also heading to points south at a leisurely pace. Mariners do what they can with the time and money they have, and then go for it.

In the first year of cruising, most of our attention was spent on the steep learning curve that accompanies any new endeavor. We learned about our boat, how it responded in various conditions, which sail configurations to use, how to navigate and provision, and keep all the systems running. There was the art of fishing and the all-important Weather. Robert and I learned how to cook in tight quarters while rolling over the waves. We quickly found out that anchoring could be stressful and how important the key elements were of knowing where it was safe to anchor and that the ground tackle was adequate to hold the boat securely. Nighttime could be a challenge. How many times did things go wrong with the boat or the weather at 0 Dark:30? Landing a dinghy on shore through the various degrees of surf tested everyone's courage. There were skills to develop that enabled us to function well as a team in new and challenging conditions. Learning to work together in all of these new situations was an interesting exercise. It was an invigorating time, sometimes overwhelming, but never boring.

Through this excitement came the realization of why we were out cruising. We found ourselves sailing along in perfect weather conditions with time to turn our attention to the surrounding beauty of the sea. The land had a different perspective viewed from offshore. All the problems, shortcomings, and hostilities of humankind faded before nature's magnitude and beauty. We anchored safely after a nice sail with time to meditate, rest, and read. The question, 'What is our purpose?' became important. Were we truly fulfilling the dream that we had on shore? Is it what we had envisioned? Were we comfortable down in that deep soul place? Did we like it? Was there no place we would rather be? Had we arrived in Paradise?

Before we left the dock there was that nagging question, "How can I be certain that I will like it?" The only sure way of knowing was to untie the dock lines and sail out onto the high seas. It's like trying to explain to an expectant couple how it will be after their baby is born. There's that old refrain, 'No risk; no gain.' If your partner has misgivings, ask them if they will take a chance. If it is not to their liking, you can always return to step one, dream, and try something else. However, when we ventured outside the box, that fearful, confining box, we became citizens of the world. While sailing through Neptune's kingdom, we gained a deep respect for the vastness and the power of the ocean, a companion, albeit sometimes a wild friend. The experience of oneness with the sea, the wildlife, the stars, new people, and cultures grew on us while we left a part of ourselves in our wake. Life did not look the same after living out on the edge. The philosophical questions take on an importance: *Can I laugh along with the cosmic joke?* [20] *Have I truly experienced that elusive taste of freedom? Am I fulfilling my soul's purpose? Am I a part of this amazing, paradoxial universe, an individual and yet at one with everything?*

Each cruiser eventually knows what is right for them and hops aboard for an adventure. On this roller coaster, we are at the controls. If we want to change course, we can. If we want a shorter or longer journey, it is up to us. We dare to take the risk, throw the dice, and embark on the ride of a lifetime.

Happiness Afloat

~ Living Together 24/7 ~

When we left San Francisco Bay on our trip south we had been together for nearly three decades. We had worked closely together raising our children and running our businesses, and knew how to function as a team. However, living together every hour of the day, every day of the week exposed issues that had not been dealt with. While our learning curve was steep aboard the boat, our relationship learning curve took a spike as well. It soon became apparent that if we were to have a *water-soluble* relationship, there needed to be some changes in order to adapt to our new circumstances and unaccustomed stresses. Trust took on a new meaning, and the value of appreciation and the art of giving and receiving suddenly felt like the most important things in the world. For starters we both wanted a higher level of respect that hadn't been there before, and we were soon amazed at the numerous topics that were coming up for discussion. Through hard work (like everything else on a sailboat) we began to make the subtle changes required for harmony on board. When the psychic dust had settled and I looked back on what it was that we had worked out, we had peeled several more moldy layers of our crusty ego off of the onion and unleashed a delectable bundle of aromatic happiness.

Appreciation created a gratitude cycle that generated positive energy like a perpetual motion machine. It has kept our marriage romantic and glittery, day-to-day, year to year. To thank each other for even the little things, like washing the dishes or changing the motor oil, brought gratitude aboard and lifted everyday chores to acts of love. When we were together every day it was easy to take our partner for granted only to have them feel cheated. Everyone loves to be acknowledged and we never failed to tell each other "I love you" every day. Appreciation is oxygen for the psyche.

Taking the time to celebrate both the extraordinary and ordinary events makes our lives and the world around us sparkle with gratitude, exuberance, and joy. Anchoring safely after a long trip was a perfect opportunity to make a regular party out of it, and if there happened to be fellow travelers in the anchorage we would invite them over to share a sundowner with hors d'oeuvres. The more we looked the more reasons there were to celebrate. One lovely Baja day Robert was fixing something in the engine room that not only required his focused attention, perseverance, and strength, but also had him contorted in exhausting yoga-like poses. When everything was back in order, he climbed out of the engine room sweaty, greasy, and breathing hard, but with a satisfied look on his face. While thanking him for his Merlin touch, I asked about the next item on my honey-do list. Silly me, I was caught up in my own work world and hadn't noticed that he needed to catch his breath for a minute, take a look around this beautiful anchorage, and savor the victory over a stubborn glitch in the engine room. When I realized what I had done, I quickly switched gears to

'Congratulations! Let me bring you some cool coconut juice. Let's take a break!' Life does not exist without those persistent problems that need to be solved, decisions that need to be made, things that break and need to be fixed, emotions and feelings that need to be dealt with. When we face these situations and actually solve a problem, make a decision, fix something, or rise above a challenge, we make sure that we take the time to enjoy the moment. An invigorating swim or a refreshing drink is just the thing.

When we are living in nature and attuned to the heartbeat of the earth, life changes from a somewhat stressed-out existence, to a life tuned in, relaxed, and aware. If we wonder why things are not going smoothly, why we do not sleep well, have high blood pressure, or other stress related problems, perhaps we are trying to dance fast to a slow song. It is necessary for us to take the time to sway with the rhythm of the ocean, the universe, and the world around us. There is never too much joy in life! When we celebrate, the world laughs, dances, and sings along with us.

With the rush of preparing the boat and then sailing off into the sunset, there was little time to worry about small annoying peculiarities that crept on board and seemed to drain the joy out of the trip. We were usually aware of these irritations but often let them pass on by unattended. Living together in such close proximity all the time shone a spotlight on habits that we'd written off as too small to matter or too large to dare mention for fear that it would start a row. When we chose to tip toe around these problems to avoid a confrontation the tension built. If we dared to talk about what was bothering us, it was more than likely going to rock the boat. When we arrived at the cruising grounds, there was usually enough quiet time to begin to deal with these potential difficulties.

You never know when something that needs changing will

abruptly present itself. I had always thought of myself as a generous and unselfish person. Raised in the traditional manner of my generation, it was expected that women would give far more than they would ever receive. It was natural for me that when our many children entered our world, for there rarely to be a moment away from my nurturing role that I could call my own. Years later, on board *Harmony* in a peaceful anchorage, Robert asked if he could bring me a glass of water. My first response was, "Oh, no, don't bother, I can get it." However, this was one of those times when Robert decided that he wanted something different. He simply wanted to bring me a drink of water and wanted me to graciously receive it. The simple, ordinary act of accepting a glass of water became a *big deal*, the beginning of a deeper understanding of give and take. I might have been magnanimous to all, but by not receiving, not wanting to be any trouble or a 'burden' to anyone, it prevented Robert the pleasure of generosity. In not allowing him that happiness, I was creating a closed or blocked channel of good energy coming from him to me. We both lost out in the interaction. When looking deep within my soul, I found a person hungry for approval, acknowledged only when I was giving and *good*. Giving and achieving were my tickets to the love and approval that I needed, but this early life lesson turned out to be a defective belief system.

Another struggle that was an intrinsic part of our modern age of feminism was the assumption that an intelligent and independent woman should be able to do things for herself. In the 21st century we are still trying to find the balance between doing things on our own, and being able to ask and receive help gracefully. In the past century women stood up to abuse and condescending attitudes. We can do it, and we can do it better became our battle cry. Men, with some lingering snorts of protest eventually began to accept this new paradigm and a majority of them, moved from being 'male chauvinist pigs' to being gentle, accommodating men who didn't mind doing the dishes or staying home with the children. Whenever I've asked an older couple what they attribute the longevity of their marriage to, the husband has often piped up with 'It's two words, Yes, dear,' or something along that line. During this recent upheaval it took a strong and courageous man to crawl back out from the dark cave that he was relegated to until he could figure out how to treat the *new* woman. He'd made a huge change and after a while, realized that there were things that he'd like to see changed with his partner as well. Could he continue following the rules of gentlemanly behavior to politely hold a door open for a woman, help her with her coat, or hold her arm across the street? And now Robert in particular was asking for the pendulum to swing back closer to center. He wanted to bring me a drink of water and it soon became apparent that there were other things that I struggled with that required his help. In my mind, requesting assistance was proving that I was dependent and needy, a negative vision of what a self-reliant, competent, modern woman should be. Acknowledging that there were some things that were difficult for me to do (especially on board *Harmony*) was a humbling experience. Rising above my stubbornness, asking nicely for help became my new practice. In this new energy pattern, I didn't have to struggle to do something that was extremely difficult or impossible for me to do. And Robert who is mechanically inclined and physically strong was given the satisfaction of helping me, a win-win situation. With the realization that it was okay for me to receive and be served, I was able to do the truly difficult work of making the actual change. Now when I hear Robert's offer to help me or bring me something, it triggers my new response of '*sure, thank you, I'd like that.*' The next step that involved even more soul searching and hard psychic work was to ask for help before I found myself struggling with something that I knew would be next to impossible. If I could only swallow my pride enough to request his help, Robert was always there to step in and make my life easier.

When someone is always giving and the other partner is always taking, the relationship becomes stagnant while the respect and appreciation levels drop. Resentment builds when generosity is overlooked. When you're living in the small space of a boat, these patterns become obvious. Working on changing these old habits brought our relationship to a higher plane of happiness and contentment. When the two-way street of give and take was opened up, the love flowed freely back and forth.

I taught Robert the sailing basics, and through practice and reading numerous sailing books, he became a competent sailor. Aboard *Harmony* we each gravitated to the aspects of cruising that we most enjoyed. Working in tandem we shared the dream. Robert changes the sails on the fore deck, hoisting them up and taking them down while I run things from the cockpit. During light airs, this often becomes a lesson in futility, but the exercise surely beats a treadmill any day. I prefer navigating, charting out our course, being the pilot of our ship. We share the day and night watches alternating every three or four hours. Robert drops the anchor and I back down on it. I steer through narrow places, and he pulls into the slips at the marinas. He winches me up the mast in my bosun's chair to do repairs while handling the safety lines on deck. Robert is the shipwright and mechanic, keeping the diesel engine firing away and I stand by like a surgeon's assistant, handing him the appropriate instruments, the wrench, the vise grips, or start up the engine, and check if water is coming out the exhaust. I manage the galley and keep the crew fed. Robert enjoys cooking and never leaves it all to me. In our little world on *Harmony*, teamwork is what keeps our journey harmonious

In a typical land-based relationship, a couple goes their separate ways for most of the day. One or both have a career and modern appliances help take on the burden of the household chores. Sometimes the woman is the primary caregiver, but today many men share that role too. Most couples become accustomed to seeing each other approximately four or five waking hours a day. We were the exception, since we owned our business and spent nearly every day working together. When we boarded our boat to go cruising, we were used to sharing time together, but not within such a confined area. Most cruising couples experience this as a major shift and the transformation can go easily, working out a few kinks along the way, or it can be traumatic. Sharing each moment can be pleasant or can be too much togetherness, overwhelming or claustrophobic. On top of this we also have to figure out how to navigate in our new environment. Where to find water and groceries, how to keep the batteries charged, lugging laundry ashore and back, and all the basics that we take for granted in our machine assisted, insulated, infrastructured lifestyle on land. Our home on the water can be comfortable with a gentle rocking motion, or it might involve dodging flying objects careening across the cabin, while bouncing and heeling in rough conditions.

Personal space became important in the small square footage that we now called home. Elbow room meant the difference between the galley and the cockpit, the cabin and the deck, or between a book and a boat project. Having time for ourselves, taking the dinghy or kayak out for a spin provided a much needed change of pace. Meeting people at an anchorage or marina, or taking a walk down a beach with a friend, gave each of us a chance to spend time with new acquaintances. More importantly we created a new comfort zone, while sharing a small space.

One of our favorite anchorages is Tenacatita, a lovely spot on Mexico's Riviera. Cruisers stop here for extended stays to swim and snorkel in the calm, perfect-temperature ocean. The white sandy beach lined with palm trees is a living postcard. Each day a group of us takes a long swim (about a third of a mile) from the anchorage to shore. Originally, our swim team consisted of a few women hungry for exercise after being aboard our boats for a long stretch. The swim became popular enough to entice children on boogie boards, men practicing for the local biathlon, dogs exercising on their way into shore, or just anyone wanting a relaxing, endorphin producing swim. Our lifeguard hubbies would escort us in their dinghies to warn pangas or the rare jet-ski that we were in the water. Bocce ball games were then casually organized on the beach. Many women preferred taking a walk down the long expanse of shoreline, talking together, getting acquainted, exchanging ideas, and telling their stories. Intense volleyball games occasionally provided exercise with everyone playing their hearts out. These afternoon gatherings were just what the doctor ordered for nearly everyone in the anchorage. People left their boats, socialized and exercised, all at the same time. These routines allowed for the stresses in a relationship to melt away, and the anchorage thrives as a favorite stopover where life long memories and friendships are created.

A crossroads anchorage like Tenacatita is a place where crews take a moment to relax and contemplate their next move. Plenty of experienced cruisers are available to compare notes with and give perspective about continuing cruising options. Time runs on a different clock and the pace slows enough to take stock. Living life in the moment becomes more important than any destination. Once we made the big rush away from home and gained our sea legs, we found that there were new decisions to make. Plans and dreams changed along the way and it's not unusual that compromise became the order of the day.

Relationship issues intensified while we lived together 24/7.

Sharing a small space tended to amplify bothersome behavior. Things that we might have tolerated in each other now loomed as something important that needed to be dealt with to both of our satisfaction. Practicing the skills of how to *work it out*, communicate, and resolve differences helped smooth out the rough edges of our relationship. If we devalued the importance of addressing the issues that surfaced between us, they didn't vanish into the pristine scenery, but lurked around in the shadows waiting for a moment to catch us unaware. By allowing the issues that arise to go unmentioned, they tended to frustrate and annoy until we had a wound that festered. How could we avoid building up resentment when up until now we had tried not to sweat the small stuff?

To accomplish our dream we had shelled out a large investment of time and money to buy our boat, equip it and sail away from the dock. It was equally important to nurture our relationship and keep it in harmony. The question was how could we take care of the essential chore of dumping the emotional garbage and cleaning the collective mind aboard our boat while living in a small space, and yet still keep the peace? When issues were discussed and unacceptable behavior altered, the air became clear of irritations, and joy entered unencumbered. Our approach to *working it out*, that we attributed to the practices learned on *The Farm*, had sustained our marriage, brought us to a higher level of intimacy, and kept our love strong and romantic. We developed a mutual respect and trust that made our adventure vibrant and fun despite the riotous weather or any unexpected problems. To delve into this nitty-gritty stuff, we had to be brave and leave our misgivings at the dock. Although I was struggling with a lack of confidence when it came to facing the ocean with its turbulent moods, I wondered if I was ready to confront my partner's occasional unpleasant behavior that I had somehow been able to live with on shore. Although these bothersome habits gnawed away at our happiness, I had never thought it was worth the conflict, and had resolved to live with it. This avoidance method of maintaining a relationship was unsustainable in our boat's small quarters (and it really doesn't work for the long haul anywhere).

We had cruiser friends, Maggie and Greg who jokingly referred to themselves as the Bickersons. They considered their contentious ways entertaining. They had their sparring routine, goading each other on with snippy little comments, unconcerned how it sounded to other people. Maggie complained to us about how difficult and exhausting these small quarrels had become for her on the boat. She had reached her wit's end and had put up with enough, especially when Greg was sitting in the dinghy, impatiently yelling, "Come on, come on, already, blankity, blank" while she was collecting their sunglasses, his hat, and bottles of water for both of them. Another cruising couple would occasionally yell at each other (you could hear it across the anchorage), and in some distorted way it sounded like their way of saying 'I love you.' These were extreme cases but we all have those unpleasant routines that we would love to be able to unload out of the bilge of our unconscious and throw to the fishes.

Our marriage contract contained the agreement to work out to a satisfactory conclusion any problems that would obstruct our happy relationship. Here is a collection of various insights and tools that have helped us answer that incessant question, "Once you have found love, how do you keep it around?"

Happiness Afloat

~ Untangling the Subconscious ~

Robert and I credit the many individuals who we lived with on *The Farm* and the strong commitment to 'working things out' that existed there, for helping us to unravel the intricacies of a marriage where the odds were against our success. Our relationship was both cross-cultural and from different religious backgrounds. I was from a conservative, missionary, Southern, Christian family while Robert came from a New York, non-religious, Russian, Jewish family. It wasn't unusual to feel like we were caught in the Battle of the Titans or were a microcosm of the Mid-east Conflict. The tools that we discovered to keep our relationship in working order have served us well over the years. We were hopeful that if we could overcome the obstacles in our individual world, maybe there was hope for humanity to peacefully resolve the bigger conflicts on Earth. When we set out for the adventure of a lifetime we carefully loaded up our boat with all the various systems, spare parts, and provisions, ready for every eventuality. Along with these tangible things, we included a collection of useful skills for keeping our happiness flowing. If you are curious about what was in our toolbox, read on.

Disclaimer: If any of these issues become disturbing and overwhelming it might be prudent to seek professional counseling. If the society as a whole was more accepting about how difficult this work truly is there would not be such a stigma against asking for help when it's needed. The advice that is contained in this book is presented for informational purposes only. The material is in no way intended to replace professional medical care or attention by a qualified psychiatrist or therapist. This book cannot and should not be used as a basis for diagnosis or choice of treatment. Please contact the author if you find something that needs correcting.

While I am not a marriage counselor, psychologist or any other form of licensed health-care professional, the following insights are borne out of a happy, fulfilling marriage and many years out at sea together. I offer these perceptions as ideas for thought, a way of understanding how we grow and communicate as individuals, and as couples, to keep the love passionate, and romantic.

The Farm that was both our home and school for twelve years was as much an ashram or a monastery as it was a commune. We called ourselves a *multi-stery* rather than a monastery, since after all we were living with several families in one house. Mahatma Gandhi referred to this practice as that of a *householder yogi*, working toward self-realization through the daily routine of raising our children and living peacefully with our partner and our neighbors. Bringing up our children in a creative environment of unconditional love and compassion required us to nurture these qualities within ourselves. Children are more apt to follow our actions than what we tell them they ought to do, so they were our teachers in a profound way.

Our practice provided a hands-on instruction to life's challenges in a chaotic world. Looking beyond our own individual self-realization, we saw value in helping our partner and children, (and eventually everyone) along life's path. Our beliefs were a composite of many spiritual disciplines, realizing that all religions at their very highest levels believe in the same key tenets. One of the basic beliefs was that *We are all one.* You breathe in my air and I breathe in yours. Scientific research continues to conclude that on the subatomic levels, we are more all one than we appear. In the Buddhist tradition there are the Hinayana, *small boat*, and Mahayana, *large boat*, paths to Nirvana or enlightenment, pure happiness and bliss. The small boat path consists of one person taking care of themselves and their piece of the universe while working toward personal enlightenment. The big boat path embraces the idea that no one can truly reach enlightenment until everyone does. If you happen to arrive at Nirvana, the next thing to do as a Bodhisattva (one who has reached enlightenment or self-realization) is to see if you can help others arrive there as well. **The practice, or the yoga, is to work towards the enlightenment of oneself and all sentient beings even though it is a seemingly impossible and never ending task.** Spiritual teacher, Stephen Gaskin, [21] used to say when describing the daunting Bodhisattva vow, "It's like shoveling shit against the tide forever." But what else are we doing here anyway?

In the early 1970's when the Vietnam War was raging, we were intent on finding a way to bring about change peacefully. We decided to embark on a noble experiment to see if we could create peace by changing the one thing we had control over, ourselves. If we could truly grasp the meaning of personal responsibility and alter our disrupting, hostile, and energy draining ways, we might have a chance at seeing our lives change for the better. And if we could cultivate and nurture our small square inch field (ourselves, our immediate family, and household) maybe we could make a difference on a larger scale as well. The specific practice that we engaged in was to live in peace and create happy homes. In order to have a harmonious household, we needed to weed out the patterns that sabotaged our progress. To have true love, we needed to first learn to love ourselves unconditionally. One of the fundamental agreements that we had on *The Farm* was that it was okay to bring to each other's attention negative habits that needed to be changed. These annoying habits were not specifically designed to provoke others, but were rather unconscious, ingrained, behavioral patterns, instilled in us from an early age, and solidified through the years. Throughout our lives we were unaware of these unpleasant mannerisms, so there was rarely a chance for us to change. On *The Farm* we allowed our family and friends to hold up a mirror to our actions so we could see them for ourselves. That we were oblivious to these disruptive or unhealthy traits was the 'sub' of subconscious, meaning beneath our awareness. We were unaware that our actions were hurtful or unpleasant to those close to us. Most of these life-long habits were our automatic, spontaneous responses to the world around us. Once we have mastered the arts of riding a bicycle, driving a car, speaking a language, or typing on a keyboard, we never forget these skills. When we do not use them for a while we may become a little rusty, but as soon as we need them they are there for us. The same holds true for the habitual reactions of moodiness, ranting, withdrawal, addiction, or any other negative characteristic within which we cocoon ourselves from the complicated and sometimes hurtful world in which we were born. Depending on our role models and how we have responded to what life has dealt us, our behavior patterns are healthy, normal activities or can be destructive to our families and ourselves. The eventual result of negative energy habits is a blockage of the love that we want to give and receive. From an early age we rationalized and allowed ourselves to indulge in anger, fear, shame, manipulation, or running away as mechanisms (to name just a few) that have protected us over the years from harmful treatment or fearful situations. In a couple's relationship, these behaviors create tension and distance and impede the love from flowing. Since there is so little physical room on a boat, the vibrations, and the emotional climate needs to feel especially comfortable. There is, however, no space large enough to fit the proverbial *elephant in the room,* that strong presence that pervades the air when the tension of unresolved problems is not discussed, dealt with, and cleared away.

Breaking down the walls and barriers to unveil our subconscious to the light of consciousness releases amazing amounts of pent up energy. ***The first step begins with a basic agreement that we want to change our bad habits, with the understanding that our partner or someone else can help bring our subconscious to our awareness. The subconscious is something that is hidden from us and prefers not to be revealed.*** When brought to our attention in a kind, loving, and compassionate manner it becomes possible for us to learn about it. We have to go deep within our souls to study its origins, see that it has become outdated and harmful, and actually determine to change these old habits. Doing this difficult work melts the ice around our hearts and frees the love that's been squelched for so long. Before understanding what my partner is trying to tell me, I usually have to be shown what I am doing several times before I catch on to what he is talking about. This is normal and both of us have to be patient. It often takes a while for me to perceive myself from a different point of view and then more work and time to actually make a change. If you are reading this before taking off on your cruising trip, practicing this skill of compassionately telling each other about the subconscious might be as important as learning about the ins and outs of your boat. This discipline can set up a working paradigm that opens the way towards breaking irritating habits. Following these steps will eventually energize your life and make it easier for you and your partner to find happiness in the small space aboard your yacht. The goal is to free yourself and toss unhealthy behavior overboard once you are aware of your subconscious self.

To dredge up the muck collecting in our emotional bilge is a touchy process. Often the tendency will be to deny it, guard against it, and counter-attack, or use any number of creative, defensive mechanisms to keep from churning up the status quo. When I step close to my partner's bad habits, he sometimes has caused such confusion that I tend to forget what I was talking about. I start to think maybe I'm the problem for even bringing it up! On the other hand, when my sweetheart brings something up that I need to listen to, I find myself struggling not to say, no, no, no! When I stop for a minute and realize what he's talking about, I know in my deepest soul that he's on to something even though I'm fighting it with all my powers of dissuasion. The important but challenging exercise is to take in the feedback and let go of the old habits.

There are several schools of thought about the nature of the subconscious. The Jungian point of view describes how our actions may vary from our conscious intentions due to the workings of the subconscious. For example, any time we have suffered and did not grieve or work through a hurt, we stashed or repressed it in the inner, locked recesses of our emotional self. That part of our self is eager to keep things as they are, not rattle any cages. It has taken a lifetime of building these walls to protect us from real and imaginary threats and only with great fear and trepidation would we want to tear them down and reveal our vulnerability! Who is this mate of mine? Do I trust him enough to let down my guard, open up my heart and soul, clear out the pain of old hurts, and leave myself unprotected and exposed? It takes courage, dedication, trust, and an open heart to say; "It is okay to go deep into these scary places."

The search for true love is not without difficulty and pain. How can I trust when my trust has been trampled? What about the anger that we feel when our souls have been violated? We struggle with our self-esteem and now are asked to face the truth of our faults and weaknesses. Only with the combination of unconditional love and truth can the fear be dispelled and like the clanging of the Liberty Bell, make us free at last. A reverberation resonates through the universe causing a crack through the hardest metal, a fissure signifying the power of truth, freedom and love, a struggle that is well worth the effort.

The following step-by-step guide will help you and your partner bring a destructive subconscious habit to the surface, and offer ways to actually change behavior.

1) The first and possibly the most important step is to make an agreement that you can tell each other about bothersome subconscious habits, with the understanding that each of you will listen and work on changing for yourself and for each other.

   This agreement has been our life long contract that was made at the time of our marriage. It has been the foundation that we have built our relationship upon that has allowed our love to deepen and mature yet maintain its vibrancy and romance.

2) Remaining compassionate, kind and patient with a large dose of unconditional love for your partner and yourself is essential for the evolution of your relationship while you go through this challenging metamorphosis.

3) Each of you will listen respectfully and hear what the other person has to say, agreeing to take notice of your behavior.

4) Make a commitment to work on changing the habit. There is a breakthrough when you become aware of what your partner is trying to tell you, while you are in the middle of doing it.

5) If you can laugh at yourself when you are actually caught in the act and stop mid-stream, you are on your way towards a happier self.

6) Recognizing and revisiting the events, beliefs, and teachings of your past that caused you to protect yourself with this unacceptable behavior or habit allows you to realize that you don't need it any longer. This may be a personal experience or an ancient memory that has evolved through generations of your family or through cultural or societal traditions. By coming to this realization, you find that your bad habits have prevented you from a more satisfying, intimate relationship in the present.

7) When you release old patterns you feel a radical shift take place deep within. Every cell moves over to accept the change. It takes place in your body and in the depths of your mind, your emotional self, and your very soul. Waves of energy flow within and around you, relieving you of this weight that you have unknowingly been carrying around for so long.

Tears can flow. You struggle to let go of an old friend, a friend who is no longer an appropriate or a healthy influence. When you confront these long standing patterns, there is a tendency to fight change with stubbornness. You clamor to find rationalizations of all kinds, going so far as to chicken out, freak out, run away, lash out in anger, come up with outlandish excuses, and deny that you ever wanted to change in the first place!

Letting go brings an amazing release. Tears of joy replace the tears of desperation, anger, and self-pity. Emotionally cleansed you feel lighter and happier. It is not unlike having experienced a storm at sea. When the dawn breaks bright and clear the day after the tempest has passed, your confidence is strengthened and at the same time you feel humbled, joyous and thankful.

8) Forgiving yourself and making the change deep in your soul, out of love and respect for your partner and most importantly for yourself moves you forward on a path to more love in your life.

9) It is possible to do away with old habits, but it is no easy matter, and then there is always the possibility that over time, in a weak or lazy moment that you will revert back to the old comfortable ways. Your loving and patient mate gently reminds you that you are slipping and to stay vigilant.

Resentment can show up when we suppress the things that bother us. Frustration can grow when we bring something up and our partner refuses to hear us out. At a low point we ask ourselves is it worth it to continue to make changes for ourselves and for each other? There is also the issue of whether or not there is sufficient trust to believe that our partner is asking us for some modifications that will improve our lives together. Putting aside our stubbornness we find strength, courage, and love and proceed to grow and change for our partner's and our own peace of mind. Discarding negative patterns frees us to find our own true identity. With the help of our partner, children, (who are mirrors of our behavior) and Farm friends we discovered the clues to weeding out our subconscious habits. With this practice, Robert and I avoided divorce court and it continues to empower us to create a warm, loving relationship.

To delve into the subconscious is a journey unto itself and not too dissimilar from the physical adventure of cruising. The commitment and discipline that the sea demands echoes the trek within. When we place as much value on the inner trip of working through our problems as we do in our seagoing experience, we develop a love-filled relationship that endures and radiates with joy, satisfaction, trust, and respect. This might be the most important part of the journey; the search for true love, freedom, and truth, which enhances our existence, and ensures that life is filled with enthusiasm while we continue down the road together.

When I walk through that dark night of the soul, that dense forest of my subconscious, and do the difficult work of changing, I notice wondrous things happening around me. Our Guardian Angel keeps us safe, the Weather Gods behave themselves, coincidences abound, and the universe dazzles us with its splendor. Magic happens!

Threatening squalls surrounded us when we jumped off from Golfito, Costa Rica on the six hundred mile open-ocean passage to Ecuador. Our route crossed through the ITCZ, the unsettled Inter-Tropical Convergence Zone. At first we were able to dodge the small, intense weather cells, but eventually we were surrounded by a long band of rain and wind. Our daughter, Olivia, was working hard to keep her courage up. Talking with her about some scary moments in my life and how I overcame my fear seemed to help. She asked me to tell her some stories about childbirth. I described how breathing slowly in and breathing out, helped to neutralize the intense feelings of the surges. Robert would sit behind me during my labor, a strong and supportive husband to push up against, propping me up, holding and encouraging me. When I breathed deeply and allowed my body to work its magic, the cervix opened and bones actually shifted to allow the baby to emerge into the light of day. Olivia and I took deep breaths and spoke of calm and tranquility. While we were watching the stormy sky, the black streak across our path slowly dissipated. When we sailed through the gap between the squalls, the synchronicity of it all held us in awe. It felt like we were walking on the edge of the world, in perfect balance. When things are working out like this it affirms the power of the strong foundation of agreements that helps hook us up to the universal flow where lies love and happiness.

Besides these basic tenets, there are additional tools in Appendix A, which might help patch up the leaks that are sapping the vitality from the health of a relationship and generate more harmony aboard.

Happiness Afloat

~ Cruising Women, Busting the Myth ~

In a challenge to the old worn out myths that women are bad luck on board, today's women play an active role in sailing the world. Their presence, intuition, and savvy sailing skills are what make most cruising voyages successful.

Out on the water, there are women cruisers who love the ocean and sailing, and then there are those who are along to support their husband's dream. Many a reluctant woman aboard, who starts out just wanting to accompany her partner on his adventure, ends up becoming an experienced mariner and falls in love with the cruising lifestyle. Sharing the dream, they partake of the myriad aspects of the ocean existence. They help do boat projects, work to pay for the equipment, practice their sailing skills, and learn about all the aspects of their boat. It may not have been their dream, but they have made it their own and are committed to cruising.

Occasionally women own their own yachts, and sail single-handed, or find a partner or crew to accompany them. They may be the exception but no doubt there will be more independent women out on the blue water in the future. Today's women have the confidence to do whatever they want, and have their own money to finance their dream. Women pioneers in cruising and racing have paved a way across the seas, participating and winning in around the world races and local regattas. Several women have circumnavigated the world solo and who knows how many more have traveled the world with their partners.

Most successful cruisers have a committed woman on board. To know if you are capable of actually doing it, testing the waters with a trial run should let you know if you like it or not. It can be a difficult barrier to surmount if seasickness or fear overrides your zeal to go cruising. If one is prone to complaining, there are a million things to complain about on board. When a mono-hull sailboat is sailing along, it is "tipping," like my kids used to say, five to thirty or more degrees. While heeled over, it becomes difficult to maneuver on deck or in the galley. There can be bruises and contusions, which we affectionately call 'boat bites.' There is rough weather and seasickness that dissipates all the fun. Frustrations surface when something on the boat breaks down, and the adrenaline starts pumping in anticipation of the worst. Tight quarters are confining especially if you have a partner whose habits tend to be annoying or overbearing. We are 24/7 with our partner, and we may have to compromise with or take orders from him/her. The anchorage is swelly, the deep water is scary, and the night watch or the rough seas cause anxiety. The dinghy, which is now the car, is capable of flipping over on a surf landing. Rough dinghy landings are a spectator sport to add humiliation to our discomfort. There can be an aversion to the ocean itself when everything becomes covered with a layer of salt. The work seems non-stop on the water and the boatyard is toxic and dirty. All the infrastructure of a town is built into our relatively small boat, and when a system fails, there is usually no one to fix it but us. Provisioning can require a long trip over rough, dusty roads to town. Then the heavy bags of groceries, laundry, and jerry jugs of water, and sometimes fuel must be maneuvered onto the boat from a dinghy, sometimes with the boat pitching and yawing. Anything to do with the head (the ship's toilet) can be annoying. It's nothing like the convenient, one flick flush we are accustomed to, but we pump, and pump, and pump some more. Mineral deposits can clog pipes requiring the system to be taken apart periodically for a thorough cleaning. (We finally, thank God, installed an electric head on *Harmony* with a push button flush. What a wonderful improvement!) The learning curve is steep. It feels as if something new and sometimes shocking waits to ambush us around the next corner. Everything was in a comfortable routine in our old life, and now it's all a challenge. It can be disconcerting to someone who is used to having it all together and *under control*. Operating a boat consists of so many tasks, from furling the sail to navigating the waters, to being in tune with the weather, which all need to be embraced and understood. Comfort is sacrificed for a wild ride of adventure with occasional adrenaline-pumping excitement.

Considering all the changes that you will have to go through, why would anyone want to go cruising? But if after looking at all the cons, the pros still hold your heart, the intriguing lure of adventure still calls to your soul, then give it a try. Perhaps it's time for negotiations and compromises. You might strike a deal to cruise for a while and help the captain *fulfill his dream*, and then at the end of a season or more return home, back to the children, grandchildren, family, friends, career, garden, and pets. When you jump into the boating lifestyle wholeheartedly, it should be fun for both of you. We often watch reluctant women grow to love cruising, and after going home for a visit, ironically miss the boat, and wish that they were back on the water, in their warm tropical paradise.

Committed to the adventure and wanting to be an equal partner on board, I began to acquire new skills like navigating, sail changes, and trying to fathom the intricacies of a diesel engine. Planning the route, acquiring and studying the charts, purchasing and making the flags of various countries, and learning about the weather were all new endeavors. Books on fish, shells, birds, and the constellations were stocked in our on board library and reading about the people, geography, and history of the places we were going to visit added depth to our travels. Provisioning for an extended passage included stocking up on those hard to find goodies like natural peanut butter, boxed tofu, nutritional yeast, sushi makings, and dark chocolate, as well as learning the tricks of how to keep fresh produce from spoiling too soon. A cool, dark shelf near the water line prolonged the life of our fruits and veggies that couldn't fit into the refrigerator. There were lists of spare parts and supplies that we needed to purchase. Keeping track of the various projects like applying for and renewing passports and fishing licenses taxed my organizational skills. Putting our affairs in order at home demanded time and patience, and placing most bills on auto- pay paved the way for a worry free journey.

Our down-sized home that we left in California had a little over 1000 square feet which isn't a particularly big house, but it had four or five times the living area of *Harmony*. We had to adjust to the challenges of living with less space while storing stuff in easily accessible places. The small boat refrigerator presents its own demands. It's not uncommon to stand on my head while removing storage containers and vegetables to get to the cold drinks on the bottom. I work around the physical confines of a boat with no square walls. On the other hand the great outdoors is our living room, the ocean, sometimes with a beach view, is the patio. Once everything is sorted out and put in its proper place, the living space for our mind and spirit is expansive.

Happiness Afloat

~ Welcoming a Woman on Board –
Clues for the Captain ~

Melanie had finally met the love of her life, but as luck would have it, Nathan lived on a boat. She had been camping and hiking and loved the out-of-doors, but she knew nothing about sailing, did not even know how to swim, and had never lived with a man, let alone in the small confines of a boat. Nathan was a savvy, prudent sailor, thrilled to have this lovely woman aboard, and did everything he could think of to make Melanie feel welcomed and comfortable. Melanie was still working full time, so he made extra space for her wardrobe and gave her the entire hanging locker and all but a couple of drawers in the dresser. She signed up for swimming lessons at the local YMCA and they went sailing together in moderate Southern California conditions where she always felt at ease. Nathan made her comfort a priority, and she has been happily cruising with him for over a decade.

Susie had met her love and the infatuation sparks were flying while their relationship developed. She agreed to move aboard his boat as a preview to his plans to take her cruising. When she arrived with her bags, the captain was busily working on an engine repair. He asked her to make herself comfortable and told her that he'd be with her soon, but it was a complicated bit of business and he didn't finish the job for several hours. From the start Kevin didn't make his sweetheart feel important in his world. He expected her to fit in and make herself at home on her own. When they left the dock on the cruise of a lifetime, as fate would have it, they were soon on a rough passage off of the notorious Oregon coast. Susie was frightened and with little sailing experience didn't have any idea what to do when things became chaotic and the captain was yelling at her to pull on this and winch in that. Suffice it to say, it was not long before she returned home. She started out as a willing partner, but she needed to be treated tenderly and given time to learn the ropes. It's important for the captain not only to make his partner feel welcomed aboard, but to allow her time to feel that it is her boat and her trip.

And then there was that young single-handed sailor, Taylor, who when he told us his tale the women moaned and the men shook their heads in disbelief. He had made a bundle of money in the high tech gold rush and his new catamaran was tricked out and ready to go with his enthusiastic partner aboard to keep him company. They departed from San Francisco on their maiden voyage and took a right, their destination the Pacific Northwest and Alaska. The plan turned out to be flawed since this particular passage traverses some of the roughest seas in the world, upwind against the swell and currents. When we met him he was sailing alone on the warm Mexican sea while his former love was living out the cold winter in Montana. Break a new sailor in gently, making it fun with low stress passages. Taking it slowly at first, her skills have time to improve, and the two of you can adventure confidently further out to sea.

The majority of men that we've met out cruising would rather have someone to share their adventures with, preferring companionship to traveling alone. They appreciate being taken care of and want the privilege of taking care of someone. To entice your matey into sharing the voyage and exciting lifestyle requires patience, probably major life changes, and new considerations that never crossed your mind. To successfully accommodate a woman, a comfortable boat is a start. Women on the most part are not as Spartan as a rough and tumble sailor and she most likely wants a refrigerator to keep the vegetables from spoiling and leftovers safe for the next day. How about ice and cold drinks and plenty of fans in the tropics? To make her feel at home, she will beautify the living space with her own flavors and storage space will need to be freed up for her belongings. An attractive working galley with plenty of storage is important, where she can safely create her gourmet meals even while heeled over at fifteen degrees.

Women in general are not culturally brought up to live a life at sea. You can help dispel the fears that abound in this unknown territory. Her confidence is boosted when she is nurtured and educated into this new lifestyle and given a chance to practice, gaining knowledge and experience. When you show her patiently and with care, you create a sailing companion who will more likely than not eagerly share her life with you, and participate in your wild and crazy lifestyle. When you make time for her to learn to sail on her own, allowing her to make her own mistakes, she becomes an equal partner. She can then help sail the boat and navigate with confidence. The stress that it takes to be in charge, with the entire enterprise on your shoulders, can now be shared by a competent partner.

Then there is the fantasy of sailing off into the sunset never to return. Your partner may have other priorities and different requirements. Her family or career may beckon her home. She may want to spend part of her year out sailing and part of it back on land. Whether the plans are for a coastal journey or a distant passage, it is not uncommon to cruise on a seasonal basis. Peak cruising times in most locations of the globe are dictated by the weather, and as a result are a part time endeavor. There are many good places around the world to stop, put the boat safely in a marina or on the hard and return home. Hurricane, cyclone, typhoon, and monsoon seasons are the perfect months to travel to reunions, weddings, graduations, and visit new babies. There is the carefree exuberance of playing with children, the rewarding satisfaction of helping care for a senior family member, and time spent reconnecting with friends and relatives. It is said that if a female cruiser can return home at least once a year, she'll remain a happy camper.

Today's independent women often have a satisfying career and a warm group of close friends. Many women earn enough money to live comfortably in their own home. The challenge for you is to entice her to join you at sea and live in a small, cramped boat that sometimes bumps and tosses about. In many aspects of life, however, women want the same thing as men. They want companionship and are willing to share your incredible journey if you make it fun and fulfilling. No doubt there will be compromises to make, but if you handle it right you are primed for a good time with someone who will share the excitement of your lifelong dream.

Happiness Afloat

~ How 'bout Alternatives ~

A captain will have an easier go of it if he chooses a partner who loves sailing and shares his cruising dream to begin with. However, most men smitten by the cruising bug have had a partner for ten, twenty, or thirty years. Often in a later stage of life a man comes up with the wild idea and enough money to actually buy a boat and sail off on the world's oceans. Cruising might not be one of those dreams high on her list and the couple then must decide what to do.

Our pal Tony chose to take a sabbatical from work to go cruising. His wife was still involved in a high-powered career that she loved, and she definitely did not like sailing. So he asked a friend to go along with him on his trip to Mexico. Throughout the cruise, his wife would meet him at various marinas where they would rent an elegant hotel room, swim in the pool, and go touring. During several cruising seasons, he was able to find a friend to help with the passage making. This arrangement enabled him to live the dream without disrupting their relationship.

Plenty of folks find the motion or the heeling of a mono-hull sailboat uncomfortable. Narrow confined spaces can also be a problem, so perhaps a catamaran with roomier living quarters and no heeling would suit your needs? They are quite popular, but can be more expensive and then there are those double berth fees at marinas. In a powerboat or trawler, you are out cruising, enjoying the travel and adventure on a boat that is spacious with perhaps a more pleasant ride. The payoff might be worth the price of diesel. Although a trawler may not be able to travel across vast oceans because of the distance between fuel docks, coastal cruising is delightful and filled with plenty of good times. If the dream is to take a long passage in your mono-hull sailboat to Tahiti or Tonga, and your partner doesn't enjoy the long passages, there is always the option of finding crew to help. They can sail with you across the Pacific and your partner can fly in to meet you in paradise.

Charlie, a friend of ours, went all out to fix up his boat for his partner but even with it in Bristol condition, she wasn't happy living on a yacht. She missed her large dining room table surrounded by her family at frequent gatherings. Her hutch filled with knick-knacks and collectables was her hobby that wouldn't hold up to the action of the waves. Even though they gave the cruising lifestyle a good try, it wasn't long before they were back on shore content to take shorter trips closer to home.

There are ways to cruise and still have time for career and family. It may be time to negotiate a sabbatical, a flextime arrangement, or telecommuting. Occasionally a woman cruiser realizes that she is done with the career part of her life and is ready for a search in new directions. Taking a break on board can be a perfect time to contemplate life and reassess what to do next. Changes in her outlook could foster new priorities and talents, and allow creative energies to surface in this lush world of innovative imagination. When we leave behind the work-a-day world it is surprising what insights await us and what new dreams present themselves along our unfamiliar route.

Happiness Afloat

~ Oh Captain, My Captain ~

There is the old saying that *he* is the captain, but *she* is the admiral. On the official Port Captain papers, we were advised to include my name as the co-pilot. If there was ever a situation when Robert was not aboard, then as the pilot I could still legally handle the boat. Another way for egalitarian couples to approach this delicate issue is for the couple to be named as co-captains. We like this set up, but there inevitably comes a time when there needs to be one captain on deck calling the shots. Usually in such a situation there can be several courses of action. When we come upon fishnets strung across our course, a quick decision by my captain for me to steer a sharp turn to port or starboard saves our propeller from becoming ensnared in the nylon lines. Valuable time is not wasted with arguing, re-evaluating, or second-guessing. If the captain's call turns out to be wrong, (oh yes, it happens) a discussion after things calm down can ensure that the lessons are learned. There is no need to lose the deep trust between us when we can turn a difficult situation into a chance to gain knowledge, understanding, and skill.

The skipper is usually the owner of the boat, but since we were both the owners and fairly new to sailing this size boat, I had insecurities knowing that my captain didn't know much more than I did. We would jibe or tangle the recalcitrant spinnaker with a hat or pair of glasses flying into the drink, which made it obvious that we needed more practice. With our trial run that included a rollicking storm came a strong sense of confidence in my captain and myself. We experienced something new almost every time we set sail, and we either handled it perfectly or we learned about managing things better next time.

Here is what happened to us when the weather turned sour and the boat needed to be brought under control by reefing the main sail, etc. Because I was somewhat freaked out and my judgment wasn't at its best, I wouldn't know exactly what to do, but I would make suggestions anyway hoping it would help. Robert, on the other hand, wanted me to trust in him and let him tell me what to do, step by step if necessary. I then would complain that he yelled at me like Captain Ahab and it made me more frightened and less likely to want to follow what he said. One problem was compounded upon another. After the sails were secured and we were back on track having a relatively comfortable ride, Robert asked me if I felt calm enough to talk about what happened. While I took a minute to center myself, it came to me how courageous my partner was. He had probably agonized over how to bring up this emotionally explosive issue without upsetting me. I had to take a deep breath to keep my emotions under control; I knew I needed to hear what he had to say. We started by agreeing to resolve the initial controversy to our satisfaction. Simply put, I needed to contain my tendency to *steer out of fear*. Trusting my captain became the obvious course. When the high winds and boisterous seas made me feel that we are in imminent danger, and fear had its tendrils clutching my stomach, suffocating my heart, what could I do? When I allowed panic and terror to grab control I felt that it robbed me of my sense of security. And then something would snap, a sail ripped or the engine coughed and my fight or flight mechanism locked into gear. I had an innate feeling that it was 'me against the world,' so I started doing things without thinking them through, to alleviate the overwhelming frantic feeling. This stealthy con man named panic enabled my fears, rigidly supported stubbornness and inflexibility, and my desperate grasping for control. If a power struggle about who was in charge ensued at this point, anger and frustration would lead to bad decision-making, distrust, and disrespect. Fortunately for me, my experienced partner would be standing next to me with an overall view of what was going on, and not feeling that crazy-making fear. Over the years I have learned to find comfort in his calm and follow his lead. When I put my trust in my captain, I was able to dismiss that old *friend*, my scared panicked self, who had been my misguided companion for so long. Fear was stealing the confidence and honesty that I shared with my partner. It required practice and discipline to work through my fear, but what a relief to give it up and let the captain steer in a tight situation. My anxiety drifted away and I wondered why I had made the process so difficult in the first place. Usually we steered by agreement and consensus, but during those high-pitched moments there needed to be a designated captain. Robert would make the call and take the responsibility for the situation.

In the new world of equality between the sexes this might not set well with the one who is not captain. I was not used to taking orders or being told what to do. In certain situations, however, this was the difference between a safe outcome and trouble. When I followed my captain's lead when the occasion arose, things went smoothly. The boat came through with no problems, my self-esteem was not compromised, and I felt a deep satisfaction in the way we handled a difficult situation. We worked well as a team and I felt confidence in my partner. Together we had created a positive outcome. When the situation calmed down I thanked him for giving directions nicely. If he fell into a harsh Captain Bligh mode, then that was another thing that needed to be discussed. However, when I followed his directions, his anxiety subsided too and his voice lost that uncomfortable tone. Avoiding bad weather helped us stay clear of these stressful situations in the first place! Impatience and schedules rushed us when we should have been comfortably at anchor. With the common trust and respect established, we each did our part to make life on board go smoothly. Sorting things through until we reached a satisfying conclusion created another building block for our growth together.

During one of our first years out, we were anchored in a small cove when a strong on-shore wind began to blow. When we stretched out on our chain, we were pushed precariously close to a rocky reef. It didn't take us long to decide that it was time to re-anchor. While Robert engaged the windlass, I put the engine in forward. Because the wind was blowing hard, he motioned that I should rev up the engine. I throttled up a little, but he needed more power to combat the wind, and for some reason I stood frozen, immobilized against my fear of going onto the rocks. He motioned for more power and I pushed the throttle lever just a bit. It was still not enough to combat the 30-knot winds. Shaking his head, he came back to the cockpit and revved up the engine to show me how many RPM's were needed. I was paralyzed with fear, a deer caught in the headlights, not listening and understanding what was really required for the situation. My anxiety was doing more to put us on the rocks than if I had trusted his simple instructions.

Finding that quiet place deep within where I could go to replenish my courage, surrender, let go, and cultivate a strong confidence that everything would be all right, created a tranquil peace of mind. **It was difficult for me since my tendency was to imagine and believe that everything would eventually end in the worst-case scenario.** I had to trust that I could handle whatever came my way, and learn to rely on my capable partner and ultimately on myself. There was a choice to make, change or return home to a comfy, safe place on land with a different set of challenges. I liked cruising too much to forfeit the entire dream for a few necessary and rewarding changes.

Respect grew between us when we saw the courage that was required for each of us to handle a rough passage, to weather the storm. When numerous situations on our trip were handled successfully, our esteem for each other increased. It was admirable when our partner shifted gears, adapted, and made difficult changes. Sometimes our approaches to a problem might be radically different, but the inevitable heated discussion would still be uplifting. Seeing things from a new angle, and incorporating the combined wisdom of the two of us often created an entirely different, but better solution. The ingenuity, perseverance, and hard work that was required by both of us to keep the dream alive and the ship in running order, bred a mutual respect that generated love.

Before a passage we talked things over, worked out glitches, and came to new understandings. There were concrete actions that we could take to keep things safe. For example, on our cruise through the islands of western Panama, I was nervous about navigating through a particularly rocky and narrow passage between islands. Robert studied the charts and stood on the foredeck. He was able to discern the shallows by watching the different colors of the water, and I safely negotiated the gap into deeper water by following his directions. We rely on each other when we feel shaky. Robert has less fear than I do when the seas are rough, and I have more patience and endurance in those same difficult conditions. Robert says he is nervous when he goes out at night to do sail changes, but he appears fearless to me. I feel more comfortable manning the helm, holding us up into the wind if we need to take down or reef a sail during those riotous situations. I keep a watchful eye on the charts making sure we stay clear of shoals, reefs and protruding rocks. Robert has an uncanny ability to fix or jury-rig a broken system while underway, allowing us to continue our trip safely into port. I have a sense of the winds and often anticipate the shifts and gusts before they hit and adjust the sails accordingly. Together we work as a team, and part of that teamwork is that I consider Robert the captain of our ship.

What happens if the captain morphs into a bellicose drunk, an arrogant egotist, a petty tyrant, a micro-manager, a yeller, or a hardheaded control freak? It is no fun to say the least. If this is the case, assert yourself while you and the boat are still safely tied to the dock. In the tight quarters and long hours together at sea, the problems will only be exacerbated.

Tales abound from the sea about the Captain from Hell, Captain Bligh, Captain Ahab, not to mention some of the vicious pirates. Here's a short tale about my captain, when he metamorphosed into his *evil twin*.

One sunny afternoon we left an anchorage surrounded by shoals and just as we were entering a narrow spot the breeze began to pick up. Since we were motoring slowly with caution, we were unwittingly blown off course onto a sandbar. I was at the helm and did not realize how much the wind had pushed us to leeward. Suddenly we were stuck fast in the sand. Robert was putting away equipment on deck at the time and was not at his usual position on the bow watching the channel. He had left me alone to negotiate the shallows. We had been in and out of this anchorage at least a dozen times and I thought I could handle it. I felt terrible that I hadn't lived up to the responsibility. Robert was furious that I had landed us on the sandbar, making us look incompetent. Fortunately it was low tide, and the water in the lagoon was slowly creeping higher. After waiting for a couple of hours for the tide to rise, several of our fellow cruisers came in their dinghies and like miniature tugboats, pushed us into the deeper channel, and we were on our way with only a minor delay. However the thought of being stuck in the mud, aground was embarrassing even though we had helped numerous people laugh off their groundings, when we had helped push them off of the same sand bank. We both felt miserable, but Robert remained in an angry pout. When we were safely anchored for the evening, our friend Sean came over for a visit and listened to Robert rant about how I had steered us onto the bar. Sean asked, "Who's the captain on this boat?" and Robert reluctantly replied that he was. Sean reminded him that he was the one responsible for our boat aground. Despite his wounded pride, Robert had to agree that the captain was ultimately accountable for all that happened on the boat, good or bad. With that understood, Robert apologized and I forgave my temporarily crazed captain. Things relaxed and we could laugh again, recalling the old saying, 'you haven't been around if you haven't been aground.'

The Fear Factor

Before we left on our adventure and whenever we return to land, people often look at us with a worried expression. They question us about how we are *really* doing? They especially want to hear it from me, because I am a woman doing this outrageous adventure and they assume that I won't hide my true feelings. They ask, 'Are you sure you really like it?' or 'Aren't you afraid?' or 'Isn't it dangerous in Mexico,' or 'What about the storms?' They seem suspect of my positive answers, doubting that I could be telling the truth. This raises the biggest question that everyone wants to hear about, the fear factor. 'Isn't it scary?'

Hope Edelman wrote in her book, *Motherless Daughters, the Legacy of Loss* [22]. "The strength we gain from confronting our fears is ultimately what gives us the self-worth, the self-respect, and the courage to love and be loved in return." These powerful words are so beautifully written. However, putting them into action is a different story, a formidable undertaking, and yet rewarding in the end. Most of us recoil in terror at the idea of facing our fears head on. It seems too difficult to fathom. The super heroes with some magic tricks up their sleeves like Herculean strength, or invisibility are the only ones that can conquer the merciless evil. But how can a mere mortal slay the scary specters along our path?

Out on the high seas, when the wind comes up and the seas start smacking us around, I had to learn how to handle my fears and insecurities. It took practice and diligence to live in the moment and stay calm. Most of the time in rough weather it was strictly a matter of hanging on, but when I had to do a simple thing like trying to get a drink of water, paying close attention not to be thrown down the stairs in the ocean's roll required all of my concentration. I tried to deal with things as they came up. It is at times like these that some people pray, chant a mantra, or behave like Lieutenant Dan in *Forrest Gump*, dangling high in the rigging of their shrimp boat in a raging hurricane. Shaking his fist at the screaming winds, he challenged God to give him more! Staying focused I became mesmerized by the incredible forces at work, the ocean in turmoil. Finding that quiet place within where I could flow with it amid the surrounding chaos was my yoga. Things seemed overwhelming if I started worrying about what dangers might lie ahead, so I worked on staying here and now and did what was obvious.

Cheryl and Alex planned to cruise the South Pacific on the *Milk Run*, as it is called, one of the longer ocean passages of approximately 3000 miles of down-wind sailing. Cheryl was struggling with a deep fear of the upcoming trip. She inspired me to write a poem in hopes of helping her alleviate the gripping apprehension encircling her heart. I woke up at three in the morning with the words pouring from my pen. If you would like to read the poem, *Caught in the Storm*, see Appendix B. I had experienced fear in that raging storm around Point Sur and I had come to terms with it. It had been a powerful lesson and I wanted to pass it on. That experience of being pushed passed my limits had a long lasting and profound effect on me.

When Alex and Cheryl began their passage across the Pacific their rudder inexplicably fell off and sank to the bottom of the sea. They were 700 miles off shore and had reached the trade winds. They tried their entire list of emergency fix-its, but in the end they had to abort their trip and were towed to port by the Mexican Navy. Cheryl came face-to-face with her worst fears and survived. She became the newest member of the hardy club, resistant to fear, retaining her sense of humor, and ready to continue the cruising lifestyle. Several years went by, and they have now cruised successfully through the islands of the South Pacific, to New Zealand and Australia and on to Indonesia and Thailand with plans for traveling further west!

* * *

The sea itself can be a source of anxiety. So much water surrounds us and what about all those critters down there, including stinging things like jellyfish and eels. Sailing off shore means that you are usually many miles away from having terra firma under your feet and anyone who has had a frightening experience around the water, especially non-swimmers, may have the surprisingly common aqua phobia to deal with. The fear of the unknown can be overwhelming to someone who has little or no experience with the sea. The uncomfortable sensations of the boat heeling, bucking and tossing might make it difficult to relax. We can feel so small in the wide, rolling expanse of ocean, insignificant and not in control. There is the apprehension of not knowing what lies ahead in this open ended adventure. All of these frightful monsters can spring forth from the deep recesses of the sea and our imagination. Paranoia lurks in our anxious minds, mulling over and over what might happen including the worst case scenarios of a sinking ship, the boat on the rocks, man overboard, a lightning strike, and, of course, those old standbys, the perfect storm, pirates, and sharks!

Fear can show up in subtle ways or in full throttle panic mode. If your partner is dragging his/her feet, complaining, and putting on the brakes as the blast-off date approaches, some anxiety or other might be the reason behind it. It seems women more than men have a reluctance to give up the security of what is familiar, homey, comfortable, and in our control. Typically the risk takers are men who seek out a chance to live on the edge, but men also can be uncomfortable in rough weather, become seasick, and sometimes do not like being too far away from a marina. They might always have one more boat project to keep them dock bound. Perhaps it is more acceptable for women to be emotional and outspoken about our feelings. Although we may struggle with being fearful, we are usually less afraid to discuss and express our feelings then our partners. The reluctant cruiser may have feelings of foreboding, but as she travels and experiences nature's beauty, enchanting new places, and the camaraderie of other cruisers, the few rough passages can be offset by positive experiences. It becomes a matter of taking each downturn in stride, being able to take a deep breath and live moment to moment. Scary times are such a small percentage of the experience that I was able to treat them as a valuable lesson in facing my fears and did not live in dread. Each time I ran into an uncomfortable situation, my tolerance and bravery increased.

Favorable weather of less than ten knots of wind was forecast for the trip around the major promontory called Cabo Corrientes, a potentially rough section of the Mexican coast up against the prevailing seas and swells. Our friends, Sam and Julia, decided to take off in the morning and because we wanted to make a night passage, we would follow them later in the afternoon. Setting up an hourly schedule on the SSB radio we stayed in contact with them and set out into good sailing conditions. What seemed like a benign weather window, however, soon turned malicious. Shortly after midnight the troubled weather system that was supposed to remain over the mainland came sweeping down the mountains bringing squalls, lightning, rain, and heavy winds that churned the seas into frothy white capped, breaking waves. Julia reported deteriorating conditions up ahead near the cape. From out of nowhere and with only a five minute warning, a 70-knot gust laid their boat over at a precarious angle. They had been motoring with only their mizzen sail and after the boat righted itself, Julia quickly brought the sail down while Sam revved up the engine to hold the boat into the wind. They kept the motor idling to assist the autopilot and were doing eight knots under bare poles. On the radar she watched while three thunder and lightning-laden squalls converged in the vicinity of their boat. They were already nearly around the cape and resolved to weather it out in 40-knot winds and ten to twelve foot seas. With lightning striking all around them, they shut down their radio, and hunkered down in their cabin until the squalls passed. For most of the long night, we stayed in radio contact with Julia, which helped keep her spirits up. The nighttime gale raged and we could hear courage and confidence in her voice when she spoke to us with humor and self-assurance. Early in the morning they arrived safely in Banderas Bay. She signed off by expressing her gratitude that she had someone to talk to during a difficult and challenging voyage. The lightning gods had given them a reprieve and left them unscathed.

In the middle of the storm when the weather was not looking better up ahead, we made the decision to turn tail and run back to the anchorage that was only six hours away. The seas moderated soon after we turned around, sidestepping the stormy front and positively affirming our choice. In our travels we have discovered there are some situations where it is prudent to abort the mission rather than risk being pummeled. Our motto is, *when in doubt, chicken out*. Two days later, after waiting for the weather to improve and meeting a friendly family to buddy boat with, we had a comfortable trip under balmy blue skies and flat seas. Sam and Julia are still out cruising with us having traded their sailboat in for a trawler.

Years later we were making the crossing from the Baja peninsula heading east towards San Carlos on the Mexican mainland coast. When we arrived we would do the yearly drill of putting the boat up on the hard for the hot summer season. If we left in the late afternoon on this eighty-mile passage, we would sail through the night arriving during daylight hours instead of having to navigate the narrow entrance of the harbor in the dark. The weather called for good honking winds, building to a brisk 20-25 knots in the middle of the sea. We were low on fuel and we took this opportunity to sail rather than use the motor. Before leaving we talked with Roger and Sally who were on a 26-foot sailboat that they had brought down on a trailer. They wanted to make the same passage and we discussed traveling across together. Attempting to discourage them by relating the weather report that it was going to be somewhat boisterous didn't change their minds. We soon weighed anchor with our new friends behind us. The first few hours were a motor sail with hardly any wind. When we ventured out from under the lee of Isla Tortuga, the skies were illuminated by the last, faint, orange glow of twilight outlining the rugged mountains, the backbone of the Baja coast. The wind picked up and for the rest of the trip we were heeled over 15 to 25 degrees blasting along in a watery groove. I was off watch and nestled in my bunk attempting a restless sleep with the broad beam waves slapping loudly against the hull. At one point the noise was so loud I bolted up into the cockpit to see if we had hit something. Thank goodness, it was only a square, rogue wave whacking us hard on the port side. In our white froth wake bioluminescence sparkled. It was wild, but okay. I knew we just had to hang on (yet again!). When we neared mid-sea, the wind and waves increased. Robert went out on deck to take down the main sail while I turned the wheel hard to port facing up into the wind. At that point things really started banging and pitching. Whenever Robert goes out on deck in rough conditions he's always harnessed on to a lifeline secured to the deck. I say; "good luck, stay safe," and I keep a close eye on him. It was dark, wet and ferocious as he fought the main down and finished tying up the sail. Soon we were traveling slower under jib and jigger, (the front jib sail and the mizzen sail or aft sail on our two-masted ketch) a less intense ride. We had been sailing so fast that we were scheduled to arrive at the harbor entrance before light, but with moderated speed we would anchor in the early light of dawn.

When we neared the calm entrance to the protected bay, there, silhouetted against the pastel colors of daybreak, was our little buddy boat motoring in ahead of us. After we set the anchor and ate a hardy breakfast, we called them to see how they had fared and they asked if we would come by later and talk about the passage. After a short rest, we launched the dinghy and visited our new friends tucked safely in the marina. Their experience had been totally different from ours. They had lived through a miserable, frightful night, motoring the entire way with waves splashing over the decks and Roger unable to go forward to raise the sails. The sails had been our saving grace. They provided balance, held us steady and kept us from bouncing back and forth on the beam seas. Sally said, "You know what I was doing? I was sitting right here at my salon table saying Hail Mary's all night long." We could not imagine being in those rough seas aboard their small boat with the outboard humming and no sails set. Despite their hair-raising adventure they had made it to port safely and in good time, Hail Mary's and all.

Courage is the ultimate cure. After confronting our deepest anxieties, fear can be worked out of our systems. In her book, *Feel the Fear and Do it Anyway* [23], Sara Jeffers describes helpful exercises to conquer nagging apprehension by forging ahead despite our disquietude. For me, a threat diminishes when I can face an intimidating situation, stare it down, swallow it, digest it, and push on past my panicked reaction.

During a typical nightmare a menacing presence chases us down a dark alley or we find ourselves falling, falling. When I found myself with a recurring, scary dream, before I went to sleep I would visualize how I wanted the scene to be played out. Reprogramming my response, I would change the pattern, and the nightmare would magically disappear. Amazingly in the dream state when I decided to continue flowing with my fall, I discovered that there was only a foot high drop beneath me. When I turned around and confronted whoever it was that was chasing me, they were no longer sinister and faded away. These disruptions to my restful sleep dared me to acknowledge them, to confront them head on. The same held true for my daytime fears. Once I accepted and even embraced my uneasy feelings, I could understand where they originated, look them in the eyes, let them go, and calm my stomach clenching response. In order to free myself from the chains of anxiety I had to take deliberate steps to conquer this dizzying apprehension. Deep breathing helped me to remain in a state of tranquility even when the seas were anything but. First, I breathed in and out deeply, consciously following my breath. It also helped to count – I breathed in for seven beats and out for seven beats. As a result, my thoughts cleared, and I was transported into that *no mind* zone far above the anxiety-causing situation. I created an overview that was peaceful, calm, and courageous. A sense of unconditional love surrounded me and I felt assured that I could do what was required in the situation. This exercise in deep breathing aided me in confronting each fear that arose from my depths. I was able to challenge its very existence and then discard it. In doing so, I stood unruffled, surrounded by serenity amidst the chaos. The Dalai Lama in *The Art of Happiness* [24] described a way to face fears and anxieties by examining the situation, devising a solution, and then working towards it. This process helped alleviate the stress so that worry would disappear. If there was a problem with no solution, than there was still no need to worry, because it would not help anyway.

Understanding that I struggled with anxiety, Robert helped by asking me to do things that were necessary for our comfort and safety, things that were routine. When I stayed busy I didn't have time to be distracted by all the bad things that *could* happen. It became easier to relax, breathe deeply, and let go.

Anxiety for someone just starting out can be relieved if they take the time to learn how to become proficient at sailing. Enrolling in a sailing class has helped many reluctant, insecure sailors. Confidence is built when they have a chance to hold the wheel and feel how the wind affects the boat. People tend to grow comfortable with sailing, surrounded by competent role models, and new knowledge and experience allows a person to feel in control. Several of our friends remarked how the camaraderie of a non-competitive, women-only training cruise was the most valuable and highly entertaining thing they did to prepare for cruising. Practicing in optimal conditions turns sailing into an enjoyable experience. When a sailor has an experienced, trusted, courageous partner aboard, fear and uncertainty is diminished and safety is assured.

While having sunset drinks with fellow cruisers, Gwen and Tim, Gwen mentioned how they had been having an interesting time buddy boating with the crew on *Wayward Wind*. Just for fun, they decided that for one day the women would travel aboard one boat and the men on the other. She said sailing without her mate aboard gave her a sense of self-reliance, knowing that she could sail the boat alone. Many cruising couples alternate roles so that the woman takes a turn at the *blue* jobs, in our case, sail changes or lowering the anchor, and the men try their hand at the *pink* jobs, which for us are piloting or navigating. The fear factor was diminished when we understood how things worked on the boat.

Drinking lots of water and avoiding fatigue helps prevent frazzled nerves. Panic is more apt to rear its ugly head when a sailor is strung out, tired, cold, hungry, or dehydrated. In any sport, nourishing meals and quick snacks are part of what keeps us going.

The perfect storm stories of disasters, near misses and death make for good reading and riveting movies, but we found that they were such a small part of cruising that it was wildly misleading. Movies like Jaws enhance people's fear of the wildlife that lives in the sea. We avoid going swimming in shark-infested waters, but there are many sharks that are actually safe to dive with. The small hammerhead or large whale sharks in Mexico or the nurse sharks in the Panamanian Las Perlas Islands pose little threat to humans. We have yet to see a dangerous shark in all of our years of snorkeling up and down the tropical coast.

It is reassuring to Robert and me to talk about the up and coming passage before we embark. We go over the charts, understand the hazards if there are any, listen to the weather, and perhaps discuss local conditions with folks who are familiar with the area. There is really no reason to go out into a storm, unless you are ready to experience it. If we are on a long passage we may not be able to avoid a rough section, but knowing the right seasons and conditions, lessens the possibility of finding ourselves in an uncomfortable or scary situation. When we made the trip from Costa Rica to Ecuador, we knew that we were heading through the ITCZ, the Inter Tropical Convergence Zone, where squalls proliferate. The spring months are supposed to have the best possible conditions so we timed our trip for mid-April. Having an idea of what to expect, we prepared by reefing the sails, and securing everything. Although we had to bash through some squalls, and the going was fairly rough, it was manageable and we had a safe trip all the way.

Jonathan and Sarah, who had sailed the South Pacific to Australia, avoided bad weather on notoriously, lengthy, rough crossings by paying for a passage router. The router was equipped with all the latest, modern meteorological instruments and could see weather systems approaching the planned rhumb line days in advance. On the particularly infamous, storm-prone, eleven-day passage from Tonga to New Zealand, they waited for three weeks for the go ahead, while persistent storms kept sweeping the area. Yachties leaving before them experienced unpleasant trips, and heaved to for days in huge seas. Some even sustained damage to their boats. Their nightmarish experiences were the opposite of Jonathan and Sarah's relatively uneventful sail.

On our trial run Robert knew deep down that he wanted to experience a storm. He wanted to know what it was like, how he would handle it, and what he could learn from it. Unlike storm-chasers, we certainly did not consciously search for a tempest, but eventually our inexperience caught up with us and his desires became a reality. The unintentional benefit was that once we had weathered big seas and high winds everything less was manageable.

One of Robert's favorite authors is Tristan Jones, a sea faring yarn teller of remarkable talent who wrote *The Incredible Voyage*. He was sailing down the coast of East Africa, covering 144 miles a day aboard his boat, Barbara, in a stiff 30- to 35 knots of wind.

On the third day they hit their first cyclone and 'within an hour we were battling winds of seventy knots with tremendous seas.... It was as if God himself was having a fit. But in *Barbara*, though uncomfortable, we were not unduly fearful... From the foregoing no one should imagine, if they have never experienced a full-blown storm at sea, that the ocean voyager becomes blasé about it, or that the living fear of Christ does not enter into his soul and emerge down his spine to his balls. Because he doesn't and it does. Every time. At least in my case. Most of the ocean voyagers to whom I have talked about this agree with me.... they (women) are one hundred percent truthful when it comes to admitting fear. I suppose some guys still have the remains of shore-side machismo in them...If they think any the less of me for being honest about it, then let them take off and navigate in a rip-roaring cyclone, with certain death under the lee in the black, stormy, rain lashed, uncertain depths... Then they can look down their noses, if they like. But don't let them tell me they were not afraid up to a certain point. I say a certain point, because there comes a time when, without any diminution of the dangers, you get beyond fear. You come to realize that it interferes with logical thought and isn't solving anything. You've done all you can do to avoid disaster, now you are in the hands of God. When this moment comes, a man feels the greatest peace of mind that is possible for him ever to experience. At that moment he realizes that death is not terribly important, even though it is inevitable, and that he has lived his life as well as he could in his own way. If this is the end, then fair enough, he's lived this life, now for the *next*. Then some regret, not at the thought of losing your life, but because you have put yourself in that situation. You determine to survive. *In extremis*, survival is the result of being angry with you for being a bloody fool! I have very often been in a situation in which I did not think I would survive, but, by God, I would go on trying - I was going to play the bloody game right down to the bottom line, because it's fun. Also it's very interesting. Also, for the time being, *it's all we have.*' [25]

The Fear Factor

~ Storms ~

Gales blow in on the Pacific west coast heralded by the weather stations' warnings of excessive winds and turbulent seas, horizontal rain, broken levees, and flooding rivers. The trees begin to rustle when the storm pushes warm, still air ahead catching everyone's attention. 'It feels like summertime,' people comment, unburdening themselves from the layers of wintertime garb. The pungent breeze turns to gusts of wind bending the trees to the northeast as the southwesterly kicks up the dust devils. A front-page section of the newspaper separated from its cocoon of classified ads, local dramas, and sports statistics, tumbles along the highway, billowing up, soaring, and then somersaulting along, not unlike the national figures on its front page.

The populace settles into their insulated homes closing the windows and doors, bringing the pets and lawn chairs inside, and stacking sandbags where needed. Commuters in their cozy cars rush home, and then rush out again, scurrying here and there to buy groceries, batteries, and flashlights before the storm hits directly overhead. The pressure is dropping and the tension is palpable, not only in grandpa's arthritic shoulder, but in everyone's psyche as they prepare for something outside of their comfort zone.

The storm finally blows in with everyone safely nestled in warm, secure, houses, listening to the rain beat down on the shingles and tiles, cringing when the thunder crashes close by. The lightning brightens the night and twinges of anxiety creep in. The first tendency might register as fear, afraid of the sheer power of nature, the loud noises, and bright flashing lights. But soon excitement takes over. Sheltered behind closed doors, snuggled up to our warm heater, we shout out oohs and aahs when the lightning flashes, heaven's fireworks. The thunder's deafening tympanic display astonishes us. Soothed by the sound of the raindrops against the windowpanes, and awed by the power of the wind in the tree branches, we soon fall into a restful sleep.

The next day the sky is a crystal clear blue. The profligate front page of the newspaper has vanished down a storm drain. Somewhere back in my mind I wish the storm water would take the sensationalized stories along with it. The pounding rain has washed away all the accumulated dust, trash, and tree droppings. Breathing in the fresh, crisp, air, washed sparklingly clean, the birds sing again, glad for another day to feed and chatter. The gentle smell in the air is like clean laundry hung out to dry on a sunny day, sweet aroma, free of dirt and pollution.

We venture out to look around and see what damage the storm has brought, tree limbs scattered on the sidewalk, overflowing streets, a fence blown down, and a few roof shingles askew. New fruit blossoms apron the orchard like freshly fallen snow. When the storm is extreme, trees fall across the road, their root systems waving in the air, and power lines dangle down dangerously.

Squalls on the horizon in Costa Rica.

It feels like we have been purified, transported from apprehension to exhilaration, from dampening tension to all-encompassing contentment. When the incoming high pushes the low-pressure system to the east, the emotions rise to embrace the new day. Old depressions and harried dramas somehow have been swept away by the gurgling streams, the flooded creeks carrying them away to the rising rivers, to the majestic ocean that is always receptive to our offerings.

A storm at sea is a beast of the same species. It comes with all the rain, the blow, the tension of low pressure, the anxiety, and the exhilaration. The big difference is that we are on a boat in the middle of the tempest, hunkered down in our heaving cockpit, rather than in a cozy, sturdy, stationary house on land. The boat is moving with the ocean sloshing under us, and driving rain is above us and on all sides. We are heeling at odd angles, spilling down a wave, not still and quiet, amidst the noise outside. Caught in a squall, the lightning flashes, and the thunder explodes in our ears, blanketing us with its loud booms.

Our mast sticks high into the sky, waving around as if tempting Thor to strike us with his fiery bolts. We become one with the storm instead of tucked away from its power and force, and one with the elements of water, wind, lightning, and thunder. The primal fears are real and acute, to be dealt with and faced in the moment, for we have a boat to drive through this confusion. Weathering a storm is one of the pop quizzes in our education at sea. Rarely does anyone rush out into a storm, but when we play this game, it is inevitable. Even after waiting patiently for a good weather window, we still occasionally find ourselves in a storm for which there was no accounting.

Usually the boat is reliable and crashes and bumps, hour after hour onward. Or if we feel like stopping for a rest, it nestles comfortably in the waves, heaved-to like a cat curled up on a bouncing couch. The boat is in her element, riding the surging water like a cowboy taming a bucking bronco. Slicing through the waves, rooster tails of white spray splash to both sides and up over the decks, and *Harmony* glorifies in her ability to go up, up, up and then down, down, down into the swirling troughs.

When we arrive at the dock safe and sound, and plant our feet on terra firma, we own a fresh outlook on life. Grateful cannot adequately describe all that we feel. There is satisfaction in having conquered our demons. We've been to the summit and back and survived. We've haggled with death and are still alive to tell our story. Relief is mixed with exhaustion, appreciation mixed with awe. Then we ask ourselves if somehow must we taste a bit of hell to truly enjoy paradise? Our dock mates swarm around us when we describe the ordeal and adventure. They struggle to grasp what we've been through listening to the hair-raising tales from real life. They are as close as they want to come to weathering a real storm when we show off our scars of battle, a bruise here, and a boat bite there. Dining with a mix of hunger and gusto, we raise a celebratory nip of grog to help ease our tired and aching bones. After a long, deep sleep on calm seas, we wake up and somehow our memory has distilled out the positive from the negative and we 'wonder what all the fuss was about.'

The Fear Factor

~ Seasickness ~

Mal de mer, barfarama, tossing up the cookies, turning green, feeding the fishes… Our kids made a long list of all the names for seasickness, but it is far from humorous to those who suffer. This malady in itself can be a reason not to go cruising. There is nothing worse than feeling ill and confined in a boat that never stops heaving, tilting, and rolling. People who battle with seasickness might think death is a more attractive alternative.

We advise friends and family aboard to focus on the horizon, to reeducate the sensitive inner ear into handling the boat's unsteady, dizzying movement. Steering the boat can also distract an unsettled stomach. Our friend, Emily kept it together by sitting quietly amid-ship until the churning subsided. Our diet when we're on *Harmony* consists of eating lightly before and during the first day of a passage, which can alleviate the problem. If all else fails, unloading a full queasy stomach over the leeward side can do wonders to settle the inner turmoil.

On a bumpy passage across the Sea of Cortez, our daughter, Olivia, felt like her stomach was doing somersaults. She bravely watched the horizon, trying not to succumb. We were sailing hard with 20-knots of wind on the beam in a light norther with plenty of white caps and choppy waves. Suddenly Olivia yells, 'There is a pod of whales directly in front of us!' We instantly turned off Piley, the autopilot, and steered up into the wind to avoid a collision. The close encounter had our daughter jumping out on the bouncing deck to have a better look at the *ballenas gigantes* while they swam close by our bow. It was an incredible nature moment and we were awestruck. In the thick of all the uproar and action, as if by magic her seasickness disappeared and never reared its ugly head for the rest of the 14-hour passage.

Bernie Siegel, M.D., the author of *Love, Medicine and Miracles* [26], describes a fishing trip that he made with his father when he was a young child. He immediately suffered from seasickness and from then on presumed he would always have this problem. The family continued to enjoy boating and he would even become ill on the drive to the boat. After watching the power of mind over matter when his exceptional cancer patients would miraculously visualize their tumors away, he decided he would not be seasick anymore. He reprogrammed himself through meditation to no longer become nauseated. This worked so well, that in stormy conditions he was able to stay out on the boat with no problems, even when the rest of his family was ready to call it quits.

Then there is the medicinal solution, ah, drugs! Medications can calm a disturbed belly when nothing else does. You may need to experiment to find which drug will do the trick, but if you suffer from *mal de mer*, hopefully you can find a cure. Taking short off shore trips to try different methods or medications can help you find out what works. There are prescribed drugs, over the counter meds, wrist bracelets, chewing gum, or ginger candies. More than a few sailors swear that Stugeron (Cinnarizine that is not available in the U.S.) is an absolute wonder drug. There is also the old mariner's assurance that on a long passage, a sailor will usually find his sea legs after a couple of days or three. Then again we know cruising friends who never stop feeling seasick until they reach port.

The only time Robert felt vaguely seasick was when we were safely anchored, but in a rolly spot with the wave sets pitching us around. He woke up in the middle of the night and had to walk around to shake off the queasy feeling. After a long stretch at sea when I find myself on shore in a small, confining space like a bathroom stall, the walls and floors start undulating and a dizzying feeling can come over me creating a reverse mal de mer that I call land sickness. I stumble out into the fresh air and breathe deeply to regain my equilibrium.

Sea-sickness has in some cases been linked to anxiety and fear, and might possibly subside when a person resolves to go bravely into that good night. You might consider the emotional connections and take a look deep within the psyche. Are there some anxious conditional responses to rough water or storms that you could discard? Do you carry around unconscious fears that hinder your enjoyment of sailing? This soul searching may be hard work, but the benefits of overcoming a fear are worth it. There is inner strength to be found there. 'Perseverance furthers', quotes the *I Ching*. If all else fails, no need to torture yourself. Pick another dream to pursue.

The Fear Factor

~ Lightning ~

With his tall, aluminum or wooden masts and web of rigging piercing the skies, the sailor has a legitimate fear of lightning. When we were first preparing to go cruising, we asked an old salt, who had cruised to Australia and back what he did to protect his boat from a lightning strike. He answered with a chuckle, that he always anchored next to a boat with a taller mast. Anchoring in the shadow of a hill or near a mountain worked as well. There has been an ongoing discussion about using heavy-duty jumper cables hung overboard into the ocean to channel the electric force back into the water, but the jury is still out on the effectiveness of that option. The intense power of a lightning bolt is so great that it tends to go where it wishes. It seems to be the luck of the draw, the gamble each sailor takes. Refraining from cruising during lightning prone seasons is one way to avoid the devastating experience. When we were in Panama we heard of several boats having a tussle with Thor's spear with damage costs in the vicinity of $10,000 each. A local cruiser estimated that as many as 10% of the boats were struck and for an old horse racing fan, those are not good odds. Of course, most of these strikes occurred during the rainy season when the majority of boats leave the region for Ecuador, Cartagena, Colombia, or the South Pacific.

Friends, Joe and Felicia of *Land's End* were sailing off the coast of El Salvador when a strike hit the water fifty feet behind them. The charge came up through the ground plane and knocked out all of their electrical equipment. When we were in Panama we heard a first-hand account of a ball of fire spewing off the mast of a neighboring yacht at anchor taking bits of wind vane with it. This voltage-laden bolt charred the rigging and fried the electronics. Random luck had the owners away at the time. And then there was Elena's catamaran, moored in Panama during the off-season, whose fiberglass decks and bottom were splattered with small burn holes after being struck. All of these incidences occurred between El Salvador and Panama where lightning laden squalls are common even during the best cruising season. The chances of being hit are minimized when you cruise in these waters from the middle of December to the middle of May. Unfortunately, this is also the season of the Papagayo winds off of Nicaragua and northern Costa Rica. The Papagayo's are the enhanced winds that blow over Lake Nicaragua from the Caribbean. The high mountains of the Sierra Madre form the backbone of the region, flattening out around the lake. This creates an accelerated gap wind that is ferocious and can blow throughout the day or rage all day and night at up to 60+ knots. We sailed this area for two years during the favorable months, and experienced localized storms with nasty squalls loaded with lightning and high winds. Somehow with the help of the mighty spirits, (there are no atheists on the high seas when the bolts start flashing) we managed to stay out of harm's way.

When threatening black clouds are in the area some sailors store their electronics in a Faraday box, a metal container, like the oven, or a cooler lined with metal screen. However, we never go near the antenna connection or touch anything metal when lightning strikes are near. In all the years that we have cruised in Mexico we have only heard of a few yachts tangling with lightening. A couple of boats were struck when an unusual weather pattern related to an El Niño year brought lightning laced tropical squalls to an otherwise storm free area. We were hunkered down near a hill, but strikes were in the water all around *Harmony*. Nearby, a foot-wide bolt shattered our peace of mind and pelicans scattered off of their perches on the pangas anchored in the bay. It was dramatic but no damage was done.

The Fear Factor

~ Pirates ~

Although piracy is not quite the oldest profession, there seems to be a long history of innocent sailors suffering at the hands of these ruthless marauders. Tales of lucrative treasure and daring adventure tempt those brave enough to risk it all. A few violent encounters make the headlines and are truly frightening, but are also rare. In our world the growing discrepancies between the haves and have-nots are exacerbated by global TV brought into the humblest villages. There is a deep divide that may tempt daring young dudes to step over to the dark side. Ships steam by their countries loaded with valuable cargo and cruising yachts seem like an enticing, floating goldmine to the eyes of impoverished folks in Third World lands. Modern pirates primarily operate in the waters around poor countries in transition, where local law and order is barely secure on land, let alone out at sea. Places in the world that have been notorious for piratical encounters are the South China Sea, the Straits of Malacca, and the Somali Coast.

Isolated incidents have been reported in scattered areas of coastline around Venezuela, Eastern Guatemala, and Colombia. In other areas petty thievery exists that can lighten a cruising boat of its dinghy, outboard motor, or things left out temptingly on deck or in an easily accessible cabin.

Mexico has been an amazingly safe arena for cruising boats. There is the occasional missing dinghy and outboard which although very annoying and distressing, is rare and easily preventable (hoist the dinghy aboard at night). The ultimate cost is often just a new outboard since the dingy *sans* outboard is often recovered. We've been approached by pangas in the Sea of Cortez who were not pirates at all, but fishermen low on water or gas. We were happy to give them what they needed. Scary stories, blown out of proportion, emanating from our hyped up media about Mexico have been a big detriment to the tourist industry and economy of our amicable neighbor to the south. When you compare the violence statistics of Mexico to our U.S. record, living in our country is far more dangerous.

In Costa Rica, for some reason, petty thievery was more common than other countries along the Eastern Pacific coast. Cruisers were advised to keep a closer watch on their stuff, especially when riding the local buses. A sad tale was told by Jordan on *SV Pegasus*, one of three young sailors who had pooled their resources to buy their boat and had traveled as far as Costa Rica from California on their way to Panama. Enjoying the nightlife ashore at a bar in Playa de Cocos, he was befriended by some local men who invited him to a party at their house. Things turned ugly when he was roughed up and robbed of his backpack, which unfortunately contained his passport and money. He emerged wiser from his experience, and his common sense quotient rose proportionately.

Our sailing buddies Donna and Don decided to rent an air-conditioned room on shore. It had been a long hot trip from southern Mexico to humid Golfito, Costa Rica and they thought a night in cool comfort would give them a taste of paradise. On Easter morning, while they were out celebrating with friends, a local bandito entered their room by breaking through the wall under an outdoor sink, and stole their computer. The boats on the moorings were untouched. Apparently there were easier pickings on land.

On our voyage from Costa Rica to Ecuador, we sailed hundreds of miles off the Colombian coast, and during the entire cruise we spotted only one large fishing boat in our five days at sea. Returning from Ecuador to Panama we sailed closer to the coast, but were still sixty to a hundred miles off shore. Early one morning while we were sailing hard downwind in 15-20 knots of wind with a two to three knot Humboldt Current going our way, we were approached by a fast moving panga with four gnarly dudes aboard. They steered close in to *Harmony* and our first thought was that these were the pirates we had heard so much about. We both came out on deck to greet them, and they yelled out, 'comida, comida,' with their hands cupped in the shape of a bowl. We had stumbled onto an offshore bank and they were hungry fishermen far from shore. I quickly went below and made up a care package of fruit, bread, cookies, and some canned goods. They thanked us and sped away. The following morning found us one hundred and thirty miles from shore and we could not believe it when two pangas approached us. Once again all they wanted was food. We made up another care package, and they showered us with thanks and then proceeded to help us navigate through their fishing lines that were dead ahead of us. Several cruisers have harbor-hopped along the Colombian coast with no unpleasant experiences, although one sailor mentioned that he was warned by the local people to be very careful in town.

Pirate encounters do happen, however. The good people on

Wandering Dream had a frightening experience off the Ecuadorian coast when their sailboat was boarded in the middle of a dark night while they were at anchor. The armed men physically accosted and robbed them. Their buddy boat heard their screams, immediately sounded the air horn, turned on their spot light, and set off a couple of flares that succeeded in chasing the thieves away. Their quick action probably saved their friends' lives. It was a very traumatic and unusual occurrence, but it made us all take our safety precautions seriously. We have heard of instances like this one that were scary and even tragic, but they are the exception to the rule. We cruisers often travel the world with a comforting sense of denial, disregarding the blaring headlines of political unrest and violence. It won't happen to us, we tell ourselves. In most cases it's like telling someone not to visit the U.S., because there are murders in the rough sections of some of our big cities. When we were on an extended stay in Buenos Aires, our landlord drew a line across a map of the city, telling us to stay north of this line and we would be safe. We were out in the crowds every day enjoying the fascinating city while kidnappings, demonstrations and riots littered the front pages of the newspapers. We never felt any personal danger in the least. Out on the oceans there is a greater chance of having bad weather than being accosted by humans. We rarely see any vessels at all except for the occasional fishermen or freighter.

A small percentage of cruisers carry weapons. If the Mexican Navy finds guns, it could be big trouble, perhaps leading to the confiscation of the boat and a jail sentence. Also the bad guys usually have bigger weapons, and we prefer not to play that game. Life on the high seas is not without risks and on those rare occasions when we might tangle with a dangerous situation, we face our mortality. In the movie, *Little Big Man*, starring Dustin Hoffman, his adopted Native American father was always talking about it being 'a good day to die.'

Traveling with one or more buddy boats, particularly in well-known dangerous areas, creates a safety-in-numbers situation that can deter problems. We watch out for one another, and when at anchor, we keep an eye on each other's boats.

The Fear Factor

~ Buddy Boating ~

Whether it was planned or we just happened to be going the same way at the same time, making a passage with a buddy boat can make the trip more interesting, safe, and fun. We gab away on our private VHF channel and if something weird happens, they are within range. Sometimes we even get caught up in the competitive spirit of racing. When we were in Ecuador we met a couple from Austria with two small children aboard. They were buddy boating with her parents which allowed the grandparents to spend quality time with the children at sea and on shore. Close friends often leave the dock together or meet up along the way. Generally we hook up with a buddy boat when we share the same itinerary. We have found it especially comforting to have company along when we leave on an extended passage through unfamiliar territory. We certainly do not mind making passages by ourselves, but the enjoyment is increased when the trip is shared.

While we were waiting out a storm at anchor, we made the

acquaintance of the good folk on *Fantasia*, our sister ship, an Islander Freeport 40'. Jeff and Annie, accompanied by their two daughters, Krysta and Julie, were sailing in Mexico on a year's adventure. Because we were both aiming for the same port on the same basic time line, we sailed together for nearly a month traveling 800 miles to San Carlos from Chamela, south of Puerto Vallarta. We were going to put our boat on the hard and they were trucking their boat home to Monterey Bay. Equipped with the same engine and sail configuration, our two boats traveled at the same speed. Even on the longer two-day trip across the Sea of Cortez, we were never out of sight of each other, spotting their mast light at night and giving each other a head's up when a lit up ferry passed us on our rhumb line. On the night watches we checked in every hour, often with a joke, trivia, or riddle that made the long passages tick by quickly. Early one morning we were sailing around the top of Cerralvo Island near La Paz when an unusual fog came drifting across our bow. The haze enveloped us in a thick gray mist and we wondered if we were in the Sea of Cortez or back in San Francisco Bay? Our trusty radar chose that moment to go on the blink and Fantasia turned out to be a lifesaver when she led us around a rocky outcropping and safely into the anchorage on the island of Partida.

In the spring of 2003 eleven boats were restlessly biding their time in Mazatlan until we could make the 190-mile dash across the sea to the Baja Coast. The weather had been particularly foul for a week or more and everyone was waiting for the northers to calm down. When the winds finally started to ease, the weathermen were still ambivalent about whether it was a good window for the two-day passage. We appreciate our trusty prognosticators and for the most part we take their advice, but our impatience and herd mentality failed to discern (or perhaps disregarded) the uncertainty in their predictions. Our penalty turned out to be a rocking and rolling trip to windward.

The seas picked up, the ride became more and more uncomfortable in the steep, square waves, and everyone was battened down. The boats sailing south had a downhill romp, but the rest of us were charging west with water spraying everywhere. We established a VHF net with the group and checked in to make sure everyone was okay. At one point when it was especially rough and fatigue was wearing us down, Robert decided to try to have some fun and declared the hourly check-in an official *bitch session*. 'Let's hear it. We want details.' Lacy was on her last loaf of white Bimbo (Mexican brand) bread, the only thing her stomach could hold down, and was cozy in her one dry spot under the dodger. Robert had sprained his ankle negotiating the step from the deck into the cockpit and that darn pin had dislodged from the autopilot again. He moaned about having to repair it underway in bouncy conditions. Karen was suffering from mal de mer and Greg's back was out. Lacy checked back in bemoaning the fact that while she thought she'd been doing reasonably well despite her heaving stomach, a big wave had just come barreling in. It splashed over the dodger, soaked her only dry spot, and salty, cold seawater was dripping on her head! The Martha Stewart of our group, Rachel checked in to say that she was baking brownies! Everyone was laughing and having such a good time comparing notes and commiserating with 'aww, that is so rough, you poor thing,' and 'I want one of those brownies,' etc., that it seemed to make the rest of the trip go easier. It wasn't long before we met up with a favorable current that hurried us towards shore. The front-runners made it into the anchorage before dark, and our buddies' bright spotlights and helpful directions aided those of us who followed.

Nothing bonds cruisers together more than sharing a passage, and becoming acquainted as the miles drift away. Sometimes we meet our buddy boats under way and although we know their voices well, we've never met them in person. Arriving at a port or anchorage, we meet face-to-face and celebrate our trip, sharing a meal together, taking hikes, and snorkeling. Once the passage making is over, we often spend a day shopping for provisions in the markets, sharing the taxi expenses, and talking. The guys help each other with boat problems, and inevitably take a break for a beer.

The down side of buddy boating unfortunately happens when cruisers become 'attached at the hip.' The constant togetherness leaves little time to meet other cruisers, and local folks. We have heard sailors complain that it can be too much of a good thing. Planned outings and meals together becomes a big commitment, and then there is the feeling that there is not enough time for just the two of you. When we return to California, we occasionally visit our cruising buddies in their land-based homes, and e-mail keeps us in touch long after we have sailed on to different parts of the world.

The Fear Factor

~ Ghost Stories ~

Buddy boating with Amy and Scott aboard *Misty* is always a blast and we've traveled together on several occasions. On one of our night watches we spent the time telling ghost stories. A ghost haunted Amy's night watches, but never Scott's [27]. When Amy was at the navigation table checking the boat's position and progress, she heard a plaintive 'Ma ma' from somewhere in the lockers! Thorough searches had turned up nothing. When she was home for the summer she mentioned this strange phenomenon to a friend and not long after that, the friend had a dream. The dream was about a boy who had a traumatic death and afterward chose *Misty* for his temporary home since he was somehow unable to move forward into the next life. She told Amy that the next time she heard the ghost, to tell him that it was okay for him to move on. Since then her night passages have remained quiet. He must have received the message.

Ghosts make their appearance at the most unexpected times, and once on a particularly riotous night passage, while returning north up the Mexican coast, Robert was on watch. In between catnaps he would pop up every 10-15 minutes to look around and check the instruments. Once he over-slept by a few minutes and he awoke with a start hearing a gravelly, grouchy voice complaining, 'I do everything around here, the watches, looking out for everything, and do I ever get one word of appreciation?' Then there was more grousing about 'everybody is drunk and sleeping through their watch!' Our ghost must have had about enough of the turbulent seas. It reminded us of the story of Joshua Slocum's circumnavigation. He was sick in his bunk and through his delirium he watched as Christopher Columbus' pilot of the Pinta, [28] a rough and tumble old salt, manned his tiller, steering him safely through the difficult night. It's somewhat comforting to know that we aren't the only boat with a ghost. One night not long after we bought *Harmony*, Robert was thrown out of our berth while tied to the dock. Our ghost also hides things and is a bit of a rascally spirit, but if we laugh about his shenanigans, the lost items soon reappear. Maybe the ancient Vikings had it right when they sent their dead to the other world in a torched long boat so the spirit could journey safely and directly to the other side.

The Cruising Life

~ Mañana Time ~

Docked comfortably in Marina de la Paz after our long trip from San Francisco, we would gather with fellow cruisers at the end of the dock each evening to take in the consistently spectacular sunsets. The evening banter would often involve each boat's plans and next destination. Major changes to the cruising plans take place in a town like La Paz or an anchorage like Tenacatita near Barra de Navidad where sailors stop to catch their breath and settle in for an extended visit. A few sailors decide to go to the South Pacific instead of voyaging through the Panama Canal and vice versa. Instead of taking the giant step to the South Pacific from Mexico, crews decide they don't want to miss Central and South America and the Galapagos Islands. Visions of going to the South Pacific end up on hold for a year or more while some mariners slow down and enjoy the coastal cruising that Mexico has to offer before sailing off to more distant destinations. Occasionally a west coast boater, on their way home will plan on avoiding the notorious Baja Bash, by returning via Hawaii, the old sailing ship route. Inevitably, crews who decide that they have had enough of cruising agree to finish out the season, sell their boat, or sail home. A few yachts with children aboard have a good time until the kids want to return to school with their friends. Mexico is a decision-making place where people slow down and plans are revamped.

A survey was taken among South Pacific cruisers a few years ago. One of the questions was "What would you have done differently?" An overwhelming majority said they would have spent more time in Mexico, some of the best cruising grounds in the world. Mariners often decide to spend another year or two in Mexico, traveling up into the sea of Cortez for the spring and early summer, and then putting the boat in a marina or on the hard in La Paz or San Carlos. The boat is then positioned for the perfect cruising weather in the Sea during the following fall. In Mexico, the fall, winter, and spring weather is perfect, and it is an easy trip back to visit family or bring down a needed part from the United States or Canada. The usual sailor's migration from north of the border begins in the late summer and fall and consists of the initial trip down the Pacific coast (the outside of the Baja) to arrive in the Sea of Cortez or along the Mexican mainland in November. This one-to two-thousand-mile trip, depending on where you depart from, might be plenty for the first year. You arrive in Mexico during the prime cruising season and have time to begin the transformation into the cruising lifestyle. By December or January the weather along the Mexican Riviera is perfect. The water is a warm eighty something degrees with excellent clarity and the gentle breezes are ideal. It is not until late February or early March before the cold north winds from the Sea of Cortez begin to cool these waters, often bringing in a smelly red tide. The cruising community is active in Puerto Vallarta, Tenacatita, Barra de Navidad, and Zihuantanejo from December through March.

Cruisers then begin migrating north to enjoy Mazatlan's Carnivale, St. Patrick's Day near Barra de Navidad, sailing races in Banderas Bay, and Easter's pageantry in San Blas.

By May the Sea of Cortez is starting to heat up and it's time to mosey north for the spring cruising season with sailing events scheduled in the La Paz area and the popular Loreto Fest in Puerto Escondido. In the late spring and early summer the sea once again has mild temperatures and clear water with pleasant southerly breezes to push us north. There are numerous anchorages to explore, fish are abundant, and snorkeling or diving among the sea life is phenomenal. The weather dictates the travel plans, and when we time it right, the cruising is continually perfecto.

A few hardy sailors remain in the sea for the entire summer, moving further north to the Midriff Islands and Bahia de Los Angeles. Puerto Don Juan provides a safe haven if the rare hurricane reaches that far north. We spent a delightful June and July cruising just a smattering of the many anchorages for a taste of this intriguing territory. The water stays cool well into the summer and this area is so secluded that you can easily spend a week or more without seeing another human being. The stark beauty of the multi-colored desert terrain dotted with ancient volcanic cones was like sailing within a living masterpiece. The rich blues of the water, white clouds, reds, oranges, dusty yellows, sage greens, and black veins of rock make up the palette of desert colors. In the mornings we watched a pair of coyotes stroll the beach, while a pod of manta rays with their wide spread, bat-like wings swam close to the boat. Pelicans soared high for the best view of a fish boil and then dove like rockets to fill their pouches with breakfast. Soaring ospreys and boobies were our companions. Traveling between islands with the strong tidal currents was ideal for watching Sei and Pilot whales up close, and they would occasionally visit us at anchor. Each afternoon we watched the clouds morph into a long elephant trunk (a developing *Elephante* wind) spreading from the Western mountains out over the sea looking for trouble. The flat-topped, anvil-shaped clouds to the east puffed up higher and higher into billowing *Chubasco* thunderheads that formed from the intense heat on land. Since we traveled there in the cooler part of the summer, the threatening clouds would usually dissipate with the evening chill. When the morning breezes swept down the mountainsides, we would wake to the strong aroma of sage and arid desert scents. The pleasantly cool and refreshing water was perfect for swimming and fantastic fishing made the trip complete.

The majority of cruisers, however, leave the Sea by late May or early June, avoiding the withering heat and storm prone months. Boats are 'put to sleep' and the sailors return home to work, see their families, or travel to cooler spots. San Carlos and Guaymas on the mainland coast along with La Paz, Mazatlan, Puerto Vallarta and Puerto Escondido are places where cruisers safely leave their boats on stands in a dry storage yard, in marinas, or on mooring balls. Hurricane season, which runs from June through November, requires the prudent mariner to cruise either north or south of the storm zone to avoid the occasional, destructive tempest. Renting a house in the pleasant, highland areas of Mexico and touring the interior has been an option for cruisers wanting to remain in the country during the summer. They often apply for a residency visa when they decide to stay longer than their six-month tourist visa allows.

From the middle of October, through November, the oppressive summer heat has passed, and once again it is perfect weather to cruise the Sea of Cortez. Sometime in late October or early November the first northers begin, and the temperature of the water and air begin to drop. By January the strong northers are blowing with pleasant lulls in between. We traveled this 1600-mile seasonal migration for five years, experiencing some of the most delightful and satisfying cruising. For many sailors a year or two in Mexico may be sufficient to prepare for adventures further from home. While spending time in Mexico cruisers not only experience another country, but they begin to find their comfort zone with the sailing life. When we decided to leave Mexico, we left with confidence gained in the years of pleasant cruising experiences.

Our cruising has been unhurried and yet overflows with unforgettable memories. Since we cruise six months out of each year, we have actually been cruising for a total of only five years over a ten-year span, and yet we are considered old timers with nearly 20,000 miles under our keel. We explored Central America and Ecuador, but for now we will forgo the Panama Canal transit and our trip into the Caribbean Sea. It was an obvious choice to return to Mexican waters when the grand babies started to make their appearances. The family beckoned when our daughter, Roseanna delivered her two babies, Toby and Coral. Then Heather, our son Brian's wife, gave birth to their son, Onyx. When our son Eugene, and his wife Tiffany welcomed Leif and Lillien, the newest members of the family, we were glad to be close by.

During the years that we have been cruising, both of our fathers and one of our mothers has passed on. The seasons have been filled with weddings, funerals, graduations, reunions, birthdays, engagements, and the birth of our grandchildren. We have made several road-trips across the U.S., visiting thirty-one states. Two summers were spent in Buenos Aires, Argentina, immersed in a new culture, language, and climate. At the same time we published my book on relationships originally written for our children, *Love, Marriage and the Art of Raising Children* [29]. The six-months-on, six-months-off cruising itinerary continues each year, while life interjects various adventures along the way. A rigid schedule would tie us down while life unfolds its moment-to-moment escapades. Who knows? Instead of sailing to New York from the Caribbean, we may decide to cross to the South Pacific, entering New York harbor the other way around.

The Cruising Life

~ Putting Our Affairs in Order ~

Cruising for half a year at a time, while managing our business and staying in touch with children and elderly parents requires that we stay connected. For the first four years of our cruising experience we still ran all of our businesses for the six months of the year that we lived ashore. Our secret was a capable bookkeeper, Elaine; salesperson, bill payer, shipper, and receptionist all rolled up in one. Elaine's loyal, honest, and efficient work handled everything that came up while we were sailing thousands of miles away. When we were near a phone we would call her to find out if there was anything that needed our attention.

Four years later after selling our business to our son, we needed someone to collect our mail, pay bills that we could not place on auto-pay, deposit rental checks, and keep us in touch with any problems that might come up unexpectedly. A former neighbor who was a good friend and someone we could trust was happy to take on the job. I signed a handful of checks and handed over a list of phone numbers to call if any problems arose. With these personal arrangements in place, we have felt comfortable cruising the seas, knowing that our business and money matters are sailing along smoothly.

Renting our properties at a slightly below market price attracts renters who are glad to have a financial break and willingly agree to take care of the little things that come up in our absence. If something major like an air conditioner, heater, a refrigerator, or a plumbing issue needs repair we have contacts to fix the problem.

For seven of the ten years that we have been out on *Harmony* we were always back home in March or April with enough time to do our taxes and put our finances in order. Cruisers often make the pilgrimage north during tax season to visit family and fork over their due to Uncle Sam. When the favorable weather season to sail to Ecuador happened to be in the middle of tax season our accountant filed an extension for us. We paid an estimated payment and even a little extra in case we owed more than the previous year.

Some of our buddies use a mail service that collects mail and sends it to various ports when contacted. However, it appears that most sailors have friends or family who take care of their personal matters. To feel comfortable knowing that your business affairs are in the hands of someone who is efficient, prompt, and trustworthy will allow you to relax far away from home.

In the not-to-distant past cruisers could be out at sea for weeks and months with little contact with their families, discouraging some sailors from cruising to distant shores. Women particularly find it necessary to keep strong ties with family and friends and appreciate the good communication systems that are now available. In this modern day of e-mail aboard, SAT phones, and the Internet, it is easy to stay in touch. Not too long ago, before e-mail, sailors might phone-patch a call through the HAM radio nets if the propagation was good. Today with the Pactor modem and HAM radio, email is free if you have a HAM license. Those without a HAM license pay $200 a year for Sailmail, a similar kind of service through the same modem attached to the SSB radio. Internet cafes are numerous in ports around the world especially in countries where most people cannot afford their own personal computer. Sailors can spend hours for the equivalent of only a few dollars reconnecting to family and friends, doing business, and making airline reservations. Wi-Fi service is common in most of the marinas, which makes it convenient to download our mail while sitting aboard *Harmony*. Today with Skype, SAT phones, and cell phones, it is possible to call home from distant parts of the globe. Cruisers staying in one country for a while purchase a cell phone with local service for a nominal fee. In 2009, while we were visiting Matthew out in one of those gorgeous anchorages in Mexico, he demonstrated how easy it was to have Internet on board. He had recently purchased a local telephone plan that uses the cellular system to give him unlimited Internet access for approximately $60 per month. Since they had Skype it doubled as a long distance phone. When we first signed up with Skype, we prepaid $10 and that amount lasted us for months. Now with a Web Cam we can see our grandchildren from miles away waving and smiling to their Nana and Bababa .

The Cruising Life

~ What about the Holidays? ~

When we first arrived in La Paz, Mexico in November of 2000, we looked forward to being tied up to a dock in a marina after traveling for 1500 miles. The next several days were spent exploring the city while we slowly put *Harmony* to sleep, preparing to fly back home to celebrate Thanksgiving with the family. The cruising season was in full swing and I couldn't help but notice that there was quite a bit of stress and even some scattered tears among the newer cruising women. They were realizing that while making their plans to travel far from home they had unintentionally overlooked how it would feel to spend the holidays away from their families. The major winter holidays of Thanksgiving, Christmas, and New Year's often fall right in the middle of the cruising season, a time when families traditionally gather together for those special occasions to share quality time. When organizing our schedule each year, we book flights for Thanksgiving during the summer to assure us a spot during the busy holiday travel season.

Virginia with her son Brian and grandson Onyx in Tenacatita, Mexico.

From Mexico it is easy for cruisers to return home for the holidays and come back rejuvenated and ready for more sailing adventures. For those hardy sailors who are far across the oceans, traveling home can be too costly and the family might have to celebrate without them for a season or two. Having your Skype telephone hooked up to a Web cam is a great way to feel like you are almost there in the midst of the happy celebrations. On the other hand it might be a once in a lifetime opportunity for family members to join you in a tropical locale that makes for the *best holiday ever.*

Instead of staying in the freezing north during the winter holidays of December, we planned to host our children aboard *The Harmony Hotel.* Our exciting holiday destinations have included spending delightful weeks in the islands north of La Paz, the Paradise Resort and Marina near Puerto Vallarta, the Tenacatita anchorage, and the laguna at Barra de Navidad. When we were in Panama, three of our children and their significant others traveled with us to the Perlas Islands, Panama City, and to the islands of Western Panama. On one of our first Mexican Christmases, we purchased a small potted evergreen tree at a Mercado and decorated it with lights. It was so cute and we thought we had it safely stowed until we were underway and the seas started rocking and pitched the tree into the cockpit, scattering dirt everywhere. Now to supply some holiday spirit, we drape Christmas lights through the rigging.

We usually fly out of La Paz or Cabo San Jose to attend our Thanksgiving gathering. Cruising down the Baja coast from San Carlos to La Paz, we have a leisurely month before we have to catch our plane, with time to play, avoid storms, and take care of any unexpected breakdowns. Back in the summer months the family makes plans for the winter holidays, choosing a nice cruising destination, and

Virginia with two of her tired grandchildren, Toby and Coral.

hopefully we are waiting there when they arrive. To avoid unpleasant sailing conditions due to a tight schedule to reach our rendezvous, we may have to travel day and night during a weather lull. Likewise when family or friends come to visit, we tell them where we will be and when. If we are held up by bad weather, they can rent a hotel and enjoy the town until we arrive.

Everyone figures out how to make the holidays special, whether in a marina or at anchor. Potlucks, lighted boat parades, midnight masses at local cathedrals, traditional processions, activities with the local children and charities can fill the calendar. Angela, an eight year-old cruising with her parents, joined a local ballet troupe in Ecuador and appeared in their Christmas dance program. A progressive dinner between four boats was a highlight of one holiday season. Cruisers create family wherever they travel, and there is often a large ex-pat community in town that welcomes sailors to their celebrations.

The Cruising Life

~ Journey and Adventure ~

Every sailor envisions traveling to enchanting places around the globe that hold a special allure. My father, Paul, dreamed of sailing to Easter Island and although he traveled the world on work assignments, he never had business on that isolated isle. Easter Island and other beckoning cruising destinations came alive during my father's vicarious voyages through his well-stocked library. He had a small sailboat on Old Hickory Lake on the outskirts of Nashville, Tennessee and occasionally sailed further off shore in his brother-in-law, Jim Montgomery's, 32' sloop *Free Spirit*. They made action packed trips to the Dry Tortugas, Isla Mujeres in Mexico and along the U.S. Gulf Coast. Several of our acquaints who we met while we were in Panama went on to make the arduous trip to Easter Island and described it as magnificent.

The sheer love of sailing, the journey to new places, and the adventure that the sea dishes up every day can be at the heart of a sailor's purpose. The final destination can lose its importance along the way. Simply preparing and sailing a boat to explore faraway places along a route serves up plenty of excitement. The unbounded exuberance of leaving the harbor, setting our sights on a waypoint, and actually arriving at the distant anchorage is a most satisfying endeavor.

On the other hand, just so we don't become too starry eyed about it, Louis L'Amour in his book, *Education of a Wandering Man* [30], said that he believed that "adventure is nothing but a romantic name for trouble." He thought the armchair adventurer with a good book and a cold drink had all the advantages, and thought that "what people speak of as adventure is something nobody in his right mind would seek out, and becomes romantic only when one is safely at home." So maybe we are just out looking for a good tale to tell, a yarn to spin for family and friends. In a lovely Baja anchorage we had sundowners with a crew who were on their third circumnavigation. Early in the morning, we watched them sail off for the next milestone. Each cruiser with their *raison d'être* weaves an intricate tapestry of adventure and discovery.

Our friends Scott Duncan and Pam Habek, on *Starship* [31], formally aboard Tournesol, dreamed of becoming the first visually impaired couple to circumnavigate the globe. They were able to see large shapes and could distinguish light from dark, but they were considered legally blind. With financial backing from groups in the States, they devoted themselves to their inspiring cause. Various obstacles, from health issues to financial shortfalls threatened to slow their passage. Their wonderful sense of humor was apparent when they warned all of us in the anchorage by VHF radio to watch out for them because they were coming in to anchor. "We like the open seas better. There are fewer things to bump into out there." When they needed assistance they were receptive to help, and while on their odyssey across the

Pacific they relayed messages from other boats over their powerful single side-band radio. The last time I checked their blog, they had arrived in Australia and weathered several exciting escapades.

Diane and Will aboard *Fancy Free* cruised when they were young and recently returned to their old haunts in the South Pacific. Their plan was to revisit places that held strong memories for them, to meet up with old friends, and introduce their teenage daughter to places they had known before she was born.

One of the more amazing cruising families that we met in our travels consisted of eleven people on board an old 64-foot wooden schooner. The parents and nine children, seven boys and two girls included four brothers who shared the neuromuscular disorder Duchenne Muscular Dystrophy. The boys had read Robin Lee Graham's book about his single-handed circumnavigation aboard his small sailboat, *Dove*. Their favorite book was ragged with dog-eared pages from being read so many times. During a long Alaskan winter when the temperature dipped to forty degrees below zero, the boys explored the Internet looking for a way to warmer climes and adventure. They found their boat in San Francisco Bay at a price they could afford, and the large family with willing hands soon brought the schooner back to life. The two eldest brothers learned about the electronics and the ins and outs of navigation, kept abreast of the weather reports, and became HAM radio operators. Negotiating in electric wheelchairs to get around the docks, they did the paperwork and helped with provisioning. The eldest daughter spoke sufficient Spanish to help interpret when they traveled south. All of the crew took their turn on watch and they ventured down the coast of California, through Mexico and Central America bringing their dream voyage into a reality.[32]

And then there was the adventurous couple, Neil and Sandy, who worked at Palmer Station in Antarctica, running the power station during the Southern Hemisphere's frozen winter. The other half of the year was spent on their boat thawing out in the pleasant waters of Mexico.

Bob and Candace spent the winter seasons in Mexico on their sailboat and the summer seasons on their canal barge in France. They discovered that both places were equally inexpensive while they plowed the Canal Midi buying their baguettes, cheeses, and fresh produce at the local, open-air markets along their route. Each evening for no charge they tied up along the canal's edge.

Is it pulling the atlas from the bookshelf, or rather exploring Google Earth on the Internet that sends us contemplating the destinations we want to visit on our quest at sea? Anchoring off of a secluded island in Panama or a deserted piece of the Baja coast that can only be approached from the sea is an unforgettable experience worth all the preparation and work.

When we were on vacation, no matter how short, I felt the satisfaction that came from a rejuvenated body and a carefree mind. It was as if I had switched into a different gear. My soul was nourished when I spent time in nature, reading a book, exploring a new place, and hanging out with family and friends. Unfortunately this mindset only lasted about a week or two and then I was back in the regular routine, engulfed in life's hurried pace. Our vacations faded away into hazy memories, pictures in a scrapbook. There is a time when nourishing our souls becomes a priority. When we are out cruising, our life metaphorically down-shifts to five-knots, the tranquil speed of our boat. The wristwatch disappears into a hidden place in a drawer, replaced by sunglasses, sandals, and a hat. A grocery run may take all day instead of being squeezed into a busy, workday schedule. Like a scuba diver plunging deep and surfacing gradually, avoiding the dreaded bends, there is an acclimating process into this new lifestyle.

Diving deeper, there is time to explore the richness of life at one with nature among adventurous people of like mind.

Unplugged from the grid in a quiet anchorage, the pervasive peace calms our jangled nerves, with no ambulance sirens, electrical hums, or traffic roar to intrude. Instead, we are lulled to sleep by the lap of water against our hull, the waves breaking on shore, the gentle rocking of the boat, and the occasional hum of the refrigerator cycling on. While cities keep all the electric, gas, water, sewage, trash, fuel, and other systems up and running, we are managing our entire infrastructure within the confines of our small vessel. The power for all our needs comes from solar panels or the generator.

Unfortunately the perpetual degeneration of everything is an intrinsic part of this adventurous journey, and has discouraged and frustrated every cruiser at some point. Living in a salt-water environment means that things rust and corrode, and critters make their homes on our keels at a furious rate. The rewarding feeling of self-sufficiency and liberation comes with ingenuity and hard work required to keep everything maintained and running smoothly. There's even an occasional patching of things together until we arrive safely at the next port.

Successful cruisers flow with the new realities of this lifestyle, live with a continuing fix-it list, and keep a positive attitude while working on the boat in exotic places. Sailors become talented magicians when it comes to repairing motors, untangling electrical and computer glitches, plumbing and sewing, to mention just a few of their tricks. If we had a somewhat limited ability to fix our boat when we left the dock, we continually learned new skills while we were out cruising. It often felt like we were taking advanced level college instruction in Adventurous Lifestyle. Thank goodness for the experienced seagoing maestros who we have met along the way who offer their expertise and give freely of their knowledge and skills.

Tradition and the written law of the seas declares that mariners give aid to those in distress. The cruising community lives by this rule and guidance and assistance are freely given. Our friends have helped us fix our refrigerator, set up computer programs to handle weather faxes, and advised us on a myriad of projects. In exchange we have run local radio nets and offered mechanical and navigational assistance. Loaning our spare outboard motor helped several couples when their *car was in the shop*. It is a true friend indeed who offers to help unclog the head! Cruisers have towed fellow sailors' for many miles to a safe anchorage when their boat lost its engine, rudder or mast. On any given day during the local net, we can usually obtain the help we need. Sharing our concerns with other sailors can make the difference between a good experience and a ride that has us asking, 'what the heck am I doing out here?' When we enter a new country, we ask how to interact with the local officials, where to find boat parts and places to provision, a good place to dine, and sometimes even medical or dental referrals. It is actually quite amazing how our cruising community runs itself with no laws or government, with only the good will of its members. Our newly chosen lifestyle comes with precious benefits and perks.

On the other hand in many practical ways we are on our own! Our partner, family, or crew shares the workload aboard the boat, taking responsibility for all of the systems, which takes up a certain amount of time. A common question from land-based friends is, "What do you do all day?" There is a romantic idea that we are sitting back sipping a Mai Tai in our cockpit, anchored near an isolated sandy beach. Although this idyllic scene does happen, a great deal of time is taken up with preparing the boat to arrive safely at that exquisite location. Commissioning and decommissioning our boat, provisioning, fixing things, and making the passage to that place of our dreams makes up the whole package of the cruising lifestyle. The more we understand what is involved, what to expect and what is required, the easier it is to cope, no matter what aspect of cruising we are involved in. The payoff is boundless. The nature moments, the feeling of accomplishment, the new friends, and experiences make it all worthwhile.

The Cruising Life

~ Healthy Body, Mind, and Soul ~

When I reached the milestone of my fiftieth birthday, my body, having weathered the strains I put on it during my invincible youth, had called in the loan. My lower back was aching with debilitating sciatic pain. Although attending yoga classes helped relieve my discomfort, living an active lifestyle in an outdoor environment was the perfect prescription. Out cruising, we take long walks in fresh air, swim daily in warm water, eat fresh, healthy foods, and have less physically demanding work. For the last ten years, thankfully my back has remained healthy and pain free.

Robert has a genetic tendency for high cholesterol levels, but after dropping dairy products from his diet, and living a less stressful lifestyle, his numbers dropped to acceptable levels. When we go for our annual physical, the doctor encourages us to keep doing whatever it is that we are doing. Cruising comes with a doctor's recommendation. For those of you who need to unwind from stress-related health

Virginia relaxing in the warm Mexican waters after a swim.

problems, cruising might be the best natural cure in the world.

Sailing is a somewhat rigorous sport, from raising the sails to lowering the anchor, and working on the boat in tight places. The physical exertion takes the place of a workout in the gym. Carrying groceries, water jugs, and laundry bags through a town to our dinghy, pulling the dinghy into the water and hoisting the bags aboard is great exercise. Putting the boat away or bringing it out of storage, re or de-commissioning, is a ton of work in hot, tropical climes. During this process we usually lose a few pounds in sweat, but it beats the treadmill. Without a car we do miles of walking when we explore new places and provision. If you have specific health concerns or prior injuries, it's always a good idea to clear cruising with your doctor.

Our friend, Allen, explained to us why he decided to drop everything and go sailing. Every year since childhood, his best friend accompanied him on an outback adventure, canoeing in Alaska, hiking in the Rocky Mountains, or rafting down the Colorado River. Recently his friend had unexpectedly died of a heart attack. Allen came face to face with his own mortality and knew that now was the time to live his dreams, not only for himself but also in memory of his friend. It was his way of grieving and finding life after death. There are cruisers who have battled cancer, and sailing for them is a healing therapy. It is an opportunity to live each day in a beautiful, natural setting.

It was important to set out on our adventure while we still had our vitality and health. Somehow we rearranged our lives, our finances, and our schedules to do what was most important to us. It might be the best legacy we can give to our children and grandchildren. We can show them by our example how they too can follow their dreams.

Our bodies are nourished in the ocean environment and when we've needed medical care in Mexico we've found it to be of excellent quality at reasonable prices. The doctors are not stressed about rules and the whims of HMO's and insurance companies watching their bottom lines. They are not burdened with astronomical, malpractice insurance and litigious lawyers. In Mazatlan, a U.S. trained doctor gave us an hour of his time when we visited him for an annual checkup. For our lab reports, we were more than happy to pay each professional his fee in cash. $25 for a chest X-ray and $30 for the EKG test, with the doctor making change out of his own pocket! No insurance forms or claims to handle. When we returned to the doctor's office, he gave us another hour of his time discussing the results and small talked about our cruising adventures and his satisfying experience of being a doctor in Mexico. When we left his office, we felt healthier than when we went in. He was truly the epitome of a loving, family healer. It's rare to find this kind of unhurried medical attention in the U.S. and we felt privileged to be his patients.

The care in Mexico is not limited to routine physicals and lab work. I had an emergency, detached retina surgery with the latest laser equipment, when a gray curtain fell over my right eye. Fortunately we were in port, and one good referral led to another until I was in painless, high tech eye surgery the following night. The price was less than our insurance deductible and the doctor was attentive and thorough, speaking enough English for us to understand the situation. When I had a post-operative check-up in the U.S., the work was pronounced excellent by a hurried doctor who spent five minutes with me, not long enough to answer my few questions, and the cost seemed ridiculously steep. The difference was never so pronounced comparing the care or the cost. For my yearly eye checkup, I return to my Mexican ophthalmologist for his comprehensive, gentle, reasonably priced office visit. He was thrilled when my eyesight results were 20/20 with my new eyeglass prescription. I am forever grateful to this doctor for my eyesight.

In parts of Mexico medical care is excellent, but there have been several cases when doctors advised cruisers to return home for certain procedures such as bypass heart surgery. Understanding the limits of their facilities and training was also a sign of intelligent health care. We have taken care of our dental checkups along the way and have received excellent care at great prices. Besides the regular checkups and cleanings, we've had root canal work, and crowns and several of our cruiser friends have even had implants.

In the southern climes, we diligently guard against skin damage due to the intense sun. With the right precautions of sunscreen, sunshades, and dodgers, staying out of the noontime sun, and wearing hats and sunglasses, we can thrive in this healthy vitamin D rich environment. UV protective clothing that is lightweight for the hot climes protects our fair skin. Bringing shoes like Crocs, water resistant sandals, or booties guard our feet from hot sand, barnacles, stingrays, and sand spurs. (Large North American shoe sizes are difficult to find south of the border.) The Sea of Cortez is a desert environment with low humidity where we have to make sure to stay hydrated. We keep our water bottles handy and whenever we think of it, we take a swig and ask if our partner has had a drink of water lately.

Before I left on our trip, I often asked cruisers, 'What about the bugs in the tropics?' The consensus was that they weren't much of a problem and I found that mostly to be true. Insects are most active at dawn and dusk. At these hours it is prudent to stay off the beaches and out of the woods, where mosquitoes and no-see-ums (tiny flying mites with a fierce bite) flourish. Certain anchorages and towns during certain seasons have a selection of biting no-see-ums, mosquitoes, bees or annoying flies called bo-bos. When we stopped at a particularly bug infested anchorage near a mangrove-lined estuary, my skin must have had an attractive taste to the no-see-ums. Robert was barely bothered with a couple of nips, but I was covered with terribly itchy, red, swollen spots that lasted for weeks. After that experience Robert built screen doors for our companionways (we call them our Tennessee screen doors because they have that down home noise when they slam into place) and velcroed screens over the hatches. Rarely are we kept awake by the constant buzz in our ear of a mosquito out for blood. Now before we go to an anchorage like Isla San Francisco or Mantanchen Bay near San Blas, we ask on the net for a bug report. If a norther is blowing it's never a problem.

* * *

Our minds were certainly challenged by the many things we needed to learn while we prepared to set off on our cruise. Robert never studied so hard than when he was working for his ham radio license, back when Morse code was a requirement. Taking Spanish 101 at the local junior college was a challenge for my brain, but that was just the beginning of expanding my vocabulary and fluency. There was so much involved in sailing, navigating, fixing engines, and gathering information about the countries on our itinerary. We became sailors, mechanics, geographers, astronomers, and meteorologists in the process. And then somehow it all came together, and we had *time* like never before. Meeting people from many nations and walks of life and hearing their stories and ideas increased our knowledge and understanding of the earth and its people. While sipping drinks and nibbling on appetizers with fellow cruisers, we have listened to tales about the long agonizing history of Croatia, the politics of South Africa, and the archeology of Ecuador. There is time for painting, beading, knitting, and crafts of all kinds, meditating, exercise, and lots of time for reading. Between the two of us we read a wide variety of books. Sometimes we find ourselves reading whole chapters to each other, laughing or exploring an intriguing thought. Long hours spent at sea allows for the creative side of the mind to expand, to explore new areas that challenge us with inventive ideas, and innovative problem solving. I like scrabble, crossword and Sudoku puzzles. When the kids are aboard there is always a card game, board game, or chess going on, stimulating the neurons, sharpening the mind's muscles, while the body takes a siesta.

* * *

Doing what we love creates a spirit that is light and full of joy. Living out in nature, we become one with the wind, seas, panoramic views, sunsets, sunrises, and night skies. These majestic elements connect us to our higher self. Mother Nature entertains us with her ever-changing weather, abundance of birds, fish, and sea life of every kind. The world unfolds its variety while we travel to new places. Deserts, mountains, volcanoes, and lush jungles intrigue us with their sounds, smells, and wildlife. The splendor and magnificence of the surrounding beauty is a constant reminder of how awe inspiring it all is. On one hand, we are impressed with how tiny a part we play in the ever-expanding universe and on the other hand, we feel that we are an intricate piece of the overall puzzle.

The veteran sailor, Charles Doane wrote, "It seems to me that the simple motion of a (mono-hull) sailboat must have a lot to do with mysticism. Insofar as a primary purpose of meditation or intensive prayer is to clear the consciousness of extraneous data, so as to exist solely in the present moment, sailing, I think, can be deemed nothing less than an enforced meditation." He continues on to describe how he is able to keep his seasickness at bay by carefully focusing on and strictly regulating his breathing. He states: (This is) a technique prominently featured in many formal meditative regimes. A key stimulant to achieving such states (mystical unitary states of oneness with the larger cosmos), according to some experts, is repetitive physical rhythms that block neural flow to certain important orientation areas of the brain and so dislodge egoistic notions of self. Sailing involves not merely the creation of rhythm, but adaptation to an imposed, often extremely pronounced, rhythmic motion, and that said, adaptation is sometimes sustained twenty-four hours a day for many days at a time." [33]

There is enough time for Robert and I to become acquainted at a deeper, more intimate level, which nourishes our souls. The romance that may have slipped away since the time we were young and infatuated, is rekindled with the fires of a more mature love. There is time, isolated anchorages, beauty, and a gently rocking boat.

The Cruising Life

~ Profound Changes in Life ~

Once we board our sailboat we feel as if we are leaving one dimension and entering another. In the beginning, the transition can be difficult while we acquire our sea legs, but when we begin the steps of making our cruising vision a reality, a change in consciousness inevitably takes hold. Pushing aside the curtains to view a different world, we learn new things at an astonishing rate. Plunking our money down for this ride of a lifetime, we hop on, buckle up, hold on, and at the same time let go, allowing the changes to wash over us.

Cruising is not all white-knuckle sailing with the rail in the water figuratively or literally. Hours under sail on a beautiful ocean, with the perfect amount of wind on rippling seas actually happens, giving us a chance to absorb the uniqueness of the trip we have chosen. When we start forgetting which day it is, we look at each other and laugh, knowing that *now* we are *really cruising*. Most people hardly notice that they are growing at an accelerated rate, growing in intelligence, knowledge, and experience. When we are out sailing we live in another world, an alternative existence. With a slower pace, comes a mellowing process where we learn to turn inward as well as outward, with time to contemplate and appreciate.

It takes a Type A personality just to pull off this wild idea, to manifest a boat with all of its complicated parts, and have the where with all to create the dream. Then when we are out cruising, we have to radically switch gears and become a Type B personality to appreciate our new lifestyle and cope with whatever comes our way. This abrupt change can make our heads spin, but when we finally *get it*, life takes on a new dimension, a new richness.

The ocean is like a report card. Sailed through easily with flags flying, can use improvement; ended up on the proverbial rocks. Uh, oh! When we persevered and made the changes required, we found that cruising and life in general became more interesting, exciting, filled with celebration, fun, and joy. It is just Robert, *Harmony*, and me. There is no shame, no blame, and no praise; the adventure gives it to us straight up. We have the choice of making improvements, the option of learning the lessons or not. Whether to continue to pay attention to the messages of nature and practice the art of cruising is up to us. Experiencing satisfaction, pride, and confidence, or frustration, discouragement, and fear are the range of emotions that can rise and fall like the rocking, ocean waves. Nature does not pull any punches. We flow with it or we don't.

When we actually become tuned to the weather, the moon, the tides, and the patterns of the sea, our heart and soul beat to the rhythm of nature, the heartbeat of Planet Earth. Our senses become acutely aware. Food tastes better. The vistas wow us with their beauty. Vivid dreams visit our sleep, like never before. Synchronicity and coincidences abound accompanied by the feeling of being in tune. We learn to play this game, discover its subtleties, unearth its mysteries, and make it our own.

The Cruising Life

~ Gifts, Gift, Gifts ~

When we departed for Mexico our pantry was well stocked with the usual wholesome provisions, and was purposely lacking in all sorts of packaged and junk foods. When we arrived in Turtle Bay, we had been so caught up with our first days in Mexico that it never occurred to us that the Halloween tradition of trick or treating would extend beyond our border. Not having much in the way of goodies to give away taught us that in the future we needed to bring a nice selection of trade-able supplies. We preferred healthy snacks, like almonds and walnuts from a local farmer near our hometown of Modesto, inexpensive in California's Central Valley and highly valued elsewhere. Packed in small zip lock bags, we gave them out as tips to fuel attendants, friends and the children. It was a sure way to put a smile on someone's face.

Since we leave in the fall, we loaded up with pencils, chalk, crayons, magic markers, and notebooks at the back to school sales and flea markets, and bring along toothbrushes, baseball hats, and clothing. Cruisers in the medical professions often bring needed supplies they have collected. Everything will be gratefully accepted and utilized. In many cruising communities, there are outreach projects for children in the barrios and schools. The yacht club in La Paz, Club Cruceros, sponsors school meals in one of the poorer neighborhoods. With donated food, the mothers of the students cook up nutritious meals over wood fires outside of their tarpaper homes. The club members also collect gifts all year long for their big Christmas bash. The party is complete with homemade tamales, a piñata, hula-hoops, and a soccer game, and, of course, a gift for each child.

At the isolated anchorage of Aqua Verde on the Baja, there is a small community that has a little one-room schoolhouse. When Anita on *Annabelle Lee* was cruising here she had taken pictures of the kids at the school, and later when she arrived in Mazatlan she had made copies for the students. When we met at the marina, she and her husband, Wayne, were preparing their boat for the Puddle Jump across to the South Pacific isles. She was looking for a vessel on their way north to deliver the pictures to the school, and we agreed. Several weeks later when we were securely anchored at Agua Verde, we dinghyed ashore and hiked up a cacti-lined arroyo to the cement block schoolhouse. The teacher, who could not have been more than twenty years old, welcomed us in. We can only imagine what the children thought of these strangers in their classroom. Each child received a class photo and they laughed and jostled each other, pointing to the pictures of their friends and themselves. We left amid cheerful smiles and adioses.

In Zihuantanejo, a regatta called Sail Fest was organized to help fund the local indigenous school. The dilapidated building had walls built of salvaged wood and tarps, and was furnished with desks, built and painted by the parents. Their books were well-worn hand-me-downs from other schools. The generosity of the cruisers in partnership with local businesses has made this a hugely profitable, fund-raising event. A parade of the fleet raises large donations by taking on paying passengers. There are sailing races, seminars, and music programs, and all sorts of fun events that bring in contributions. The cruisers spend time working on building and painting projects to improve the school. The thrill that comes from children surrounding us with smiles of gratitude is more than enough payback.

The Cruising Life

~ Fixing the Boat in Exotic Places ~

Before we leave the dock, we make sure the engine is sound, the rigging is safe, and all the major systems are up and running. By the time we reach a distant destination, the pounding seas have usually taken a toll. More than likely, the problems are minor, which require some time and a touch of ingenuity. A major problem with the engine or transmission, broken rigging, or blown out sails, can cause a longer delay, especially in a remote location.

Even after years of cruising we spend most mornings doing repairs or maintenance, chipping away at the inevitable *somethings* that happen while living in sea water's corrosive environment. Boat improvements and projects continue as the budget allows and *Harmony* continues to be a work in progress.

While we cruised in Mexico Robert installed four solar panels over several years. We never installed a water maker since our boat has two large water tanks (160 gallons total) that lasts us for at least four weeks. So far we have always made a stop in port for fresh provisions and water within a month's time. If Robert and I were sailing out on a long passage far from coastal waters, we might consider purchasing a water maker. However, in many tropical climates, it often rains enough to collect a tank full of fresh water in one major downpour.

During our travels in Central and South America, we have been lucky to find knowledgeable mechanics. In most countries of the world the local people keep their highly prized vehicles running on a modest budget by rebuilding the parts. If Robert does not have the expertise to repair something there is a good chance that a local mechanic in a small, dark, greasy, back alley shop will have the broken part fixed in short order. Cruisers have spent weeks waiting for replacements to be shipped from home when they probably could have had it manufactured locally in just a few days. On the other hand, some components, especially if they are still under warranty, must be replaced by the manufacturer or from a reputable source in the U.S. While waiting for the package to clear customs, savvy cruisers settle in and enjoy their down time. There are always numerous adventures to fascinating inland destinations that await us ashore. Not allowing impatience and frustration to bring us down, we experience the local history and culture that we might have bypassed if it weren't for this minor inconvenience. When first arriving in La Paz, we were able to have both our starter motor and fresh water pump fixed within a week for around $35 per part. The bushings were replaced, the motors were cleaned of rust, and other parts were replaced as needed.

The following year after a successful 1600 miles of Mexican cruising we ended up in the La Paz area again. We were enjoying ourselves in the islands north of La Paz, an enchanting stopover on our way to San Carlos to again put the boat away for the summer season. When Robert went to check the transmission oil before continuing north, he discovered that a foamy, white, mayonnaise-looking substance had replaced the thin, red oil. Somehow water had worked its way into the transmission. Fortunately the gentle north wind blew us on an easy downwind sail back into La Paz. We started the engine for a moment to maneuver into our slip and then immediately shut it down. By some miracle the transmission still worked. Apparently any fluid works for a little while. A bit of detective work soon found the source of the problem. In our particular configuration, we have a transmission cooler that is in line with our heat exchanger for the engine. It is a mini heat exchanger, and the corroded inner tubes were leaking salt water into the tranny's oil. While we had a local welder work on the transmission cooler, we also had him fabricate a new riser since ours was rusty and needed replacing. Apparently a thirty year old boat, especially one that had some seawater spraying around inside, is likely to have some rusty parts that need attention.

The transmission cooler was easy to remove but the riser was another issue. It was 125 pounds of rusty steel nestled in a tight place under the cockpit sole. Robert rigged a pulley and hoist system using the main halyard and he guided it while I slowly cranked the winch and hauled it up and out of the engine room. The welder, Chiquita, meaning tiny, came with a good recommendation from a local cruiser. He turned out to be a large man sitting in a wheelchair in his open-air shop in the backyard of his home. Chickens pecked in the dirt, birds sang from the mango trees above our heads, and children ran around playing while he and his men worked on fabricating and welding parts. He told us that he could do it with no problem. When we asked him when he would have it done, he said, "Mañana". We had heard rumors about mañana. It can mean tomorrow morning or sometime tomorrow, or it can mean several days from now. Robert said, "Mañana?" with a question on his face. Chiquita said in English, "Do you have a problem

Robert at work on the transmission.

with that?" "No, No, No problemo," was Robert's quick reply and Chiquita laughed his deep belly laugh. Leaving it all in his hands, we left to explore the tranquil town of La Paz. It turned out that we set sail in four days and the parts cost us only $160. We felt incredibly lucky to have had two totally new manufactured parts built so quickly and inexpensively. Of course, there are some nightmarish tales from people who were plagued with shoddy work and problems that seemed to go on forever with one thing after another. Asking for recommendations from cruisers who have been satisfied with an honest and skilled local contact is a key to a successful fix.

Years later we were anchored in Playa de Cocos where we did our official check in to Costa Rica. After a few days of provisioning, and meeting with the port captain, customs, and immigration officials, we were ready to continue our travels south. We looked forward to spending time in beautiful anchorages along the tropical coast. Robert pulled up anchor and I put the engine into forward. A screeching, whining noise ripped through the cockpit, and I quickly shut down the engine and Robert re-anchored. It sounded like a blown transmission, and my Merlin mechanic went below to prepare to pull the transmission out of the depths of the engine room. We knew this was a potentially serious problem that might take a long time to fix. We hauled the transmission out of the depths of the engine room with our halyard pulley after Robert unhooked it from the shaft, couplings, and engine. He found a power plate with smooth, shiny metal instead of a toothed spline. Here was the source of the screaming sound. The transmission checked out okay and it looked like we had dodged the bullet. Dinghying ashore, we asked around about transportation to a larger town and the helpful locals told us about the early morning bus to Liberia. The town was only an hour away and people said we could find a reputable machine shop there. The next morning Robert and Olivia, with her fluent Spanish, hopped on the bus with the power plate wrapped in a plastic bag. As fate would have it, a few blocks from the bus stop in Liberia was big, beautiful 'Precision Machine Shop.' The machinist fabricated new teeth in a matter of hours and the victorious crew was back on *Harmony* by twilight. By the next day the transmission was nestled back in its comfortable hold, and we were making preparations to sail the following morning. Once again we had weathered a major problem and were able to have it repaired in a day for only $44 dollars. If that wasn't some kind of miracle, I don't know what is! The engine started up and the transmission slid smoothly into forward, reverse, and neutral amid a chorus of cheers and high fives.

Over the years sailors have had to use their ingenuity while underway to ensure a safe arrival into port. A jury-rigged boat limps along to the next anchorage where parts and expertise await. On our return trip from Ecuador to Mexico we once again found ourselves with transmission problems in Costa Rica. This time it was the same heat exchanger that our friend, Chiquita, had rebuilt eight years before in La Paz. It is salt water-cooled and apparently electrolysis had once again corroded the tubing and allowed seawater to enter into the transmission oil. We were anchored in tranquil Ballena Bay and lucky for us, Punta Arenas, a hub of boat repair shops, was only twenty miles away. To preserve our transmission, first we used our supply of transmission oil and then bought out the small local shop's supply and changed the oil until it was clear of the delectable strawberry milkshake looking mixture. We had disconnected the heat exchanger and had a lively discussion that night with some fellow sailors in the anchorage to come up with an innovative solution. We connected a length of hose to the oil lines and placed it in a bucket. (There is very low pressure on these lines.) Then, we ran a hose from the salt-water faucet in the galley sink down into the engine room and into the bucket to cool the oil filled hose. The water would overflow the bucket and drain into the bilge, which would then be expelled by the bilge pump every ten to fifteen minutes. The transmission stayed cool and we called it the '*Harmony bucket method.*' Our jury-rigged repair worked like a charm for about ten miles and when the wind piped up, we sailed the rest of the way to Punta Arenas. We put the engine on again when we neared the dock. Our transmission was safe. After we had the cooler rebuilt and purchased another rebuilt spare for $45 apiece, we were on our way again after only a four day stopover.

A few weeks later while crossing the Tehuantepec in calm waters, our transmission over heated and a safety valve released, spilling out all of the precious transmission fluid. We shut the engine down and started sailing at one knot with barely enough steerage to avoid a fishing boat in our path. On the morning Single Side Band (SSB) net, Robert asked the fleet what he could use for transmission fluid since he did not have quite enough to refill it again. Apparently anything from motor oil to vegetable oil would work in a pinch. We had plenty of motor oil so we watered it down with diesel fuel to make a thinner mixture and refilled the transmission. We hooked up the *Harmony* bucket system again and were on our way. Robert then had to solve the problem of why the new heat exchanger wasn't working. A blocked water hose was the culprit this time, something totally unrelated to our new part. After he sucked the crud out of the hose with a vacuum cleaner, the water ran smoothly through the coolers. When we arrived safely in Huatulco, Mexico, we loaded up with fresh transmission fluid and had no more trouble for the rest of the twelve-hundred-mile trip north. (Or for four years of cruising since then. Knock on wood.)

On our five day trip north from Ecuador to Panama, we noticed that our steering cable to the rudder was slowly unraveling. Over the course of the trip the nine-strand line splayed apart like Medusa's hair of snakes. Robert would hacksaw off the wayward pieces so they didn't become entangled in the steering apparatus. Preparations were made to deploy the emergency tiller in case the cable snapped. By the time we dropped our anchor at the hooked-shaped tip of Isla del Rey in the Perlas Islands, the cable had two strands holding everything together, but we had made it to this lovely isolated anchorage. Once settled in Isla del Rey, I called up the only other boat in the anchorage to say hi and invite them over for dinner to share the biggest sierra mackerel that we'd ever caught. While we were enjoying the evening meal the conversation turned to how happy we were to arrive with our frayed cable. To our amazement our friendly neighbor had recently replaced his steering cable with a new one and still had his old one on board. It was not worn out but he had just wanted to update it, (like we should have) and he was happy to give it to us along with just the right couplings. Another magical fix showed up when we least expected it.

Inevitably there are times when major mechanical problems present themselves. We've known cruisers to return to the U.S. from Mexico, to do complete engine swaps and other major repairs. They choose the often rough trip north up the Baja coast or have their boat trucked from Mexico. We also have friends who have done this same work in yards in Mexico, making a few overland trips to the U.S. for parts. The job is eventually done with less expense, and they are still in their tropical cruising location. Whatever you decide, breakdowns do not have to be the end of the dream, but become merely a side trip, an additional adventure, intrinsic to the cruising life style. All cruisers have been there before, and perhaps one day we will be there lined up in the work yard next to you, fixing our boats in exotic places

The Cruising Life

~ The Yard of Tears ~

Futility, despondency, and the immensity of it all define the yard of tears! Hundreds of beautifully equipped cruising boats are lined up in a storage yard hoping to return one day to their beloved ocean. Varnish on the wood is chipping away in the hot desert sun. Engines are seizing up. A woodpecker is pecking holes in the wooden masts, and wasps and birds are making homes under radars. Like many active cruisers we leave *Harmony* on her stands for each hurricane season, before releasing her for another cruise. However, there are hundreds of boats waiting patiently year after year, a part of a fading dream. Perhaps one day, their owner will return to cruising with health restored, cruising kitty replenished, family obligations taken care of, or vacation time accrued. The numerous masts in a marina represent the dream to go cruising. These boats in a storage yard in a foreign country represent a journey taken for a while, but interrupted by one of life's curve balls. An evening walk through the rows of boats, high on their stands above

Virginia and Robert in the work yard at Marina Seca in San Carlos.

the dusty ground, reveals many of our old acquaintances. Year after year for two, five and even ten years, these cruisers continue to pay the storage fees. We wonder if they will ever return, or will they put the boat up for sale so it can be made seaworthy again and carry some avid sailors on a new adventure?

When we have a long list of projects to do before launching, our boat is towed to the work yard. The vast distance from our enviable life at sea and the harsh reality is exaggerated when we are *on the hard* with the launch ramp into the water just a short distance away. The yard is one of the most toxic places that we have ever visited. We tangle with dust, fiberglass, varnish, and paint fumes, sweat, blood, and tears. Dangers are everywhere and can inflict serious injury. Suspended in the air with a twelve-foot ladder to climb up and down many times a day, we remind each other often to be 'careful, nareful' way up there. The enormous amount of work boggles the mind, trying to tear us away from our hopes that someday we will be able to relax again in a calm, pristine anchorage.

Putting *Harmony* away on the hard for the summer season and commissioning her again in the fall is some of the hardest work we do while cruising. We call it 'paying the piper.' We've had our fun and now the bill comes due. At the beginning of every cruising season in Mexico, we spend three days to a week painting the bottom, and although it is hot, dirty, strenuous work, it is not unbearable. Leaving our boat on the hard in the sweltering, arid, Sonoran desert each summer takes its toll. Our routine consists of sanding the bottom, and slapping on a couple of coats of bottom paint, before splashing her back into the water. We usually stay aboard in the work yard with our little air conditioner keeping the aft cabin cool. But if the weather turns unbearably hot, we'd rather not sleep in a pool of sweat with mosquitoes buzzing in our ears, and it is definitely worth renting a room in a small hotel that has a nice shower, a small kitchen, screens, and air conditioning.

Our old boat always begs for something to be fixed, replaced, repainted, or improved, besides all the regular maintenance. After our shakedown cruise to Mexico, we had to replace a handful of parts, but for these jobs we stayed clear of the work yard. After three years of cruising we had to replace the cutlass bearing. After six years, it was obvious that we needed a complete new set of rigging. These jobs had not been done since the boat was new, thirty-three years before, and it was time to bite the bullet, and head into the yard. The cutlass bearing was so imbedded in its casing, and the coupler so rusted into place, that Robert spent three days tugging, banging, hack-sawing, and drilling them apart. He suffered the usual bruised and blistered knuckles, and sore shoulders, while he worked in a compromised position in the small confines of the bilge. All around us were friends struggling with a wide variety of boat maladies, such as blisters on their hull, replacing chain plates, repairing a rudder damaged from a run-in with a reef, or repairing an engine that would not turn over. Rick and Angela were entrenched in the yard for two years installing a new engine, and remodeling their interior. Vince was replacing segments of rusted plate on his steel boat. Several boats that had weathered a disastrous hurricane in the Sea of Cortez were lined up for major plastic surgery. Jerry was lowering the mast, preparing his boat for a truck ride back to his native waters in the Northwest.

The yard is a place where real men cry. There is never a shortage of sympathetic shoulders while we all struggle with our projects, stranded far from our beloved cruising grounds. However, even in the yard, the camaraderie of the cruising lifestyle shines through. We are constantly borrowing tools from one another, and asking for advice or opinions from our neighbors. After the day is done we compare stories

Virginia touching up the bottom paint before launching Harmony.

and laugh together over dinner and a cold drink. With persistence, we eventually bust out of the grime, dirt, and dust to set sail again. But in the yard, it takes all of our fortitude to keep the picture of the clear blue water in focus. The vision drives us, keeps us rising early each morning to put our shoulders to the grindstone, working late until it is too dark to see, long past the hour when the day laborers have gone home.

A few boat owners travel to foreign lands and plan to have the work done where labor prices are less expensive. A certain number of cruisers have all of the work done for them, with hefty withdrawals from the cruising kitty. They no doubt have the wherewithal to pay, but their headaches might revolve around a job that is not exactly what they wanted in the time frame that they had in mind. There is also the uncertainty of an engine fixed by someone who might not care about anything but being paid. Most cruisers do the work themselves, and call in an expert when needed. When we take an active part in maintaining the boat's systems we gain not only the satisfaction of doing the job, but also an intimate understanding of our boat and its secrets. Often a successful voyage hinges on the ability to make repairs while underway. This close relationship with our boats can be the deciding factor when things break down.

When the day finally arrives when the lowboy pulled by a tractor (or in some yards, the travel lift or railway) comes to haul *Harmony* back to the water, we have a boat that is raring to go and seaworthy. After we splash, the first order of business is to motor out to a slip in the marina or to the anchorage and set the hook in order to check out all the systems. After making sure everything we have done actually works, *Harmony*, in appreciation of all the attention, reciprocates by performing her carpet ride magic, bounding across the waves, back in her natural habitat.

The Cruising Life

~ Anchoring Tales ~

When a group of cruisers hang out together, it isn't long before, the anchoring stories start making the rounds. Everyone has a tale or two. On a typical winter afternoon in Barra de Navidad the winds were whipping across the anchorage at up to 25 knots. We were relaxing and reading after lunch in our aft cabin when we heard a faint voice calling, '*Harmony, Harmony.*' When we poked our heads out to take a look at what was going on, a small trimaran had dragged down on our anchor chain and our 3/8ths inch chain was slowly sawing away on the port alma. Robert quickly jumped in the dinghy while I put out a call for help on the VHF. Neighboring inflatables joined in to push the errant tri into safe water and re-anchor. Later that same week in similar winds a small sailboat dragged anchor to the far, shallow end of the lagoon. The bottom is a mucky, thick mud and the CQR anchor, known as the plow anchor, has a tendency to plow through that muck when the daily winds pipe up.

Friends of ours, Don and Sheila, told us of the time they disconcertingly awoke one morning to find themselves a mile and a half offshore with their anchor hanging straight down. They had dragged, but fortunately their boat steered herself straight out to sea avoiding a nearby reef. Usually anchoring problems result either from heavy winds and insufficient scope, the wrong anchor for the conditions on the bottom, or an anchor that is not dug in securely.

Isla Isabella, a wildlife and bird sanctuary documented by Jacques Cousteau is not to be missed. The isolated island over twenty miles off the Mexican coast is the home to frigate birds, also known as man-o'-war birds, the blue-footed boobies, and various species of gulls. Anchoring there, however, can be a challenge. The ocean floor is sandy, with pinnacle rocks scattered about that an anchor can become trapped in and chain can wrap around and become difficult to hoist. It becomes really dicey when the seas build and the crew needs to make a quick escape. When visiting there we make sure there is a good weather window or we pass it by. After setting the hook, a dive in to check that the anchor is set in a safe sandy spot, reassures us. Several boats have donated their anchors to the reefs when they became entangled in the rocks and the crew had to cut the chain. A few years ago an unfortunate cruiser lost his boat at Isla Isabella when the hook became ensnared in the rocks. A large, onshore swell from a southerly storm made the anchorage untenable and he was unable to quickly release or cut the chain and barely escaped with his life.

Another anchor story comes to mind when recalling the time our anchor wouldn't grab. It was at a charming little anchorage in between two small islands where we attempted to set the anchor, but we continued to slide backwards thumping along the bottom. When the anchor was pulled up to reset, we found a large stone nestled in the cup of our Bruce anchor, and naturally that was keeping it from digging in. It was no easy task to reach out over the bowsprit and dislodge the securely wedged rock while making tight circles in the narrow space.

Delivering *Harmony* north in the spring of 2005, to put her to sleep in San Carlos, we had a beautiful weather window for the five-day passage. Only in the final hours of the trip did a storm begin to build. When we finally arrived in the San Carlos Bay anchorage, we dropped the hook in a wide-open space and we were soon asleep. When we awoke, our neighbor, Gene came over to tell us that we had slowly dragged one hundred feet or so during the gusty afternoon winds. He had been about to come over and warn us, when our anchor reset and held. The locals all knew, and now we did too, that in the center of the bay there is an area with a thin layer of sand over shale rock. Not long after that with winds gusting up to 35 knots, we helped a catamaran re-anchor when he experienced the same problem.

The Cruising Life

~ Setting the Anchor ~

There are a few basic guidelines to setting the hook that allows us to rest easy. When there is good communication between the person on the foredeck dropping the anchor and the person on the wheel, things are more likely to go smoothly. After hearing couples yell at each other while anchoring, we made a resolution to use hand signals for forward, backward and stop. Holding up our fingers to indicate the depth, communication was easy with our new sign language. Crews can use hand held radios to simplify things while setting the hook. Creating a workable system for anchoring peacefully takes the stress out of this potentially challenging procedure.

The anchor is set with a scope of from five to seven feet of chain (all chain rode) for every foot of water depth. Marking a link with a plastic tie every twenty feet makes it easy to keep track of how much is running out. The *cantenary* (the extra slack in the chain that runs along the ocean floor between the hook and the boat) relieves the stress on the anchor. The freeboard on our boat is calculated in and we let out some extra rode. If we put down the hook in twenty feet of water, we add the five feet of freeboard to equal twenty-five feet. Twenty-five feet times six feet of scope equals one hundred and fifty feet. If we are in tight quarters, one hundred and twenty-five feet will do, but if the wind pipes up, there will be peace of mind if we have set out that extra twenty-five feet. In some places, significant tides are a factor. Adding this component into our computations prevents us from ending up high and dry, or with insufficient scope.

While making sure that there is a safe distance from rocks, reefs, and neighboring boats, the helmsman (usually me) keeps an eye on the depth sounder waiting for the right spot. Once we've located a space and the depth sounder says, for example, twenty feet, I first turn the boat into the wind, and put the engine in reverse. *Harmony* has a tendency to walk her aft end over to starboard in reverse, so in tight places I add some extra angle, or point the bow more to starboard to compensate. When the boat is nearly stopped, Robert splashes the anchor. Once the hook hits the bottom, he lets out chain while I back up until the anchor grabs with a secure hold. When sufficient chain has been let out, I rev the engine until the chain straightens out and pulls taut, and the anchor digs in. With the engine back at idle we make sure that it looks and feels safe and secure. Like most cruisers we use a bridle to relieve the stress on the bowsprit or windlass. At this point anchoring is completed. I turn off the engine, shut down the instruments, and we celebrate our arrival!

In case of engine failure, we thought it would be valuable to know how to anchor under sail. At first Robert and I started practicing in mild conditions until we felt comfortable with our abilities. Being extra cautious during our first tries, it was surprisingly easy in light airs. It wasn't long after that first try that our propeller snagged a tangle of seaweed and we shut down the motor to keep it from overheating. Since we were just a couple of miles away from our destination and a mild breeze was blowing from the right direction our new skills came in handy. We successfully anchored under sail using the back-filled jib to dig us in. Then we dove on the propeller and cleared it of a huge ball of tenacious strands of kelp. Now that we have done it a few times and know the drill, we feel confident that we can anchor under sail, but it's just so much easier using the motor to set the hook.

The Cruising Life

~ The Radio Nets ~

The morning VHF radio nets at marinas and large anchorages are informative and the variety of characters who participate is always entertaining. The VHF radio, with a reach of only twenty-five to thirty miles, keeps the local boating community abreast of all the activities, while hooking sailors up with necessary assistance. After the scheduled net, the VHF returns to its function as a telephone between boats, and keeps us in touch with our friends. It's reminiscent of a party line, like the old style phone system that I had when I was growing up in Korea. These systems entice 'lurkers' to drop by and listen in on the conversations. Instead of the Morse code letters that we would dial on our black, rotary phones (ours was dah-dit-dah), we use our boat names to hail each other. We've been amazed when occasionally the unusual atmospheric conditions in the Sea of Cortez have allowed us to have a conversation with friends hundreds of miles away, their voices booming in like they are anchored next door.

Local radio nets like the Gold Coast Cruiser's VHF Net is spontaneously established when a quorum of boats collects in the Tenacatita/Barra de Navidad area in December. The relaxed and entertaining nature of this local net keeps everyone tuned into the community activities. Unlike the big town nets, which have a set schedule of net controllers, this anchorage is largely made up of transient boats, so the net depends on a different person volunteering each day. The Gold Coast Cruiser's Net is especially entertaining when children take control, surprising the entire anchorage with their abilities to handle the rapid-fire traffic. Occasionally a shy person dazzles us with their eloquence, humor, and a display of latent public speaking abilities. Cruisers are given the chance to air creative new material. Sometimes members will give a short Spanish lesson, a bit of Mexican culture, or interesting trivia. Poets come up with limericks and a songwriter will try out his new creation. A bay watch announcement might report sightings of whales or dolphins in the anchorage or rare glimpses of birds like the roseate spoonbill. When an unusual low came through and gave us a week of rain and storms in an otherwise dry, sunny season, beautiful purple and yellow blooms coated the surrounding hillsides. When someone asked on the morning net what the colorful tropical vegetation was, a horticulturist in the fleet had the answer: jacaranda and tamarind trees.

In marinas amid a forest of aluminum masts and electronic interferences of all kinds, the static and extraneous noise often makes it impossible to hear the long-range single-side band nets. However, the SSB/HAM radio is our lifeline when we leave on voyages. Weather reports are broadcast and we are connected in case of trouble. It is strictly a cruiser run endeavor where the men and women and sometimes, children of the fleet volunteer to be net controllers and coordinate the daily traffic. On every net the first order of business is to listen for emergency traffic. On most days the radio is silent, but with the number of people sailing the open seas in small boats, there is bound to be some action from time to time. Emergency traffic is a rare occurrence, but we do take off on trips assured that the nets are there if we should need them. The next order of business is hearing from those vessels that are underway. Cruisers let the net know their location and destination and give on-site weather reports. By looking at our weather info and then comparing that to a report from someone on the scene, the amateur weathermen try to keep current. After the reports from vessels underway, the weather reports, and general announcements, the nets open up to general traffic and give everyone a chance to pass messages, greetings, and news. Days out at sea seem to revolve around the radio schedules. These nets are a great tool used to stay connected to the community.

On a five-day passage from Ecuador to Panama, off shore from the Colombian coast, there was no one leaving to buddy boat with us. Pat and Carrie, moored in Ecuador, checked in with us in the evenings on our own special SSB radio schedule. We looked forward to their friendly voices following our progress north. Glenn and Pamela with their two young adopted Chinese girls traveled from Panama to the Galapagos Islands, on to Easter Island, and then to Chile in South America. At a certain time each day, we were able to give them updated weather reports during their long, rough, up wind passages, not to mention some needed encouragement. What excitement to hear of their arrival in the Galapagos Islands by Christmas Day where the girls were able to celebrate with the iguanas and large tortoises. When they left for Easter Island, it was not long before radio propagation made connecting with them more difficult. Reverting to our HAM radio e-mail, we stayed tuned in to their progress and unique experiences on shore. We traveled vicariously with them through the long days and nights across oceans that we will probably never travel ourselves.

Infrequently when the call goes out for emergency traffic, the customary moments of silence are shattered by a voice. All ears immediately tune in and the radio operators whip into action. One fellow cruiser reported that his rudder had been whacked in rough seas and was jammed to starboard. The boat was making lazy circles sixty miles off the coast, drifting helplessly to the southwest away from land! Knowledgeable shipwrights in the fleet came on the air to give advice on possible courses of action like how to rig a spare rudder. However, since the rudder was hopelessly bent nothing worked in the tempestuous sea conditions. Eventually a cruiser fluent in Spanish came on the radio and was able to contact the Mexican Navy. They were able to orchestrate a rescue of the disabled vessel and coordinate a tow to the nearest anchorage. When the two boats arrived in Chamela, an anchorage south of Puerto Vallarta, the exhausted sailors and Navy men were welcomed by the cruisers in the anchorage with a warm meal. The Mexican Navy, which over the years has been an outstanding aid to disabled cruisers, then towed the damaged boat to Puerto Vallarta where repairs were soon made in the yard.

On another balmy evening while we were tuned into the Southbound Radio Net, *Harmony* began to shake and rock. The water was rippling, churned up with small closely spaced waves. People listening on shore passed on the TV's bulletin of a large earthquake that had occurred with its epicenter in Guatemala. Conflicting news reports filtered in, and it turned out not to be in Guatemala at all, but the epicenter was in Colima, 60 miles south of where we were. We immediately grew concerned about a tsunami wave! Several boats by that time had already pulled anchor and sped out to open waters. A tsunami travels at around 600 miles an hour and by the time we did the math we realized that we were late and would have been swamped before we stowed the anchor. In 1995 there had been an earthquake in this same area and the water in the bay had actually emptied out, and then came rushing back in. Two large tourist hotels crumbled and the nearby town of La Manzanilla was flooded. The local inhabitants ran to higher ground where the school was located to find their children safe and dry. This night on the net, information was passed continuously to the fleet and luckily a giant wave never materialized. A record number of boats (78) checked in to the Southbound Net. The drama continued when Philip, a single-handed sailor, set out of Banderas Bay fearing a tsunami wave. When he heard the 'all clear,' he set his autopilot for the anchorage. Exhausted, he fell asleep in the wee hours of the morning and ended up driving onto the rocks near Punta de Mita. With a rapid response from the local port captain and several cruisers, his boat was saved and towed into dry storage, rebuilt, and eventually was back on the water again. The next morning's news reported that the earthquake had been quite destructive in the town of Colima with structural damage and loss of life. We placed a call on the HAM frequency phone patch to our son to let him know we were all right. 'All right from what?' he asked. Apparently moderate earthquakes in Mexico receive little attention in the U.S. media.

While on the subject of earthquakes, when a serious temblor shook El Salvador, several coastal towns near where cruisers anchored were isolated by road closures. Help was requested via radio and boats in route from Mexico carried extra clothing and medical supplies with them.

From time to time HAM operators in the United States or the U.S. Coast Guard pass on bulletins requesting "health and welfare" reports for missing boats. Not everyone has e-mail on board and they can be out of communication for weeks at a time. Frequently a sailor listening to the net has seen the 'missing' boat in a secluded anchorage and the 'all is well' message is relayed back up the line.

More than anything our radio nets are entertaining, not unlike listening to the old time shows of radio's heyday before television. In a quiet anchorage far away from the swirl of city life, we wait for the clock to inch towards the top of the hour when our favorite radio host with the velvet voice welcomes the audience, and proceeds with an hour or so of diversion. Someone always has a new tale to tell that can be exciting, inspirational, or funny enough to make us laugh.

The weatherman is also one of the daily stars of the show with his tales of highs and lows, tight millibars and catabatic winds, chubascos, and elephantes. Some days we are treated to a discourse on the weather from our professor of meteorology who enlightens us on how a distant weather system can ricochet and domino effect the weather in our small corner of the world.

The actors and boat names are always changing, but the drama of vessels under way never fails to intrigue. From Mexico we can follow the travels of boats on their way to Pitcairn Island, Hawaii, the Marquesas, or the Galapagos. It's not uncommon when the traffic has dwindled to nothing and the net controller finally signs off that we go out on deck to relax and talk about what a great show that was.

The Cruising Life

~ The Weather Gods ~

After a few boisterous passages, trying to understand the weather patterns became my obsession. By carefully exploring the climatic idiosyncrasies along our routes, we hoped to have a cruising season free from some of the angst and torment of slosh, bump, and crash. We have met ex-cruisers who have returned to a land-based life because the rough weather was more than they could bear. Perhaps with a better understanding of the weather, I could achieve a bit of control over how enjoyable our time at sea would be. By studying the GRIB files (weather charts that we can download onto our laptop computer from our HAM or SSB radio) and talking to other cruisers who were savvy weather watchers, I gained an understanding of what was going on, but what I was wishing for was an intuitive telephone hook up to the Weather Gods! Waking up with the sun, we tune up the radio and listen to our weather gurus on the Mexican SSB nets. There are several to choose from, and we generally check in to the Sonrisa Net with our friends, Rick and Geary, and the Amigo Net with 'The Professor,' Don Anderson of *Summer Passage* transmitting from Oxnard, Ca. They give us informative, entertaining, and, more often than not, accurate weather reports.

Along the United States coastline, professional meteorologists prognosticate the weather, pinpointing the conditions down to small local areas. Continuous NOAA (National Oceanic and Atmospheric Administration) weather forecasts that extend out three days to a week are easily obtained on the VHF weather channels. When we sailed out of U.S. waters it became more complicated since the English language broadcasts ended near the Mexican border. This is when the single-side band weather gurus fill a significant void. In an archetypical sense, they represent our protectors and our most esteemed guides. Focusing on Mexican waters, they give detailed forecasts for both the inside and the outside of the Baja Peninsula, the mainland coast, and south to the Gulf of Tehuantepec. Predicting the tropical storms and hurricanes of the summer season is essential for cruisers' safety. On other frequencies and nets, the weathermen foretell the notorious Papagayo winds off the Nicaraguan and Costa Rican coasts and the fickle ITCZ (Inter-Tropical Convergence Zone) squalls on the passage to Ecuador, Hawaii, or the South Pacific isles.

We huddle around the radio in our aft cabin, listening to the weathermen forecasting their daily reports. Believe it or not, we take detailed notes during the broadcasts because they often rattle off the specifics in rapid fire (the pressure gradients, the high and low pressure systems, the wind speeds and directions, and the wave heights). We refer back to our scribbling when discussing future passages.

Around the world there are many dedicated amateur weathermen who provide an invaluable service for small craft operators who brave the seas and oceans of the world. Former cruisers know the value of accurate predictions and are aware of the conditions that affect our lives on the water. Several of them, when they settled back on land, set up powerful radio stations and compile and broadcast the daily weather reports.

Everyone becomes a weatherperson with varying degrees of competence and a certain percentage of us become weather junkies, thinking, talking, and agonizing about the weather. The modern weather faxes and GRIB Files make forecasting easier, but still Mother Nature never fails to remind us of who is in charge. The weather is always unusual. The El Niño and La Niña weather patterns create noticeable effects. One year the rainy season was late, and another year the cooler weather lasted far into the summer months. The wily weather gods love surprises, have a rascally sense of humor, and don't want us ever to become complacent. They were smiling upon us one year when we were able to spend ten lovely days in the Baja with our children during the Christmas season without a *honking norther.* Some years cruisers have sat in anchorages on the Baja for up to three weeks, waiting for decent weather. Celebrating Christmas with fellow boaters, they would rather wait to go north to La Paz or across the Sea to Mazatlan or Puerto Vallarta, than be beaten up by steep seas.

When we heed the warnings we generally enjoy gentle seas and pleasant sailing. If we bow to our own imperfections of impatience or cockiness, the sea is likely to make us suffer with a taste of its angry, violent, and unforgiving moods. Alas, these weathermen are also human, and, even when they attempt to demystify or translate all the weather charts, miscalculations and uncertainty does occur. Then we all learn something new about the weather.

The Sea of Cortez has predictable weather patterns. Also known as the Gulf of California, this sea has been created over eons of time. The tectonic plate that is holding the Baja Peninsula slowly grinds its way northwest. Old dormant volcanoes line the coast and have left behind perfectly protected anchorages in the middle of ancient calderas. An occasional earthquake reminds us that the seemingly solid earth can tremble beneath our feet. This body of water stretching between the Baja Peninsula to the West and the Mexican mainland to the East is 700 miles long and up to 200 miles wide. During the autumn and spring, the weather is fairly benign with beautiful, sunny, clear, warm days balanced by pleasant, cool nights with mild, sailing breezes. There are times when the wind is so light we have had to motor-sail all day. The weather changes dramatically in the late fall and winter months. Stormy lows, one following another, make their way into the Gulf of Alaska and then slam into the Pacific Northwest and California. During these lows the weather remains lovely in the sea. Once the low passes on to the East, however, a high-pressure system sets up over the four corners region of Arizona, New Mexico, Utah and Colorado and a different weather pattern emerges. The Santa Ana winds start howling offshore in Southern California, and the system known as *northers* begins roaring down the sea, the high flowing into the consistent, tropical low. Strong, cold, blustery winds that blow a steady 20- to 35-knots, funnel down from the north. The high wind velocity causes a rapid buildup of steep, square waves galloping down the narrow, shallow sea. Going south in these conditions is fast and furious, but can be rather uncomfortable due to the short wave intervals. Unless your boat has a powerful engine, it is nearly impossible to pound north, and even then the progress is slow, battling miserable conditions. Tacking back and forth across the sea is an uncomfortable option with steep beam seas slapping the boat around. Once the high-pressure system moves on to the East, pleasant winds return. This on again, off again cycle continues until late spring when the prevailing southerly winds flow north to the persistent, summertime, thermal low near Yuma, Arizona.

Besides the seasonal highs and lows, major promontories always present a weather challenge to the mariner, and Cabo Corrientes is no exception. Situated along Mexico's mainland coast south of Puerto Vallarta, this cape lives up to its Spanish name of *currents*. The jutting protuberance of land creates its own weather, not unlike Point Conception in California or Cape Hatteras on the east coast of the U.S. The currents are strong, and when the winds rise in intensity, chaotic seas are kicked up into a froth. With a northerly component to the wind and swell, voyaging south in the winter can be a rollicking, downhill sail. Even then the stronger winds around the cape can churn the waters with a washing machine effect that can make for an exciting ride. The currents have an uncanny way of changing abruptly. At times, we will be sailing at a swift six or seven knots when suddenly the GPS reads three knots and we are left wondering what happened. When we sail further south around the corner to the Chamela anchorage, the winds moderate and the weather becomes a delightful tropical temperature. It echoes the dramatic climate change that exists sailing from Northern to Southern California. At Chamela, the water is warm, much to our delight, and after anchoring, the first thing we do is dive overboard.

On the other hand when we try to push north into rough conditions around Cabo Corrientes, we wish we had stayed at anchor! Most boats wait in Chamela, eighty miles away, for a weather window and then go when the weather calls for light airs. Whatever the wind speed is in Chamela, you can count on it blowing twice as strong at Cabo Corrientes. Waiting out the weather becomes a lesson in patience for all of us. Tight schedules to pick up visitors or catch a plane add to the pressure to wait for a favorable passage traversing this rough area. For visitors with a plane to catch, there are frequent buses driving up the coastal road to Puerto Vallarta. It helps if the patient half of the cruising couple can keep his or her foot firmly down when the more restless half urges them to go out too soon. The old power struggle can erupt over whether to go or not. I jokingly call Robert my Diva when he is restless and urges us to go out anyway. And then he complains, 'Why did you take me out in such nasty stuff?' I've learned over the years to be assertive and insist that it be a nice ride for both of us. If we take our boat out in inclement weather, we either have a miserable trip or end up returning to the anchorage to wait for the right window. This becomes a humbling learning experience. When the boat stays put until a favorable forecast we celebrate the gloriously smooth passage. A tight little cove called Ipala located in the shadow of the cape provides shelter. Sailors take the long day sail from Chamela to Ipala, rest overnight, and round the Cape in the early morning calm. An alternate plan that we like is leaving Chamela in the afternoon, proceeding to the Cabo on an overnighter and rounding the Punta or point at dawn. This cape might seem like such a small matter, but it has seen its share of broken equipment, roughed up crews, and damaged relationships.

After our first season of sailing in Mexico, we were beginning to get the hang of cruising during the pleasant weather windows. Not bound by schedules, we would wait patiently, and were rewarded with optimal sailing conditions for the six months that we spent on the water. On our entire eight hundred mile trip north from Barra de Navidad to San Carlos/Guaymas, we avoided being beaten up in rough seas. When at the end of one season, we jumped on a mild southerly breeze for the two-day passage to Mazatlan, it proved to be a profound contrast to our first year of stoically pounding north. While on a week stopover to wait out a norther, we were able to provision and enjoy the town during Carnivale. We then had a perfect window for another three-day passage to Aqua Verde, making good distance up into the Sea of Cortez. After several weeks of sailing the deserted Baja, we jumped on another southerly breeze for an overnight passage to San Carlos, sailing most of the way on a broad reach with a light, southerly swell. In rhythm with the seas and the weather, in the flow of the wind, the tides, the moon, the currents and swells, we settled into a comfortable pattern on our watches. Since the seas were gentle it was easy to cook and all went well. With a sense of gratitude we arrived at our destination rested, and refreshed. Maybe we had to experience a big storm, a Sea of Cortez norther, turning back in rough weather again and again (no one said that we were fast learners), to fully appreciate pleasurable passages. It seems like it is necessary for us to have an intimate knowledge of adversity to appreciate the finer things that life has to offer.

The Cruising Life

~ Gone Fishin' ~

The old instinct of an ancient hunter emerges during the primal fight, when a struggling fish is finally brought on deck. A small towel is placed over the fish's eyes, we pour some cheap tequila into the gills to calm it down, and pay homage to the spirit of the fish that will grace our table. We feel like a part of a traditional culture and this intimate process that we have with our food brings us an awareness of our close relationship with nature and our small place in the vast scheme of things. Nothing could be tastier than a fresh cooked catch just reeled in aboard *Harmony*.

One of our first entanglements with a fish was while sailing south, paralleling the deserted, western coast of Baja. Our fishing line, quietly trolling behind the boat, suddenly snapped violently. Several boat lengths behind us a two or three-foot narrow fin sticking out of the water glided stealthily by. When we hailed friends ahead of us on the VHF, they echoed our story. They had just lost a big one too. There went one of our new cedar plug lures to a monster fish going around snapping lines right and left. And there went our dream of having fresh fish for supper.

While quietly reading in the cockpit on a passage, the waves splashing against the hull, a screaming line running off the reel announces a possible fish for dinner. I jump up and slow the boat down by bringing her up into the wind or throttling back on the engine. Robert slowly tightens the drag and begins to reel in the fish. The skipjack or his cousin, Bonita has a large muscular body and pulls hard against a fisherman's line, giving him an exhilarating fight. On one passage we hauled in and released nine *skippies*, one after the other, and decided to pack up our reels and forget about it for the rest of the day. We were played out.

Early on in our cruising career, on a trip with our kids aboard *Harmony*, our sons hooked a large skipjack that was hunting for his

Virginia and Robert's son, Saul, with a spiny puffer fish on the line.

breakfast in the early morning. We were inexperienced fishermen without a clue about which fish is prized and which to throw back. After a hardy fight, it was pulled aboard. When we slit it open eight undigested little fishes slithered out accompanied by shrieks from the girls. After carefully cleaning it, we put it away in the fridge to be made into a tuna salad for the potluck that evening. When we brought our rather dark meat contribution to the party, only a couple of people dared to take a bite. They politely remarked that it was a good tasting salad, but finally a friend let us in on the fact that skip jacks are a bit too fishy for most people's palates. When the pickings are thin and all we catch are Bonita, we sometimes marinate it for two or three hours in lime juice, soy sauce and spices. When cooked with onions, garlic, potatoes and carrots it resembles beef stew.

At one secluded anchorage Randy and Will were new to the fishing game and came over to ask if they could borrow our fish book to identify their catch and see if it were edible. It was a good thing they asked, because they had hooked a puffer fish, also known as fugu in Japan. This fish has poisonous parts that if not carefully prepared can cause sickness and even death. We offered them some of our marinated skip jack stew and after polishing off a big bowl, they vowed that if we had not told them to watch out for bones they would have thought it was beef.

For many years although we had recipes for skip jack tuna, it was not our favorite and we usually released them after a tough battle, until recently! We were anchored next to a boat with fairly new cruisers aboard and they introduced us to their method of preparing the tuna. The results with a freshly caught Bonita turned out to be some of the best sashimi ever. We couldn't believe we'd thrown back so many, missing out on this delicacy and we immediately turned our longtime friends onto this delightful culinary discovery. They were similarly impressed. The new instructions were to cut the choicest quarters of the fish and put them in the freezer section for about four hours. After that, roll small cuts of fish in sushi-flavored rice and Nori seaweed or place a piece over a ball of rice with pickled ginger slices. It melted in our mouths like in our favorite sushi restaurants.

The yellow-spotted sierra mackerel, tender yellow tail, and colorful, distinctly shaped Dorado (Mahi-Mahi) are our favorites. These fish are usually abundant during the cruising season. It is not uncommon to hook a Dorado in the early morning or at dusk, when sailing near Isla Isabella. When we tie into a Dorado we immediately recognize its iridescent, day-glow, blue, turquoise, and green colors flashing in the sunlight. This powerful pelagic fish leaps out of the water somersaulting and twisting, and with a back flip, can often throw the hook. Hooking a Dorado signals a gourmet meal if we can only bring it on board. That is the challenge; the subtle pulling and relaxing of the line to bring it in. After a protracted fight, hauling it steadily in, this beautiful fish freaks out at the sight of the boat hull and begins to thrash about all over again. Aboard *Harmony*, there have been many a vision of fresh mahi-mahi tacos only to have it free itself at the last minute before we could pull it on board. Robert has learned over the years to keep *Harmony* under way, to keep pressure on the line. When the fish is brought in close to the boat he shoots it with his spear gun so that he has two lines attached to the fish with little possibility of escape. As soon as a Dorado is pulled aboard, its fabulous rainbow of colors turns to a dull yellow.

The sierra or Pacific mackerel and the yellow tail are smaller fish and put up less of a fight. We usually hook at least one whenever we sail through certain shallow areas near a Baja reef. Once we caught two with a fish on each line a moment apart. The sierra and yellow tail have a tender and mild tasting white meat that is used in Mexican cerviche.

One winter holiday we had eight people aboard the *Harmony Hotel* and several of our avid fishermen were becoming discouraged that no fish were in sight. The water was too cold, the sea had been fished out, or they had the wrong lure. Fishermen always need a respectable excuse for meager pickings. Just a few miles from one of our favorite anchorages, the reel went spinning out. The boys had caught a large Christmas sierra and those were the best tasting fish tacos ever.

On another visit to these enchanted isles, a serious norther began to blow. In our usual, comfortable anchorage a cross swell began to build and crash up against the sides of the steep hills, creating an uncomfortable back wash. After calling up our friends in the next cove over and hearing that they were having a calm, mellow time of it, we upped anchor and motored around the corner to the longer, narrower inlet. On the short but roaring trip around the point our reel screamed out. We were pulling the fish in while holding the boat steady in the busy seas, and noticed it was a long slender needlefish. The four-foot long fish was larger than any we had ever seen, and we had no idea if it was edible or not. I left the helm for a second to grab our fish identification book, thumbing through to find that it was one of the tastiest fish in the Sea. We pulled it in, anchored and then began the messy business of cleaning it. The meat turned out to be a light blue green color which had us questioning our trusted reference guide. After searing it lightly on both sides, the strange colored meat turned white, and we agreed with our fish book that the needle fish is one of the top best tasting fish. This fish has an added bonus. The bones are a blue color like the lids on our Tupperware so there is little chance that we would catch a bone in our craw.

Buddy boating with several of our fishermen friends aboard their

Robert with his beautiful dorado catch.

trawlers, we picked up new tricks and tips from experienced hands. They knew which lures worked best for which fish and what speed to travel to hook a Dorado. They generously shared tips on good fishing locales and the most successful way of bringing a fish aboard. Ed, one of these aces, swore by his Coke bottle. If you put a coke bottle on a line and drag it behind the boat, it churns up a wake that entices the fish to come have a look. Sure enough one of the boats with a Coke bottle caught a big Dorado that we all shared for dinner that night. We also lucked out and landed a Dorado *sans* Coke bottle, while Ed and his bottle came up empty handed.

Unfortunately from time to time, we have caught things that we were not fishing for. The fish below the water are looking for food and so are the birds circling above. Often a gull, pelican, or booby will circle the lure, think it is a fish, and will dive on it. At various times we have landed each of these birds and that was not a fun experience. One poor gull drowned while we were sailing hard, and we felt terrible for the rest of the day. Even after we put the anchor down in the next cove the gulls on the nearby rocks scolded away at us for killing their cousin. Since that experience, now we quickly stop the boat and save the bird. Early one morning we caught a young pelican that ended up with the hook in its neck. Robert donned his gloves and carefully removed the hook, dodging its flailing wings, feet, and long beak before it flew away. The boobies are the worst. We often sail near islands where they have their nests and nurseries. Two or three will follow us diving for the lure and we have to quickly pull in our lines.

Birds are not the only bane to a fisherman. We have lost many a lure to a fish that we never see. They must be huge because the line squeals out and snaps right off and we are using eighty-pound test. Once on a long passage a huge fish grabbed our lure and gave us a tremendous struggle. When we brought it in close to the boat we realized it was a sailfish with its long bill and beautiful colors. We had no qualms about releasing this spectacularly beautiful catch back to the sea, but extricating the hook from its mouth was no easy task.

Recently while anchored in Tenacatita we noticed a pelican flapping around in the water, struggling for its life. When we approached it in the dinghy we realized it was bound up in a fishing line with little fish hanging from the hooks. Robert and our son, Brian were able to free the bird and it took off flying, swooping down over our boat in a grateful, farewell gesture. We left to take our visitors to the airport and on our return a week later, the pelican searched out our boat and floated happily around us as if to say thank you.

On *Harmony* a ritual is performed for each fish that honors us with its presence. When it is brought on deck, we thank it for coming to nourish us. I put the boat back on course while Robert cleans the catch and washes down the deck. The inedible parts go back in the water where the sea recycles them. Nothing goes to waste in nature's world. Catching only what we will eat, when we have a fish in our small refrigerator, we pull in the lines. When we reel in a larger fish, it is shared with our neighbors at the next stop.

A Few Fishy Tales

When the fishing is exceptional there are letters sent home to share the story. Below are a few e-mails that Robert wrote to the family about our fishing adventures.

The fishing has been terrific. On both of our Sea of Cortez passages this season, we have caught enough fish to feed not only ourselves, but also friends in the anchorages. Today, making the relatively short, twenty-mile trip from Chivato to Burro Cove in Conception Bay, the first thing we tied into was a good-sized sierra mackerel. We have caught sierra in this neighborhood before and I was hoping that we would catch one since we had eaten and given away all of the Dorado from our crossing. That Dorado, by the way, was one of the fiercer battles I ever had with a fish. The boat, sailing along at five knots, added to the pressure. When we finally brought it on board, cleaned it, and put it away in the frig, I was exhausted, and had to take a nap.

During passages I am never particularly hungry but when we arrived, we immediately cooked up some Dorado with onions, garlic, and oyster sauce and oh, mi Dio, did it taste good. Then we made our famous potato-fish burgers for a potluck on shore. Friends on another boat made Dorado sautéed in sesame oil, ginger and garlic. So I was hoping for a sierra and zing went the line. They don't fight like Dorado and Virginia thanked and blessed it as we brought it on board. Pacific Sierras are never very big so I thought I would try for one more and

I put my lures back out. Pretty soon zing went the new line on my new flea market reel and brand new lure, and the fight began. I knew almost immediately that it was a skipjack. They have this way of going straight down to the bottom, pulling, and fighting. When we finally fought it up to the boat it had practically swallowed one of the hooks and it took a bloody while for us to unhook it and throw it back to the deep. He must have been twenty-pounds. Well, that Skippy sort of took the fun out of things and we had enough sierra so we reeled in the lines. We soon anchored, had a swim into the beach, and visited our friend and weather guru, Geary at his palapa on the shore. Geary told us about his son who is a chef at an elegant restaurant in San Francisco where an average dinner is $700 per person. Wow! When the sun was setting, the mosquitoes and no-see-ums came out and we made a run for our dinghy and safety away from their bites that don't bother me very much, but blow up into big red welts on Virginia. We returned to *Harmony* where we proceeded to make sierra ala souse chef. I chopped up some onions, fresh green pepper, garlic, Mexican chili pepper and oyster sauce with fresh tomato, olive oil and two squeezed limes. I steamed it all for about three to five minutes on each side. Who could put a price tag on the delicious meal of fresh sierra eaten aboard *Harmony* that night, anchored in that calm, star-studded anchorage?

To the genuine fisherman: The hits are becoming less frequent as we head south through the Sea of Cortez. Now that we are approaching La Paz, except for 'three Skippies in a row,' there has been nothing. After the three skippies we stopped putting the lures out and there are no hits if our lures are sitting on the deck. This morning a sierra decided to hook up on that well-worn path from Isla Partida to La Paz, right by the whale-shaped island where sierras hang. It fought like a Skippy and I thought 'oh, no,' but then again it had been two days at anchor, and I was ready for a tussle with this fish. When it popped to the surface about half way to the boat, I thought maybe I was lucky and had hooked a large sierra. It had the characteristic, beautiful, yellow spots but was snagged by only one barb and that was holding very precariously. I brought it on deck and tried to hold it while Virginia raced for the knife, only to have it flop away, but it was still on deck! Flap, flap, flap, grab, grab, grab, gone, gone, gone. I had never lost a sierra, ever. Virginia calls it the learning curve of the Zen Fisherman. And now that we are crossing the San Lorenzo channel into the bustle of La Paz, the chances of redemption are slim. Oh, the life of the genuine fisherman!

Later in the season I sent the following e-mail home entitled **the yellow fin redemption...** The jury is still out on what tastes better, yellow fin lightly seared with onions on tortillas or barbecued with pad-Thai sauce over rice.

We are off sailing south down the Mexican mainland coast on a new adventure to Central America. As soon as we left Acapulco the wind characteristically picked up from the West, which meant that *Harmony* was wing on wing going due east, our heading at 90-degrees. When we arrive in Ecuador, we will be more or less due south of Miami so we need to make some easting, but probably not as dramatically as going due east like we were on this trip. The wind held until late into the night, and piped right back up the following day, so we've been sailing most of this passage. In the middle of the night we had two close encounters of the freighter kind. We just couldn't get away from these bad boys bearing down on us. Finally revving the engine up and taking a 90-degree turn saved us. It was scary. We were ten to twelve miles off shore trying to avoid these shoals that stick way out and we were obviously in the shipping lanes. After evasive action we steered in closer to shore, and the big freighters quietly passed outside of us.

We've never been visited by so many pods of dolphins. They cluster around us to ride the bow waves, including during night watches when they look like luminescent torpedoes shooting forward to the bow and then darting back to zoom up again. Awesome! Not to mention the shooting stars, and the sliver of an orange moon rising at 3 AM. Spectacular!

Early the next morning the wind piped back up and *Harmony* once again was doing six to seven knots, jib poled out, wing on wing. The fishing line went screaming out, the eighty-pound test line broke and so we knew we were on to something big. Rob tied on a new lure and soon had another strike, which once again broke his line. Even though this was an eighty-pound test line, we had been using it all season and it might have become brittle from sitting out in the sun. So he cut a fresh piece of line and tied on two new lures, rebuilt with new hooks. When we were about ten miles out of Puerto Escondido, our scheduled stop north of Hualtulco, both lines went zinging out. We were still sailing hard, and the tension from the boat coupled with the weight of the fish created a huge pull. Rob worked really hard reeling the first one in, and it was a good-sized yellow fin tuna, big and round. Its broad body was an easy target for the spear gun, and we heaved it on board with the requisite 'thanks for coming to feed us.' Some tequila poured over its gills and a towel over its face slowed it down, but we were still sailing hard and approaching our port of call. We dropped the jib, and then started cranking in the second line. This one was even larger than the first, and we already had more fish than we could possibly eat so we didn't want to land it. We just wanted our lure back. When the giant catch was reeled up close to the boat, it was fighting hard, and all at once the line broke and off he swam. This was the first time we had snagged a yellow fin tuna, let alone two.

The seas were churned up with the waves on our beam when we made the turn into this anchorage to investigate a good spot. People had mentioned that it was crowded, but with the swell running it was nothing more than a tight little rolly hole in the wall filled with pangas with no room for us at all. We turned around and crashed out through the waves, pointing our bow to the next anchorage, Puerto Angel, thirty-seven miles away. We had never gone into an anchorage and not put down the hook, another first for *Harmony*. In and out of the harbor we negotiated our way through a huge fishing fleet with the largest, most modern equipment, including helicopters aboard that can spot the large schools of fish. We imagined that they are able to rush their yellow fin quickly to the airport and on to the sushi bars of Japan and the U.S. Having anticipated stopping for a late lunch at about three, now we were tired, and hungry. As soon as we were out of the rough swells of the harbor we cooked up some of the fish and chowed down on lightly seared yellow fin tuna tacos.

Puerto Angel has a small, narrow opening into a tiny bay, and it was obvious that we were going to have to negotiate this one in the pitch dark of a moonless night. We've made instrument landings before, but usually we had been to those anchorages or ports once or twice before in the daylight, and knew the lay of the land. Inching our way into this small bay, it looked like we were steering straight into a steep rock wall. Somehow we managed it with Robert standing on deck making sure there was water in front of us. We followed our GPS headings from our cruising guide, and had the radar and depth sounder all conspiring to land us safely. We were so happy to finally anchor after thirty-seven hours of riotous passage making, but it had been one of the best and most exciting sails ever. Needless to say the crew slept well.

In the morning we awoke to find ourselves in a most enchanting spot with two other sailboats and the usual fleet of pangas. A single-hander on one of the boats said he'd been here ten years ago and nothing had changed. We have never heard anyone say that about any other part of burgeoning Mexico. Life seems to pass by at a mellower pace. On the other boat in the anchorage was a couple from Croatia returning home after living many years in Canada. They have been broken down for weeks working on their transmission. We handed out Ziploc bags of yellow fin to our new neighbors, who were overjoyed to have fresh fish for dinner. That evening we had beet soup (borscht), fresh salad, and paella rice. Rob fired up our new BBQ for the first time, and seasoned the tuna with oyster sauce. This meal nourished the lean, hungry crew and we felt rested and revitalized.

Cruising Options

A variety of choices, each with a distinct character and flavor, present themselves along the ocean's highways; passage making, secluded, out of the way spots to drop the hook, busy marinas, and protected anchorages that can hold enough boats to resemble a village on the water. Passage making carries us to a new country or a distant destination. There are plenty of hardy sailors who favor the longer passages and stay at sea with only short stops for repairs and supplies. When we finally arrive at the cruising grounds we can choose to stay at a pleasant anchorage or stop in a marina to provision and take in the local culture in town. We prefer to remain in the pristine areas as long as possible and when the fresh fruits and vegetables run low, we always appreciate our time at the docks. Most of us prefer a little taste of each.

Cruising Options

~ Passage Making ~

Numerous times I had stood on shore and wistfully watched a boat sail away, disappearing over the horizon. When we were departing on our extended passage I was the one now sailing to a distant shore. Passage making is long distance cruising where you might be at sea for a couple of days, or spend more than a month without seeing land. When we journeyed from San Diego to Cabo San Lucas, Mexico at the tip of the Baja Peninsula we made the customary three jumps of one overnighter for each leg. There are not many comfortable hidey-holes along the miles of isolated shoreline, but there are three or four well-spaced, protected anchorages. For those sailors leaving the west coast of California this can be their first overnight experience and they begin to flow with the rhythm of watches and sailing out at sea day and night. Our voyages continued to lengthen when we sailed from southern Mexico to Ecuador and at one point we were over 250 miles offshore during one 600-mile, five-day journey. That was the extent of

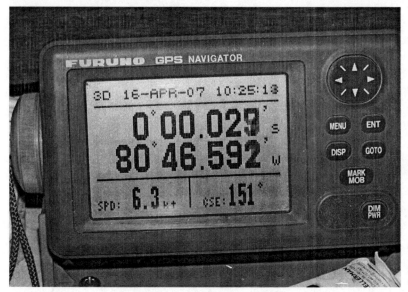

The historic moment of crossing the equator on the passage to Ecuador at 4 am.

our longer passage making, but many of our buddies have made the nearly 3000-mile trans-Pacific voyage to the Marquesas in the South Pacific in anywhere from nineteen days at sea to over a month. To cross the Atlantic usually takes a minimum of two to three weeks with favorable winds.

Before we begin a passage, we are usually well rested and psyched for the adventure. The lockers are well provisioned and I have prepared ready-to-eat food. Even though we don't struggle with sea-sickness, I prefer to have some meals cooked until I become accustomed to the roll of the sea. While we rarely have big dinners underway, the food seems especially tasty with the salty sea breeze for flavoring. When the seas are rough we eat lightly, but one of our friends says that he has a hearty appetite in all conditions.

Passage making allows us constant interaction with the sea and we catch a glimpse of its subtle and not so subtle incarnations. We are the small fish in a big pond engulfed in the beauty, solitude and excitement of our surroundings.

When Olivia crewed with us from Mexico to Ecuador in the spring of 2007, she wrote several colorful letters to her family and friends. Here's her take on a stretch of passage making along the Central American coast encountering the blustery Papagayo winds.

"For the last three weeks, I've been venturing with my parents on their sailboat, *Harmony*. Huatulco, Mexico was where I initially met up with them, and our final destination is Ecuador. We plan to be sailing together for the next 2 months or so and already it's been a wild adventure! Here is a taste of the past few weeks".

'We just landed in Nicaragua. We passed through Honduras late last night during the wildest night passage I've ever had in my life. I think Rob and Ginn have been through this kind of adventure before, but man, it was INTENSE!!! It was never bad. It was always exciting. But there were definite times when I was physically shaking, and couldn't speak without a quiver in my voice because it was so wild. Shiver me timbers! That's all I can think to say. This expression alludes to an old wooden ship striking HUGE WAVES and massive SWELLS so hard that the boat's timbers actually shiver. It was like riding a bucking bronco for seven plus hours! Yeeeeehaw!

So here's what happened. In order to leave Bahia del Sol, El Salvador we had to cross over the shallow sand bar through the huge waves that guard the entrance to the anchorage. Due to these high seas breaking across the bar we were basically trapped like a lobster in a cage for the last five days. Things finally '*calmed down*' and we drove *Harmony* up and over these monster waves and out to sea. Free at last!! Whoo hooo! And then we turned our bow southeastward. Initially in the afternoon along the El Salvadorian coast, we had ten to twenty-five knot winds and a bouncy sea. After the sun set over a beautiful extinct volcano, and the night turned pitch black, we crossed the mouth of the Gulfo de Fonseca, the border between El Salvador, Honduras, and Nicaragua, and the winds started to build. The seas grew to a steady six to eight feet and the winds cranked up to a sustained twenty-five knots gusting up to forty. This was HUGE wind. The rockin' and rollin' carried on for hours from about 6 PM to1 AM. Seven hours of you-cannot-go-from-the-cockpit-to the-galley-to-sip-some-water-without-getting-knocked-on-your-booty-kinda of rocking. *Harmony* was just bouncing, banging, dishes flying; one particular wave sent our recently collected shells crashing to the floor, and I was vacuuming up little pieces of shells this afternoon. During the trip the autopilot acted up a couple of times and we found ourselves unknowingly off course in the dark night. Rob did late night electrical work to get the auto-pile-ee to work again. We ripped the main sail, and tangled the rigging. It was non-stop! No one slept or ate much.

Once we were on the other side of this slot, the entrance to the Golfo de Fonseca, the raging winds and seas calmed down. I was on watch from 12:30-3:30 AM and I guess Rob and Ginn had a break and slept a few winks. The seas were much calmer, but the wind was still strong and fierce. I listened to a pod cast of This American Life, on my mp3 player to try and chill out during my watch and that was wonderful, great radio. All night long we fought our way through the kicked up seas, completing the passage this morning. The rest of the difficult 230-mile trek from Nicaragua to Costa Rica through more Papagayo wind-blown seas still lies ahead!

There was one thing that was amazing. Last night was by far the most incredible night sky of stars I have ever seen in my life. It was a dark night, no moon, and absolutely clear and there were no cities around. No lights from the land, and the stars were all so bright and seemed to never end. Not to mention there were stars in the water. Phosphorescence would light each wave *Harmony* crashed through, each splash a disco ball of water. So maybe not a pleasant ride, but it was still pretty magical. After my shift ended around 4 AM the seas started to build again. Never did they actually totally chill out, but by around 6 AM, we landed outside Puesta Del Sol in Nicaragua under a red morning sunrise. The seas were SO rolly while we waited to get into the marina. We flopped back and forth for several hours until high slack tide when we could enter over the bar, but now we're finally here. And it's heaven. Seriously. We are at the marina of a small but luxurious hotel, where we walk down flower-lined paths and take perfect temperature showers on solid ground. Finally I was able to wash all the salt out of my hair and crust off my body in a continuous stream of water. There are endless empty pristine beaches here that are Nicaragua's best, complete with great waves. I was out on the boogie board this morning and this afternoon I went for a dip in the infinity pool overlooking the ocean with volcanoes in the distance. Since we are at a marina, we have access to electricity and Rob has rigged our little A/C unit above the hatch to my cabin. A/C here on the boat! This is sheer bliss. A/C is a miracle. I've often thought that air conditioning is not something that I'm into, and I've bad-mouthed it for years, but this is special. Our thermometers have clocked temperatures of 100-110 degrees with the humidity levels up to 90%. A/C at this point is pure gold turned into sweet, sweet cold air. It's 6:15 PM and already the parents are sleeping. We are just exhausted. It's been a day for licking our wounds and chilling.

Good times!
Love you all so much,
Olivia'

Cruising Options

~ Passage Making – On Watch ~

With the autopilot in charge of keeping us on course and the sails adjusted for the wind direction, the GPS is dialed in to our next waypoint, and we are underway. It takes a little while for everything to settle down before we remember to plan our watch schedule. When we are off on a longer passage we love having an extra crewmember to share the watches allowing each of us plenty of sleep every twenty-four hours. On our two-month cruise from southern Mexico to Ecuador, Olivia was a great help, especially on the two five-day passages. Each of us was able to have six hours of sleep at night and a nap during the day so it was quite comfortable. When we are just a two-person team we are sailing shorthanded and have devised a watch system that limits sleep deprivation. A three-hour shift works for us during the daytime and on the night shift we each do one four-hour shift, and then alternate a two-hour shift in the early morning hours. This four-hour shift hopefully allows for a longer, deeper REM sleep each night, and then a nap or two during the day keeps us from arriving at an anchorage tired and frazzled.

Harmony has made one particular four hundred mile run several times over the years. It consists of four days and three nights, most of which is sailing out of sight of land from the Southern tip of the Baja Peninsula to the Chamela anchorage one hundred miles south of Puerto Vallarta on Mexico's mainland coast. We have sometimes done this run in consistent twenty to twenty-five knot winds, an exhilarating, downhill sail. And then there was the year we had a flat calm and ran the motor for most of the trip. The last time we made this passage we experienced a combo of mellow sailing with some of the roughest forty-five knot wind, twelve-foot seas that we have seen in a while. The weather report warned of a rough spell coming up on the fourth day, but we thought that we would almost be at our destination so we went for it. The chaos broke loose in the last one hundred miles, and what an incredible day it was. The sun was shining and we were off of the well-known Cabo Corrientes with its conflicting currents and big seas. We surfed down the waves with the wind behind us. We shot a foaming rooster tail off each side of the boat that was blown off in white spray. Large bearded white caps broke around us. Unfortunately one of those big following waves pushed us sideways and its big sister threw us over on our ear. Frothy seawater was churning over the rail into the scuppers and our two solar panels on the starboard side took a short holiday through the crest of a wave. We both held on and watched while the boat righted itself, unscathed and then the main sail tore with a loud rip. A shackle on the jib broke and the foresail started flapping and snapping hard in the wind. We thought that it was prudent to fire up the motor to help hold us into the waves to take down the errant jib. But our trusty motor sputtered and died. There we sat in the deep troughs of the waves, lying a hull, slowly floating down wind. I remember us looking at each other and having a moment of laughter, feeling that even though everything was screwed up, it was going to be all right.

Who could think about a watch schedule with all of this going on? Both of us swung into action to bring things back under control. Robert went out on deck and started to sort everything out, pulling down the main, and hanking on a smaller jib while I hand steered, surfing *Harmony* down the large swells. He then went below to put the engine back in running order. In the time it took for us to recover from our slew of setbacks we had worked our way under the cape and things had begun to moderate. Amazingly enough, in these tumultuous conditions, I wasn't scared for the entire wild ride. At least the rough weather had hit us during daylight hours when we were rested and could both be on deck during the fiercest moments. When conditions had mellowed out, we went back on our watch schedule allowing each of us a rest. In the middle of the night with the help of an instrument landing we arrived in Chamela, and the next day we put the boat back in order and began to unwind.

During one of those fluky weather years, a trip that generally consists of a series of short day sails and harbor hopping turned into a six hundred mile passage. Stopping by the Mexican Riviera on our way north from Panama, we were waiting for the right weather to journey north from the Chamela anchorage on our way to San Carlos. The dry storage lies north of the Tropic of Cancer, a safe spot to put the boat away for another hurricane season. Our son Eugene was getting married and he and his fiancée, Tiffany, had a bachelor/bachelorette party planned in Las Vegas. We knew we would be there for the wedding but we didn't think there was a chance of actually making it to their Vegas party too. With the prevailing northwesterly winds and swell, it usually takes a month working our way up the mainland and then we cross the sea and gunk hole up the Baja coast before sailing back across the sea again to the mainland. But the weather guys' forecast for a two day window of southerlies had us packing and on our way. The balmy winds carried us to Mazatlan where we listened to an updated weather report calling for another three-day window of good weather. We topped off the fuel tanks and continued north on an unprecedented five-day passage. Following the mainland coastline we stayed between ten and twenty miles offshore.

Often on the first night out to sea falling asleep can be difficult. We tend to lie in our bunk and listen to every creak and hope that everything is in order. By the second day we sleep soundly, our bodies adjust and the two of us easily establish a comfortable rhythm of night and day watches. After checking in with the weathermen, we knew that we were just going to make it. We were forty miles out from our destination and the favorable weather window began to close when the northerly winds began to fill in. I came on watch at 2:00 AM to find us pounding into steep, square waves, making little progress. Robert was tired and strung out after his watch in the difficult, worsening conditions. With a fresh, rested viewpoint, I made the obvious decision to tack off to starboard on an exhilarating six-knot sail toward the bright, revolving, Guaymas lighthouse beam. Ducking in under the point, we eventually reached calmer seas and were able to bend our angle of sail closer into the wind. *Harmony* scooted into the anchorage of San Carlos in the early morning with the wind howling at our heels. Thanking our lucky stars and the weathermen for their help in accomplishing a most pleasant and speedy trip north, we put the boat away and made it to both parties in plenty of time.

Extended passages became more common the further south we sailed in Mexico and still longer distances between ports existed on our way to Ecuador. After a delightful week's visit with our daughter

Caitlin, and her future husband Tad, exploring the many beautiful bays of Huatulco, we prepared for our straight-shot journey across the notorious Gulf of Tehuantepec. The carefree cruising with the family, fishing, swimming, and snorkeling was the perfect way to rest up for the five-day trip to El Salvador. In Huatulco's Chauhe Marina on the edge of the Gulf, we waited for the green light (a calm weather window), to avoid the serious winds that can blast across the Tehuantepec through a gap in the Sierra Madre Mountains. There are two options when crossing the Tehuantepec. The preferred itinerary has the sailor going straight across on a mild weather window that can be accurately predicted. The other choice is to hug the coast, with 'one foot on the beach' as they say, and if the blast of wind does come through the pass the fetch will be manageable and you can anchor or sail in the fierce blow. With this second option it is possible to stop each night and drop the anchor off the beach in sand. If the wind is howling up to fifty plus knots, it may not be the most comfortable night's sleep, but with good holding you should be safe with maybe a bit of sand on the deck. Our forecast was for a five-day stretch that was so calm that we 'could have paddled a canoe across,' as our weatherman, Don Anderson, likes to say. We picked up Olivia from the airport and that night with our diesel tanks filled, we followed our rhumb line directly across the Gulf. With three people on board, our watches consisted of three hours on and six hours off, allowing us plenty of good rest. It was a piece of cake. Without the breeze however it was so hot that near the Mexico/Guatemala border we stopped *Harmony* and dove into the clear, green ocean for a refreshing swim. Our plan was to bypass the expensive marina in Guatemala making our destination Bahia del Sol in El Salvador. One dark night off of the Guatemalan coast, our way was sprinkled with what looked like starlight for as far as we could see. All of us stood on a nerve-wracking watch for several hours to negotiate our way through a large panga fishing fleet, each one displaying a small light on board. Closing in on El Salvador the following morning we heard a single handed sailor calling for help on the SSB net. He had lost his engine and in the calm conditions he had sailed for days with little progress, and had drifted close to a rocky shore. Our buddy boat, Sea Peace, was a few miles in front of us and graciously volunteered to give him a tow. They finally reached him on this moonless night and we followed them along the coast to the waiting room anchorage. When we woke up the next morning all we could see was a threatening line of white, frothy seas breaking across the sandbar entrance and wondered how and where we would enter through the rough surf. A call to the marina on the VHF connected us to the local guides who instructed us to wait for the afternoon slack tide. It was a most uncomfortable wait bouncing around in the swell, but the crew was tired and we all slept anyway. When the afternoon slack rolled around, much to our amazement, the white line of crashing waves subsided and like the parting of the Red Sea, flat water appeared in front of us. A former cruiser in his panga came out and guided the four waiting boats through the shallows and gave continuous instructions over his hand held radio of more to port, now a sharp turn to starboard, straight ahead. We were on full alert, paying close attention to our guide's instructions when we surfed over the treacherous bar into the calm, river anchorage. With pangas and dinghies standing by in case of trouble, there was enough wind coming from the right direction for the engine-less boat to sail in successfully under his own power bringing up the rear of our small flotilla.

A peculiar weather pattern occurred the year that we made this passage south. Major storms in the South Pacific created an unusually large southwest swell. The surfers were out in force but it made for dicier bar crossings and left us little protection in several of the southwest facing anchorages along the Central American coastline. On our return trip the following year, we had calm anchorages and easy bar crossings, a real contrast from the passage south.

After our inland escapade to San Salvador and Guatemala we once again set sail and battled our way south through the raging Papagayo winds along the coast of Nicaragua and Costa Rica. On one long, moonless night we experienced consistent 50-knot winds and by midnight we had endured about as much as we could stand. The logical choice was to fall back on Plan B, stepping off the carnival ride from hell, and clawing our way into what is mysteriously called No Name Anchorage. For two nights we hunkered down while the winds raged, the anchorage white with kicked up seas. The main sail had a tear along the reef lines so we put in the second reef (Yes, we should have had the second reef in when the winds started to howl) and when the winds let up a bit, we had a lovely broad reach sail in 20-25 knots into Costa Rica's tranquil and pristine Santa Elena bay. Our next long distance passage was a five-day, off shore, up wind trip from Golfito, Costa Rica to Bahia de Caraquez, Ecuador. On this nearly 600 mile run we tasted a smorgasbord of weather, sailing through squalls, rough seas, flat calms, and even a day of sunny skies while making our way through the ITCZ (Inter Tropical Convergence Zone). One of our buddy boats traveling a day ahead of us had a squall system sit on top of them for thirty-two hours. In this area, several degrees of latitude on either side of the equator, the weather, currents and swell from the northern hemisphere meet up with weather, currents and swell from the southern hemisphere, creating these hodgepodge systems. During the nastier conditions all three of us would be on watch to check the radar, steer clear of the worst squalls, and ensure that everything stayed tied down. There would be plenty of time to catch up on our sleep once we arrived in Ecuador. Even when the seas continued to bounce and heave all night long eventually sleep would overtake us.

It is said that on a long passage like the downwind Puddle Jump from Mexico to the South Pacific or from the Mediterranean across the Atlantic to the Caribbean, sailors can experience boisterous seas, consistent trade winds, and the doldrums where there can be days without a breath of breeze. The longer passages are for the serious sailors who have prepared their vessel, provisioned, collected the appropriate charts and visas, and taken care of their affairs at home. These hardy mariners find a comfortable routine of watches, which generally consist of three hours on and three hours off with naps during the day although each crew finds the schedule that suits them best. Long distance, cruiser friends, Charles and Anna sailed north from South Africa through the South Atlantic Ocean to the Caribbean Sea. To accommodate the fact that the captain had a difficult time sleeping during the day while his wife was a night owl, they adopted a four-hour on, four hour off watch schedule. If he was sleeping soundly during the night, she would do a longer stretch of up to six hours. Then he would take over while she caught a long snooze during the day. It's not uncommon for cruisers to have friends or family along to share the watches to distant destinations. Everyone has an easier trip when there is ample room for the crew and everyone enjoys each other's company.

When we pick the right season to make the longer passages, the winds are usually favorable and the watches tick by uneventfully. The gorgeous surroundings dish up *nature moments* with periodic visits from the dolphins, turtles, and whales plus an occasional fish on the line. On a long ocean passage, while sailing along in the consistent trade winds, the sails are set and only small adjustments need to be made for days at a time. Keeping a lookout for any chafing is par for the course.

On a coastal trip however, we often spend our time setting the sails, and then fiddle with them for the rest of the day. The wind varies from morning to evening as the dance of the diurnal, thermal pattern shifts over land and sea requiring sail changes and adjustments. In the morning the off shore breezes send us off at a pleasant clip. Following a mid-morning calm, the winds shift to onshore for the rest of the afternoon. Nearing sunset the winds and seas calm again. There is still plenty of time to read, cook, make radio contacts, write, and nap.

The SSB and HAM radios are our connection to the outside world when we are at sea. Happy to be checking in as a vessel under way on the morning and evening nets, it is reassuring to know that our friends are following our progress. Over the years Robert has had a good time as a net controller on both the HAM and single side-band radio nets. When his scheduled show comes up while we are underway, we shut down the engine if it is on, and disengage the autopilot. I hand steer the boat while he runs his show. We also turn off the refrigerator and any fans, inverter or neon lights since all of these appliances can create loads of radio noise and static. Nets can often run for over an hour. After Robert signs off, we take showers, do our routine checks, and then put the autopilot and fridge back on and continue on our way.

After we watch the big red sun melt into a puddle of gold at the rim of the ocean, we prepare for our night watch by first adjusting or reefing the sails. Since we don't have a roller-furling jib and we would rather not make sail changes at night, we set it up for a comfortable ride. All the navigation lights are switched on, along with the radar, which goes on standby. I usually take the first night watch while Robert sleeps during his down time. When my shift begins, I plot our position on the chart, take a 360-degree look around the horizon, and check the radar. We are usually traveling at a speed of five to six knots, which equals approximately one nautical mile every ten minutes. The radar is set to the six-mile mark, and we flip on the twelve and sixteen mile settings to see if there are any large, fast moving ships coming our way. When we check every ten minutes we have sufficient warning even if a ship is traveling at twenty knots or more. Every hour we check all the systems on board and take the boat's bearings off the GPS and record our latitude/longitude position on the paper chart. If the motor is on, the hourly check-up consists of looking at the oil pressure gauge, water temperature and fuel gauge. In between keeping an eye on everything I like to star gaze, play solitaire, do yoga, meditate, and catnap. It is a great time to bring out the guitar and sing to the sweet spirits of the night.

If the weather changes or there is any reason to question what is going on, we call for our partner to help with what needs to be done. If we become fatigued, we call for a new watch shift no matter what time it is, or how long we have been on deck. If someone is sick or otherwise indisposed, it makes the strain on the other partner that much more difficult. One person can manage, like many single-handed sailors do, but there's nothing like having someone along to give us a break. I once asked a single-hander friend of mine who had sailed all the way from Alaska how he managed to sleep while under way. He had a relatively simple solution. When he was well offshore, the radar alarm was turned on and he would go to sleep. The alarm would sound if the radar encountered any target, ships, land, or buoys.

Despite my initial trepidations about making long passages, when we were actually underway, I became enthralled with the wide ocean in all of its mysterious moods. I was swept along with the flow and rhythm of its awesome expanse. With a change of attitude and a dose of courage, the night watch was transformed into a magical experience.

All the noises of the boat's movements, groaning rigging, and wave action seem exaggerated at night and often made me wonder if everything was okay. When I became accustomed to the night watches, I could recognize the difference between the normal sounds and something that should grab my attention. An engine sputter, the autopilot not holding its course, or a torn sail can fire up my adrenaline. All of these things and more have happened aboard *Harmony*. We either fix them underway or jury-rig it with a touch of ingenuity until we arrive at a marina for more serious repairs. On a stormy passage, a wave can knock the boat sideways or slap our stern with a loud explosion. These waves create a noise that has us both at full alert wondering what we hit, or whether we have a gaping hole in the hull! We're always relieved when we realize it is only one of those rouge, square waves. Back to sleep everyone. Off of the Colombian coast, we hit a log that had come down from some rushing river during the rainy season. It bumped against our hull from bow to stern. Thank goodness it caused nothing more serious than scraping off some bottom paint along the water line. If the weather is unsettled or stormy, we trim the sails, and hang on just like we normally do during the daytime. If the seas become rough and fatigue sets in, heaving-to in order to take a rest can recharge the crew for the next leg of the journey.

Out on the ocean we rarely see another vessel at night unless it's our buddy boat's lights. On a clear night a ship's lights can usually be spotted before they show up on the radar and there is plenty of time to track their progress and direction. Occasionally we'll pass a fishing fleet or a big lit up ferry will appear and then recede over the horizon. In certain areas we have to keep a closer watch for pangas that carry only a small light because the fisherman may be sleeping, not watching out for us. If we cross a shipping channel we make sure we are out of harms' way. Sailing at night near the Panama Canal involved keeping a close eye out for huge container ships and tanker traffic. We watched as the red or green navigation light of a moving vessel approached and then passed us, and then their white stern light bid us goodbye. A freighter or cruise ship looks like a lit up city and we can see them from a long way away. The further off shore we ventured, the less traffic we encountered. It's a big, wide, empty ocean out there.

The night watch is often a bedazzling array of the moon rising and setting, stars drifting across the sky and the luminescence in the waves. The chance to watch the sun set to the West, while the full moon rises in the East is one of those unique events that is difficult to capture on film. On a few occasions the full moon began to disappear without clouds, mountains, or fog to obscure it. We laughed when we realized it was an eclipse and imagined how unnerving such an event must have been for the mariners of old. Stargazing at night gives us amateurs a chance to identify the constellations. Orion the Hunter stealthily stalks his prey along the Milky Way, bow and arrow at the ready, and the Big Dipper pivots around the North Star. The Pleiades's, or Seven Sisters, are our companions, and have helped guide us through a dark night. Sirius, one of the brightest stars in the sky, twinkles red, green and white, like a patriotic Mexican disco ball when it first rises above the horizon. The Southern Cross was our constant night companion when we sailed south towards the Equator. It shone brightly directly in front of our fore stay, a guide leading the way. We keep *The Stars* written by H. A. Rey [34] of the *Curious George* series handy to understand how mankind has interpreted the night sky for millennium. The occasional meteor shower, comet, and space shuttle add another dimension to a night watch.

Without a moon the night watch can be extremely disconcerting and provided me with a good opportunity to deal with childhood fears of the dark. The uneasiness vanished when I understood that the nighttime sea was the same friendly place that we experienced in the daytime only with the lights out. At first I felt uncomfortable and anxious being on watch alone on the night sea. When I let go of my fears and concentrated on the beauty of the stars and the moon glow sparkling in the waves, the feelings of dread were replaced by awe and enchantment. I now look forward to the night watch, a quiet time to spend with my thoughts, feelings, and dreams. The muse of poetry has visited me on beautiful, night sails. Those long, nocturnal passages have become an opportune time for me to feel at one with the big outdoors and commune with nature.

Cruising Options

~ Passage Making – Nature Moments ~

When visiting with our friends on board *Mija*, Terry interrupted our conversation to point out a group of silver and black rays jumping like Jack in the Boxes between the boats in the anchorage. 'Nature moment, nature moment,' she exclaimed exuberantly, and we've been calling it that ever since. Rarely does a day go by without an endless stream of nature's entertainment. Sailing along the coast of Baja, the spectacular scenery stretches on for miles.

In the early dawn on one of our Sea of Cortez crossings our raw water pump that cools the engine started to leak and spewed salt water around the engine room. We shut down the motor and hoped for the wind to make its appearance. We were becalmed forty miles from Mazatlan where the blue, distant mountains were seen rising out of the morning haze. Just then a large pod of *circus dolphins* surrounded *Harmony* and gave us a riveting performance of twists, back flips, jumps, leaps, a veritable water ballet. Our guardian angel put on a show for us while the wind gods cranked up the fan. Before we knew it, the breeze filled in (on the nose, wouldn't you know), right out of Mazatlan harbor, but we were sailing on a tight reach toward our destination. It was a magical moment and we were underway. The wind shifted when we approached the mainland, which allowed us to bend in towards the marina and a safe haven.

Later on that season we were crossing the Sea of Cortez, the eighty-mile trip from Punta Chivato on the Central Baja to San Carlos on the mainland side. The skies were a rare overcast reflecting gray in the water below and we spotted as many as twelve pods of whales on all points of the horizon. Twice we had to slow the boat down to let the leviathans cross our bow. It was their ocean and we were just passing through friendly territory. When they came close by to check us out, spouting a huge spume of fishy smelling spray into the air, we sailed up wind avoiding the stench. Their unique, fantastic noises filled the sea air and we were mesmerized by the beautiful sounds.

A huge blue whale, which the zoologists say are the largest mammals ever to exist on earth, nestled up close to our starboard side on another passage. This extraordinary mammal swam downwind of us and spouted out of its wide blowhole. It was steel-gray-blue in color and one large eye looked up at us for what seemed like a timeless moment. This gigantic creature was at least twice the length of our boat and slowly swam alongside and across our bow, before it disappeared gracefully into the depths. Astonishment mixed with awe surrounded us and we sat in silence, reflecting on the privilege of observing such a rare sight.

Magical nature moments continue to follow us from sea to land. The day my father passed on in the Blue Ridge Mountains of North Carolina, there was a huge storm. Bright, sunlit white clouds interspersed with dark, ominous gray ones, swirled in all directions while forming up over the mountain crests. Before the rain came down in a major deluge, rainbows refracted the afternoon's sun's rays sparkling off of the moisture in the clouds. The dancing prisms seemed to swirl upward to form a colorful, spiral staircase to heaven. Double rainbows then arched across the sky in brilliant hues. Several years later leaving Barra de Navidad for our distant destination of Ecuador, a rainbow glistened a Bon Voyage, and I was reminded of my father and how lucky we were to be living his dream of sailing the high seas.

While snorkeling among the numerous reefs, an entire world of underwater life reveals itself in Technicolor. It often feels like we are swimming in our own, giant, private, aquarium, floating weightlessly along amidst the schools of fish swimming all around us. The variety of sea life is abundant, from little turquoise fish to puffers and yellow tails to pargos, groupers, triggerfish, sierra, urchins, snakes, rays, and lobsters. During a memorable dive, I counted twenty-two different species swimming by my prescription dive mask in one afternoon of exploration under the water's surface.

Isla Isabella, the famous bird sanctuary, holds a bounty of awesome nature moments. This is the home of the large, ominous looking frigate birds, the bandits of the sea, that swoop down with their forked tails skimming the ocean and swipe fish from other birds. The black, male birds perch atop stunted trees attracting mates by puffing out their bright crimson throat pouches in a courtship display. The boobies nest on the ground next to the rocky path that ascends up the cliff to the lighthouse, and squawk loudly to warn us to keep a safe distance away. The newborn babies hide under their mother's feathers and the teenagers, decked out in a most fashionable, white fuzzy, feathered look, eye us curiously. Huge, orange and green iguanas up to five feet long lounge lazily in the sun around the new visitor's center. Research scientists and students spent months camped out in rustic tents, studying the habits of the bird life. The waters teem with exotic reef fish and numerous whales swim close in to shore feeding in the nutrient rich waters.

From Isla Isabella to Puerto Vallarta and on south to Acapulco, we have seen large numbers of huge turtles floating in the water, some with boobies perched on their backs taking a rest, miles from shore. When we sail close by, they dart quickly into the deep, their flippers defying their reputation for being slowpokes. In recent years there has been a concerted effort by Mexican ecologists to safeguard the declining population. They collect the newly laid eggs from the nests on the beach where the mother turtles deposit them above the tide line, and fence in the eggs to protect them from scavengers. On each mound of eggs is a tag with dates noting when they were laid and when they are due to hatch. When the baby turtles emerge from their rubbery eggs, they are held in a ventilated cooler until they can be released at night when the predator birds are roosting. We know of at least four places where this is being done. Various species are studied and counted each year, and the work is going well. Each year we see an increasing number of these interesting creatures in the ocean and turtle tracks on shore.

When we travel through humpback whale territory, a nature moment stretches on and on while we watch them breech, slap their fins on the water's surface, and dive with their flukes bidding adios. Each time we arrive or depart Banderas Bay, near Puerto Vallarta, a welcoming committee of three or four humpback whales greets us at the entrance with their breaching, cavorting, and splashing performance. They are there waiting for us like sentinels whether the seas are kicked up or calm. Banderas Bay is one of those places in Mexico where the humpbacks come to hang out each season after having migrated thousands of miles from cool Alaskan waters. We usually spot at least a dozen whales on a day sail around the bay.

There is rarely a passage, when dolphins don't come to play. They cavort in *Harmony's* bow waves, or surf down the faces of large waves displaced by our full-keeled boat. Several dolphins compete for the best surfing position, squeaking, playing, and jostling. Then they fall back only to rebound to the front again. We have had as many as fifteen playing at our bow, ranging in age from babies to adults. It is not uncommon to see a dolphin with a striped 'tattoo' on its back, possibly a battle scar from a boat propeller. When they first approach, dolphins often swim up alongside our center cockpit to signal to us that they are there before they head to the front. We love to go out on deck to watch them and I sing to them a slow rhythmic chant. They whistle, arch out of the waves, and turn to look up at us, as if to communicate their delight in our company.

Each year when we anchor at Tenacatita or Chamela we look forward to a visit from Chippy, the dolphin with a notch missing from his dorsal fin. He's been a fixture in that area for all the years that we've been cruising, and old timers remember him from before we arrived on the scene. On several of my swims into shore, two or three dolphins have accompanied me, squeaking and swimming nearby.

The entertaining needlefish hurriedly darts away from our boat, balancing on his tail, like a stone skipped across a pond. Schools of flying fish sail through the crests of waves. It's not unusual for our deck to have several aboard after a boisterous night. One morning Robert went out on deck and came back into the cockpit with black footprints following his every step. He had unwittingly stepped on a squid that had launched itself onto our deck during the night and its black ink was tracked everywhere!

A large bill fishing tournament was underway when we made our way north on an overnight passage from Isla Isabella to Mazatlan.

A giant marlin with its electric blue skin shimmering in the morning sunlight, jumped as high as the deck of our boat. Then, in case we didn't believe our eyes, it leaped again. It somehow knew that we were not after it, but only wanted to watch its spectacular dance on the top of the waves. It was not long after the marlin sighting that the wide-winged rays began to perform their jumping exercises. They flew from two to six feet above the water's surface, and then splashed back down, loudly slapping the water. Their aerial antics were so full of exuberance and they seemed to be having such fun or is it just trying to rid themselves of parasites?

Mother Nature works her magic when we sail across open waters. Whenever she feels like it, she pulls out her bag of tricks to entice and delight, frighten and intrigue. The swell of the Pacific Ocean, generated thousands of miles away from Hawaii, Alaska or New Zealand, lulls us to sleep at anchor. The winds that fill our sails arrive from fronts located hundreds or even thousands of miles across oceans. We watch the moon through its phases from full to new and back again, the tides bending to its magnetism. The days in Mexico and Central America during the winter season are generally a bright, beautiful, sunshiny blue. The nights are a mixture of warm darkness dotted with a brilliant light show of stars or a moon which lights up the sea with its silver-yellow glow. Sunrises and sunsets, The Artist's brilliant display in bold strokes, splash across the sky and are reflected in the ocean in a vivid palette of coral, gold, orange, pink, and purple. In certain areas, under the right conditions it is not uncommon to see the green flash wink its emerald glow at sunset when the big orange ball dips below the horizon.

In the tropical climes, the nighttime light show displayed in the thunderheads is awe-inspiring. One stormy night along the Costa Rican coast, we traveled mile after mile alongside a wall of clouds filled with squalls and lightning in pink and gold brilliance. The spectacular jagged spears of raw, electrical power ricocheted between clouds, often finding their way to the water. Fortunately the squall line stayed a healthy distance away on our port side. Wonder can become mixed with 'uh, oh' when the squalls start moving in our direction and our mast pointing straight up into the sky is the highest thing around for miles.

On a more pleasant note, there is nothing quite as invigorating as riding the waves hour after hour, with all sails set on a beam reach or wing on wing with the wind behind us, far out of sight of land. And after days at sea the faint outline of land appears on the horizon, and we experience the thrill of 'Land Ho!' Eventually we make out the landmarks and it's not long before the anchorage or breakwater comes into view, with a mast or two rising above the water.

Robert enjoying a refreshing waterfall in the Perlas Islands, Panama.

Nature sometimes meanders in intriguing directions and traveling out in the wilds, we are privileged to partake of its mysteries. While we were nestled in a small, desert anchorage north of San Carlos, Sonora, Mexico, a few bees began to buzz around our screened-in hatch, attracted to the fragrance of fresh water, a rarity in this arid land. Bees were always considered our pets when they would visit our booth on a sunny day at an art and craft show eying our brightly colored tie-dyed clothing in search of sweet nectar from these unusual flowers. When a customer would start to wave wildly or freak out about the bee, we would try to calm them by saying, 'It's okay. It's our pet bee-bee coming for a visit.' The children would gather around to watch our pet walk up and down our fingers before it flew away, not finding any tempting juice around. On this warm, sunny day, we welcomed the bees and invited them to the aft deck where we put out a bowl of fresh water. Soon there were hundreds of bees jockeying for position along the water's edge, and with their full bellies weighing them down, they were barely able to lift off and fly away. We watched them for a while and then returned to what we were doing. Several hours went by and again a few bees started to buzz around Robert who was working on deck. He checked their bowl and sure enough it was licked dry. I called out to the scouts who were buzzing around the screens that we had given them water and they could go home now. Amazingly enough in a short while, there was not a single bee around and in the four days we were anchored there, only an occasional scout showed up and then peacefully left.

This outback anchorage seemed to be the center for fascinating natural phenomenon. We were visiting with friends one afternoon when we noticed hundreds of big, blue and white, bowling ball-shaped jellyfish bobbing around the boats. When we looked closely, they had short white tentacles that propelled them through the water, often careening into each other like bumper cars. Some mix of water temperature, delectable food, or mating season conspired to fill our waters with these intriguing creatures. Even though we had to restrict our swimming for that day, Jordan, our five-year old pal from the neighboring boat and I spent a long time watching the funny blue balls bump into each other, laughing at their comical antics. When we returned to our boat in the dinghy, we inched along slowly in order to navigate through the swarm of underwater visitors without nicking them with our prop.

As twilight approaches and we are nestled in a desert anchorage the lengthening shadows create images across the rocky cliffs that tower high above our heads. We pull out our folding chairs and sit on the forward deck and adjust our vision to see what's hiding, like in those double image pictures that were such a rage back in the '90's. And then we see him, *the man in the mountain*, nature's guardian spirit, watching over land and sea. He might be sleeping or gazing up into the heavens or if he's the humorous sort, he'll wink at us.

Each tranquil anchorage encircling the Sea of Cortez has its own pristine beauty of tawny-colored mountains filled with cacti and unusual rock formations, surrounded by clear turquoise and green water. The binoculars are kept nearby to watch an osprey swoop down, catch a wriggling fish, snake, or mouse in its talons and devour it perched atop a saguaro cactus. The parent ospreys take turns hunting and then sitting on their nests atop a rocky pinnacle. Occasionally a bandito frigate bird battles an osprey for his catch. We often feel as if we're watching a live showing of the Discovery Channel on a very wide screen. The community of gulls perched on a craggy island indulges in a lively conversation. Whenever we throw scraps of fish to a lone gull, it's not long before his buddies come join in the free food giveaway, squawking and fighting over each morsel. The statuesque blue herons stalk the shores looking for small fish for dinner, and the pelicans and blue-footed boobies go into dive-bombing mode along the rocky cliffs at breakfast and dinner hour. On one quiet afternoon we watched a rare, red beaked oystercatcher picking its way along a deserted beach.

Time seems to take a vacation when we become immersed in Mother Nature's awesome extravaganzas. These over the top production numbers fill our lives with fascination, wonder, and excitement and when we are engulfed in such beauty, privy to the magical events of nature, we know that any uncomfortable moments are an inexpensive price of admission.

Cruising Options

~ Secluded Anchorages ~

A pleasant anchorage every twenty to forty miles apart makes for easy daytime hops along the eastern coast or the inside of the Baja. In the right season, the Baja becomes a spectacular cruising ground, where the water is warm and clear, and the weather is benign. North of the old mission town of Loreto lies the magnificent, rock encircled anchorage of San Basilio Bay, known to us cruisers as San Juanico. Aside from being incredibly scenic, it also is home to a cruiser's shrine that has been there for, no telling how many years. A hardy but scrawny tree sits at one corner of the beach and is decorated with various cruisers' ornaments displaying their boat name, date and maybe a poem or saying. There are shells, wine bottles, bits and pieces of boat, laminated boat cards, and a lone shoe. The surrounding sandstone is also artfully engraved with boat names. When we dinghy into shore on our pilgrimage to this monument, we locate our friends' names and read the poetic and humorous inscriptions. The tree used to have a four-foot high rock wall leading up to it with a stone lined path. Several years ago Hurricane Juliet tore through the area scattering the rocks halfway down the beach and blowing away many of the hangings. We were one of the first boats to arrive after the destructive storm and when we walked the beach we began to pick up flotsam that used to belong on the shrine. In a rather futile gesture, we stacked them around the weather-beaten tree. Among the beach detritus, we found what must have been a piece of whalebone, and since our tie-dyed offering was in tatters, we decided to use this large, white vertebra as our new contribution. We painted "*Harmony*" in bright red with our names and date and I climbed into the top branches to secure it with fishing line. As the seasons went by and cruisers replaced their lost ornaments, the shrine honoring the cruising lifestyle once again appears respectable and festive. Before the hurricane tore things apart we had discovered inscriptions dating back to the 1980's. The rare hurricane makes sure the shrine stays current and refreshed.

Harmony *at anchor in the natural hurricane hole of Puerto Don Juan in Mexico.*

During one of our visits to San Juanico we had a memorable Halloween party on the sandy beach. There were three boats in the anchorage and a lone camper van set up on shore that had managed to negotiate the tortuous road to the bay in their four-wheel drive truck. Under a full moon we gathered around a roaring bonfire, played music, sang, and munched on goodies. One of the campers turned out to be a talented performer working out of Nashville, Tennessee. Her music was a special treat and serendipitously that night she met a single-handed sailor at the party. They fell in love, were married, have a daughter, and are living the good life.

Arriving at one of our favorite spots, we stay for several days, sometimes a week or more. We fall into a pleasant routine of watching the sunrise, working on boat projects for a few hours in the morning, and spending the afternoons swimming and snorkeling. If there are other cruisers around or an outback NOLS adventure group sails in on their small, Shackleton-style ketches, we can usually drum up a bocce ball game on the beach. Later we might hang out and trade tales over a sundowner, or have a potluck on shore followed by music around a bonfire.

On the Baja coast far away from the Pacific swell, the dinghy landings are benign and we take long walks along the pristine white beaches, or hike the trails through the desert. For the amateur archeologist, early petrographs can be found around Conception Bay and there are caves of early inhabitants scattered among the cliffs of Aqua Verde and on the islands north of La Paz. Outside of one cave opening far above the waterline, oyster shells are piled several feet high and inside there is a blackened ceiling from cooking fires that tell an ancient, tribal tale. Flint is scattered about collected from a rock strata on the island. In one cove not far off the beach is a sailors grave and shrine dated 1806, an interesting destination for an afternoon of exploration.

The shell collecting is often excellent, since there is little surf to pound them into tiny bits. One beach dishes up white pooka shells, another, conchs and cowries and at the north corner of Bahia Conception the shore is covered with, what I call jingles. Each yellow, white or orange potato chip-looking shell has a small, white baby's footprint etched on the inside. When you shake several of these together, they make that jingle sound. On our walks through the hills around San Juanico, we find God's or Apache tears, small black drops of obsidian. The rare and delicate, paper-thin nautilus that washes up on certain beaches during a particular season is a real trophy.

The islands north of La Paz called Espiritu Santos and Isla Partida have many pristine inlets where we drop our hook. The name Espiritu Santos fits this island perfectly since it is filled with spirit and magic in the sheer beauty surrounding the clear, turquoise waters. There are usually a few other boats in each anchorage, but during certain months we have had them to ourselves.

On the shorter daytime passages in the sea, we travel through spectacular scenery. Striations of different colored rock rise above us and it feels like a sail through the Grand Canyon. The mountains surrounding Puerto Escondido are exquisite in their towering, craggy grandeur and the radiating sunbeams at sunset have a stunning, illuminating glow. Beautiful and even more isolated areas exist north of Santa Rosalia near the Bay of Los Angeles and the Midriff Islands. Only a few cruisers reach these northern islands but those who weather the long summers in the numerous anchorages know the secluded beauty that exists here. The entire Sea of Cortez is a magnificent place and together with the bays along the mainland coast makes Mexico an enchanting cruiser's paradise.

The only places on the Eastern Pacific Coast that we found that rivaled the cruising experience of the Sea of Cortez was the

Western Islands and Perlas Islands of Panama where each island has its own unique flavor. In the warm, glass-like waters of Panama, we would often see the anchor at the end of our chain. The jungles of lush vegetation are home to howler monkeys, pairs of beautiful green parrots, and an assortment of waterfowl, cranes, herons, and pelicans feed in the abundant waters. Fresh water is often available, running from pristine waterfalls or springs, and in one anchorage we spent an afternoon snorkeling in an undisturbed coral garden. Few settlements exist in these Western Panama islands, and the clanging noise of distant civilization rarely reaches these secluded locales. Occasionally a fisherman/farmer would arrive in his panga to offer us freshly caught fish or produce. Once in a while an iguana would be for sale along with mangoes, papayas, or a whole bunch of bananas grown in his small family garden.

Cruising Options

~ Marina Time ~

After weathering a long passage or bobbing at anchor for a while, nothing is more gratifying than docking at a marina. Nestled calmly in a slip, we hook up a hose to wash off the accumulated salt crystals that have encrusted everything. Then we indulge ourselves in a luxuriously long, hot, shower under strong water pressure. We provision, top off the fuel tanks, fill up with water, wash our laundry, and do boat maintenance. Nearby towns are usually equipped with parts stores and services and friendly neighbors are glad to help us find what we need. The radio nets crackle every morning with information, announcements, services, and trading possibilities. Before we've even caught up on our sleep, friends are knocking on our hull, and the social calendar fills to overflowing with various activities. With our boat safely docked, we spend time away from her to explore the town and its cultural treasures. Beach excursions, language classes, potlucks, jam sessions, dances, and games of Mexican train (dominoes) fill our schedule. Seminars are held on topics ranging from the Puddle Jump, or a trip through the Panama Canal, to the mysterious workings of a water maker. Charts and information are exchanged for our next destination, and we often connect with cruisers going our way. Friendships are renewed with nights out tasting the local specialties, or watching a recently released movie. When the persistent fix-it list requires skilled attention, a willing assortment of ex-pat technicians and local repairmen are standing by to help us do everything from fiberglass to engine work, stainless fabrication, and sail repair. These services are almost always at a reasonable rate and we make sure to agree on a price before any work begins. Several marinas have facilities for a haul out to do bottom work and the usual yard projects. For those interested, occasionally a HAM Radio license test is given so sailors can acquire their license and join the friendly fleet of 'HAMsters.'

Cruisers often discover that when we left home we packed too much of some things and wished we had stocked others. There are frequent swap meets at various marinas where the *treasures of the bilge* are exchanged. We look for that special something that we need and try to rid our boat of some dead weight. These maritime garage sales are similar to an old-time community social.

Depending on who the entertainment organizers of the fleet are, various docks have a weekly get together where everyone brings hors d'oeuvres and drinks to share. Stories are exchanged, talented musicians entertain us, and we bask in the friendly camaraderie. A certain number of cruisers become comfortable with marina life and stay for long periods of time. Sailors coming in from a long trip may spend time in a marina, splurging for a few days or weeks, and then return to their frugal ways at anchor. Anchorages are available if funds are low, and one can still take advantage of the town's resources.

An intricate part of the cruising experience is the opportunity to explore the surrounding areas around a marina while meeting the local people. During our first years on the water, La Paz provided many wonderful opportunities to explore a Mexican town. Many days were spent walking the streets of this small city whose ancient historical roots extended back to the native peoples who were pearl divers before the Spanish priests, and later traders and merchants set up shop. We hopped aboard a bus for a scenic ride to the west coast of Baja and the artist's community of Todos Santos. An active community of local artists and expatriates make their living creating beautiful arts and crafts. This out of the way spot lies awash by the Pacific swell for those inclined to surf.

The riot of Cabo San Lucas' party atmosphere with the airport close by was only a little further down a two-lane highway. It was a quick jaunt through the forests of saguaro cacti where the highway is bordered with yellow signs warning of cattle in the road. Several times we had to stop to let a herd of cows amble nonchalantly across the busy road. On a journey following the eastern coast of the Baja from La Paz to Cabo San Lucas, we traveled over the mountains to Barrilles, stopping at El Triumpho, where the French mined silver in the late 1800's. A towering brick smoke stack at least ten stories high dominates the rural skyline where it was used in the ore smelting process. While investigating the deserted ruins we met an old man collecting sticks of firewood in a woven basket. He told us the story of how the plata (silver) used to come out of the mine long ago. The quaint little town harkens back to older times during a flourishing silver rush.

During the winter of 2001, we traveled as far as Mazatlan, Mexico and had a chance to become acquainted with this quaint old town that transported us back to a classic, Spanish colonial era. Mazatlan's buildings were built by explorers, merchants, and priests who settled this thriving port. Spanish ships provisioned and loaded here and among the many items they traded were gold and silver. Houses were built high on the hills with tall stonewalls and stairs leading up from the low-lying streets to protect them from the high waves, or *olas altas*. Stormy seas from occasional summer hurricanes give the Olas Altas section of the town its name. A towering cathedral anchors the downtown area near a sprawling Mercado or marketplace where we provision from the wide assortment of locally grown vegetables and fruits and tasty smoked marlin and tuna. The meat section is brutally honest with every part displayed (not for the faint at heart!). We watched deliverymen hauling in entire halves of beef on their shoulders. Provincial style government buildings encircle a large plaza nearby with the traditional gazebo in its center. Local men gather to play dominoes or chess and young folk flirt under the watchful eyes of their elders.

On our early morning entrance into the marina, we had negotiated our way through Mazatlan's huge fishing fleet. Shrimp, mackerel, marlin, and tuna are brought in daily to the restaurants that are famous for their fresh fish entrees. The galley slave deserves a holiday and we treat ourselves to the local cuisine, which is not only delicious, but also reasonably priced. It's never hard to find a group of cruisers to accompany us for a night on the town.

Since we arrive on our boats with maybe a bicycle for land travel, the local transportation system is one of the first adventures that we encounter. A common sight all over Latin America are the inexpensive, brightly painted buses that seem to always be chugging by to whisk us on our way. In Mazatlan, taxis and VW bugs that have been converted into open-air tour-cars are conveniently everywhere if we need to lug groceries back to the marina. Taking a nice break away from the boat, Robert and I spend hours wandering through the narrow, cobblestone

Live chickens for sale at the farmer's market in Sololá, Guatemala.

streets of the old part of town. Hidden treasures are discovered like an art gallery featuring local artists, a small museum displaying the early history of the region, and a vegetarian restaurant.

The newer section of Mazatlan down the road from the marina was built up around the tourist trade. Travelers from the cold climates of Canada, Europe and the United States, flock to the white, sandy beaches of Mazatlan during the winter months. In this *Gold Zone* we did a shopping run to a huge, modern, grocery store for the items we couldn't find in the Mercado.

While staying in the marina, we attended several sporting events, including an evening baseball game at Mazatlan's comfortable stadium. The modernized venue included everything from a wide screen TV and boisterous fans to cotton candy and peanut vendors. Lucky for us we were in town when the world class Mazatlan Marathon passed by the marina. Standing out along the route we cheered the Olympic level Kenyan runners who outdistanced everyone. Persons with visual impairments were also well represented, each with a white scarf held by a sighted runner. Fathers pushed children in strollers, paraplegic athletes in wheelchairs impressed the crowds with their speed, and people of all skill levels attended.

There are numerous opportunities to engage with the local population, and the cruising community has a social calendar that can be daunting. Before we knew it, we had so many places to go and things to do that we had to make some choices between concerts, horseshoe tournaments, sailing races, weekly potlucks, a Mardi Gras parade, a bullfight, trips to the beach, and inland tours. This is in addition to all the things that require attention on our boat, provisioning for the next leg of our journey, or collecting charts and guides for distant destinations.

It is no wonder that a certain number of cruisers find that a town around a marina fits their idea of a home community. Many ex-pats and cruisers have settled in towns like Mazatlan, La Paz, San Carlos, or Puerto Vallarta and a newcomer can fit easily into their midst.

Cruising Options

~ On the Hook ~

By late November northern winds start blowing in the Sea of Cortez and the water temperature drops. Most of the cruising fleet starts to gravitate south to enjoy the tropical conditions along Mexico's mainland coast south of the Baja. Because the Baja Peninsula is no longer protruding out to block the Pacific swell, this section of the coastline has fewer calm anchorages. These protected spots become popular places where cruisers can tuck in around a corner out of the lump. At the peak of the season, the equivalent of a small village materializes in these peaceful locations where boaters plan on staying for a week or more. We drop our hook and meld into the cruising community. A local VHF radio net spontaneously develops to let everyone tune in to the daily news and social calendar.

Several of these winter anchorages along this Mexican Riviera are Tenacatita/Barra de Navidad, Zihuantanejo, La Cruz in Banderas Bay and the bays north of Manzanillo. A more distant, southerly destination that draws a few cruisers each season is the lovely nine bays of Hualtulco. Beautiful Tenacatita Bay is a favorite spot that offers a tropical climate during the winter months with provisioning nearby. The small town of Barra de Navidad, which is only fifteen miles away, has a protected lagoon for dropping the hook. A local resort named the Grand Bay also boasts a large marina with slips available. An ideal combination of tropical weather, secluded anchorages, town amenities, and a marina makes this area one of the best cruising grounds once you leave the Sea of Cortez. For many years we have spent from one to three months on the Mexican Riviera during the winter season.

When we first arrived, Don from *Windward Luv* was the Mayor of Tenacatita having succeeded the mayor, another Don, aboard the boat, *Black Swan*. With Don's first lady, Lena, they were the honorable first family for seven years presiding over this spontaneous village on the water. They would announce to the fleet when the vegetable truck would arrive up the mangrove jungle run and led the traditional Friday Night Mayor's Raft-Up. For this event all the cruisers in the anchorage were invited to tie up their dinghies to his anchored, pink flamingo-bedecked inflatable. Everyone brought hors d'oeuvres to pass around, and then the mayor would direct the group to introduce themselves and tell a bit about their adventures. Mariners are a collection of fascinating characters from all over the globe and from many walks of life. Rarely is a sailor without a dry wit, a raucous sense of humor, or a hidden talent. Circumnavigators brought amazing tales of their passages sailing the South Pacific and through the Indian Ocean. They told lively stories of foiling the pirates by traveling in groups around the Horn of Africa and then sailing north through the Red Sea into the Mediterranean. There were also intriguing tales of traversing the Panama Canal, sailing up wind along the Venezuelan coast to the Caribbean, and one tough, salty couple had made the raucous trip around Cape Horn at the tip of South America.

A community spirit develops in these popular anchorages, that reminds us of the *good old days* on *The Farm*. Cruisers make up a generous, cooperative group, sharing and helping one another. At the same time, part of what makes life on a boat unique is how separate we really are. There is always plenty of room to be alone. When anyone needs help, mechanics lend their expertise with engine repairs. Rigging skills have come in handy, and dragging boats have been rescued. Doctors and nurses give consultations, sew up cuts, or graciously answer questions with no insurance forms or HMO's to deal with. When an emergency strikes, the entire community is on alert and everyone does what they can to help the situation. Sometimes it is no more than listening every day for a progress report and sending out good wishes. Still, the feel of the community is so strong and all-embracing that it makes any tough situation better.

This cooperative effort was never so apparent then when everyone came out in force to help rescue a sailboat that had washed ashore on Tenacatita Beach. It was a nasty sight watching a beautiful sailboat being tossed around in the rough surf. Cool heads mobilized the anchorage, and a former fire chief coordinated the rescue effort to minimize confusion. Powerboats volunteered to help pull a long towline and dinghies hauled kedge anchors out passed the surf line to keep the boat from being swept further on shore. One of our fellow cruisers was a hero when he went inside the boat while it was heaving side to side with each breaking wave. He closed the portholes and hatches and prevented more water from entering the yacht. His wife stood on shore and yelled, 'Here it comes,' allowing him time to brace himself before each wave crashed. A 45' twin-engine cabin cruiser tugged against a 300-foot long, one-inch line, and was finally able to point the distressed vessel into the waves, slowly inching her away from shore. A coordinator on board the motor yacht with a hand-held VHF radio called out when to power up after each wave broke, maximizing the tugging effort. The errant sailboat was finally pulled out to deeper water where she was safely anchored. A bent rudder and a salty interior that had knocked out some of the electronics was the extent of the damage. The quick, voluntary action of everyone in the anchorage had prevented the boat from becoming a total loss. In grateful celebration, the skipper and his matey ordered up a catered feast for everyone in the anchorage. Shortly thereafter, the owners, accompanied by two buddy boats, successfully made the one hundred mile passage back to Puerto Vallarta to a safe haven on the dry dock. A potentially devastating event came to a happy end, and today they are out cruising again.

Cruising Options

~ On the Hook – Dinghy Landing 101 ~

In the Sea of Cortez, gentle waves lap softly against the beaches making dinghy landings about as easy as a dinghy landing can be. When we approach the shallows, we lower the wheels, jump out, and pull the dink up on shore. Taking note of the tides, we drag our car above the water line and set a small anchor for good measure. Robert and I are careful to watch out for the stingrays that hide under the sand near shore. To avoid the dangerous and painful stings, we wear a pair of Crocs, sandals, or booties and shuffle our feet in the shallows. In some northern Baja anchorages where the skates are plentiful, Robert likes to collect rocks on shore and has them in the dinghy to throw out in front of us to scare them away.

On the mainland coast, in contrast to the Sea of Cortez, the Pacific swell builds up on the beaches and the surf landings become more of a challenge. In a corner of a protected bay, a slew of moored pangas often mark the safest spot to land. The art of successful dinghy landings takes time to master and we had our share of soaking, sand-filled escapades. It was exhilarating to get it right. The dinghy rode atop a wave, balancing gracefully, and then set us down gently onto the beach. When leaving the shore, we catch a lull between steep waves with a speedy departure, slicing buoyantly through the crests of the breakers. If things go well, we exchange celebratory fists with the spectators watching the antics from shore.

Tenacatita is one of the spots in Mexico that provides varied surf conditions allowing us to hone our skills. On one big surf day, Robert miscalculated his exit through the sets. The next thing he knew, a huge wall of water loomed menacingly in front of him. He powered up and raced towards the face of the wave. All of us on shore held our collective breath, waiting to see if he would make it or be thrown over backwards! At one with his flying machine, he soared off the top of the wave crest taking air, with the tip of the prop slicing a white trail. He landed safely on the other side to the amazement and cheers of everyone on the sidelines.

Another memorable moment occurred when we visited La Manzanilla, a small village a few miles across the bay from Tenacatita, where fresh produce, Internet access, and a pay phone can usually be found. Dressed for town, we boarded the dinghy to go ashore. Because this beach is more open to the swell, the waves are steep and close together, making the surf landings sketchier than on the more protected Tenacatita beach, but we made it into the shallows with no mishaps. When I jumped out, a short following wave hit the aft end of the boat and knocked me down, with the dinghy landing on top of me! I came up laughing, unhurt, but dripping wet. In the future I wore my bathing suit on all dinghy landings to La Manzanilla, and brought dry clothes in a plastic bag!

Having the right equipment can give you a better chance for

A line of dinghies with hinged wheels on the beach at Tenacatita, Mexico.

a safe landing. An outboard engine capable of pushing the dinghy onto a plane will give you enough power to keep up with the speed of a wave. Our medium sized inflatable dinghy has an 8 horsepower outboard motor, which is enough to do the trick. When we approach the shore, we lower down our hinged wheels that turn the inflatable into an amphibious craft, making climbing out of the surf and hauling the dink up onto the beach a relatively easy exercise. When leaving the beach, once we're out of the surf, we have to remember to pick up our wheels. If we don't, we wonder why we are riding so sluggishly and can't get up on a plane.

Surfers are usually quick to learn the moves of a safe dinghy landing in big waves, having spent all those hours gauging the heights and rhythms of the sets. When we are riding a wave in, we wait patiently outside the breakers for the right swell. On a typical trip into shore we will see three or more larger waves in a set, and then a quieter period. Once we make our choice, we power up and stay right behind the crest of the wave. We try to travel at the same speed as the wave, allowing plenty of water beneath us when our wheels touch the sand. Next we hop out, catch the dinghy and pull it up away from the water's edge. If our timing is off and we fall behind the crest, the following wave catches up to us and breaks over the aft end swamping the dinghy. If we don't have enough power to stay on the wave's turbulent edge, we can be thrown sideways, where bad things can happen in the surf. Our old hard dinghy with a 2 horsepower engine once became a submarine. It nosedived under the water, was turned broadside to the waves, and ended up half-filled with sand and seawater. If we find ourselves ahead of the wave, there is not enough water under the dinghy and we can be slammed down hard onto the sand, with a wave breaking over us!

One day Robert invited a new friend to experience a dinghy landing to 'see how it's done.' Unfortunately Scott was a bit heavier than I am and he sat a little further forward than I usually do. With this altered weight distribution and a poor choice of timing, the dinghy careened sideways, banging hard on the beach, and they each received several bruises and scrapes. If our new friend had sat further back it's possible they might not have veered off the wave. The science of balance and gravity are also an important aspect of a safe dinghy landing. Having a cocky, blasé, or fearful attitude can also produce uncomfortable outcomes.

Flowing with the waves when we go into shore is the easy part compared to heading back out into the breakers. In the warm water and balmy air, we strip down to our bathing suits and brace ourselves for the possibility of a wet ride. It's not uncommon for a wave to splash over us before we are out of the surf line. Pointing the dinghy into the swell, we hold on to it with our feet planted firmly in the sand in hip deep water. The engine idles, the prop is lowered into the water and everything is ready when the lull comes. Both of us quickly jump aboard, put the engine in gear and speed full throttle over the incoming waves into open water and safety. There are certain notoriously rough surf beaches where the wait is longer before a lull arrives. It is not unlike deciding when to hop into a twirling jump rope. Wait.... wait.... wait....., now jump!

One of our fellow cruisers with his brand new dinghy and outboard demonstrated a spectacular wipe out in unusually tumultuous surf at Tenacatita. All hands were soon helping him. Several of us pulled the dink to shore while other folks scanned the shallows for his lost prescription glasses. While the glasses were miraculously recovered, (one year the tally was eight lost pairs) the mechanics were already speeding back to their boats for tools. They checked the vital fluids of his outboard motor and removed the salt water and sand. In no time they had it purring again.

Avoiding a dinghy outboard wipeout, cruisers who have kayaks often paddle into shore, practicing their white water surfing skills or row their dinghies in like an oversized boogie board.

Our dinghy transports us into shore for provisioning, to the beach for fun and games, and scoots us to our neighbors' boats for a visit. It carries us to optimal snorkeling spots, and can be used as a backup if the big boat's engine should die and we need a push. Kids are allowed to drive the dinghies long before they are of legal age to drive a car and occasionally, the guys have races to test the performance of their rigs. The highlight for every dinghy is the Friday Night Raft-ups in Tenacatita where a community of inflatables (sometimes as many as forty) tie up and spend an evening together.

Each night we raise our raft onto davits to keep any slimy growth from making its home on the bottom, and to prevent the chance of it being stolen. If we leave our dinghy in the water, the small waves slap against her all night long, and in the middle of the night she bangs against the hull when the wind or tide changes.

The Mayor of Tenacatita

When cruising season rolled around again and we were on our way to southern climes, we stopped off at the Mazatlan Marina. Don, the mayor of Tenacatita, approached Robert and said he was not returning to the anchorage that season and would we please take the *McHale's Navy* video with us to pass around to the cruisers. Hardly a thumbs-up movie, its sole attraction is that parts of it were filmed in Tenacatita. If you have not seen enough of this beautiful area au natural, you can watch it on this B-rated video. Stowing the cassette carefully in a dry spot, we carried it with us to Tenacatita. When we arrived, there were a dozen boats, but no local net and no mayor.

With Friday rapidly approaching we needed a mayor to run the traditional Raft-up. While we were dinghying around the anchorage, we met Valerie who had served on a city council in Canada. She would have volunteered for the Mayor of Tenacatita position, but she planned on leaving the next morning. Catherine, on *Solstice*, had actually been mayor in her California hometown, but gracefully bowed out saying she was taking a break from such duties. When Friday came around with no emcee in sight, Robert volunteered to be the acting mayor. When no one else came forward to shoulder this responsibility, he eventually dropped the acting to become the official mayor. We went to the usual spot and threw out our 10 lb. dinghy anchor and before long we were surrounded by approaching dinghies that were tied off to first our dinghy and then to each other creating a large circle. After everyone had arrived it was time to begin the first order of business, passing the hors d'oeuvres. The raft ups became a showplace for the gourmands in the fleet to entice our taste buds with their best recipes. After the culinary specialties made their rounds, and our plates were full, it was time for the evening entertainment. Everyone introduced

Robert and Virginia with their grandchildren, Toby and Coral, on a mangrove jungle run in Tenacatita, Mexico.

themselves, told who they are, where they were from and where they are going. Wanting to know more about our fellow cruisers, a theme for the evening was presented, such as how did your boat get her name, what was your wildest cruising experience, or your 'how did you meet your matey' story to celebrate Valentine's Day. Talent night was a riot of music and all sorts of imaginative fun. People lingered until darkness fell over the anchorage before drifting back to their boats. An itinerant British couple who had traveled over 60,000 miles in their wooden sloop said, 'They enjoyed themselves immensely, never having attended a dinghy raft-up in all of their travels.

`A politician never had it so good; no elections to win, no polls, no taxes, no cost overruns, and rarely a problem to solve. Coordinating the Christmas potluck at the palapa with the owners supplying delicious shrimp and rice dishes was the mayor's biggest task. With valuable assistance of other long-time cruisers, there was plenty of information for newcomers who wanted to know where to provision, how to check in with the local port captain, and the waypoints to safely navigate the sandbars into the nearby Barra lagoon. The mayor might make an announcement about where to observe the crocodiles or how to avoid a nasty sting by the skates that hide under the sand in the shallows. Every season a new arrival would tell about scurrying into the engine room in the middle of the night searching for what sounded like an electric motor running in the bilge. The mayor would give a head's up on the morning net that the noise, as strange as it may seem, is coming from the Jack Crevalles, a large fish from the grunt family performing late night chants under our boats.

When we left for Central American, we passed the office on to other cruisers, who continured to carry on the tradition. Now that we are back, it looks like we are up for a second term and we will save you a space if you are ever passing through.

Cruising Options

~ On the Hook – Lifelong Connections ~

One of the luxuries of the cruising life is having time to relax and share drinks and meals with fellow sailors. We compare notes, exchange stories, and have a common understanding about our shared lifestyle. Each person that we encounter has a stash of interesting stores to tell about their incredible lives, unfamiliar places that they have traveled, or interesting work that they used to do during their other life on land.

Besides the usual carpenters, firemen, doctors, and engineers by the dozens, we've had the pleasure to meet rocket scientists, gold miners, bush pilots, Alaskan fishermen, actors, marine biologists, traveling nurses, boat builders, and other interesting characters. A South African couple had been squid fishermen for ten years traveling the dangerous currents and boisterous seas off the African coast. A music teacher and her vocalist husband taught and performed on the U.S. and European summer concert circuits. Phil was one of the most courageous daredevils we ever met, smoke jumping into wild fires that were devouring Western forests. Everyone brings their interesting slant on life along with tales of the itinerant traveler.

Wherever women gather, they love to engage in heart to heart 'girl talk.' One afternoon while hanging out with some friends in the fleet at Tenacatita, someone mentioned that it would be fun to have a women's get-together. A meeting was planned to take place on one of the more spacious powerboats in the anchorage and sixteen women convened with plates of delectable snacks. After the introductions, we sat around and talked about what it was like to be cruising women. The conversation even included some anchoring stories and how to do perplexing knots. We had to laugh when a worried husband called on the VHF radio to find out when we were coming home. A few men imagined that we were having a bitch session all about them, but it could not have been further from the truth. The party extended well into the night with all of us weaving our tales and bonding, so that by the time we went back to our boats, we all felt a jubilant connection.

Not to be outdone, the men called their own gathering on the net the following morning. They also partied late into the evening talking about engines, sail configurations, fishing, and entertaining each other with their tales of storms at sea.

A week later, another woman's gathering was announced, and this time we met aboard a sleek Santa Cruz 52. Twenty-two women filled up the large cockpit and the cabin below. The party turned out to be more than just a good time. Candice, who had been a nurse in her other life, noticed an open sore on Jenny's leg and treated the infection with supplies from her first aid kit. She continued to visit Jenny's boat several times a day until she was out of danger. Jenny had been afraid to make a big deal of her health problem for fear that she would interrupt their cruising plans. We left that meeting feeling that we had made a difference in her life, and realized the importance of a strong, closely-knit community of women. From that time on it was easy for us to communicate about what was important and make the anchorage feel like home.

Every afternoon several of us would swim the third of a mile from the anchorage to shore, talking and exercising. Those who didn't swim met us on shore for a half-mile walk down the beach and more conversation. Mexican train games, bocce ball, volleyball, card games, yoga classes, and hanging out at the palapa continued throughout the afternoon until the sand fleas made their appearance around 4 P.M. Women, both shy and gregarious, became close friends, while we learned more about each other's worlds. I found this camaraderie essential to my happiness during my cruising experience; a chance to talk with those who were going through the same experiences, changes, and emotions. When an anchorage gels into a warm, unified, healthy community of cruisers, everyone feels contented and energized.

The brotherhood also flourishes everywhere that boats gather. In Tenacatita they play bocce and volleyball in the afternoons and hang out at the palapa over drinks. Groups of musicians convene for an evening jam session and there's the occasional card game aboard someone's boat. Sailors circulate around the anchorage helping with things that need fixing and spending time shooting the breeze.

In Mexico everyone participates in the friendly greeting of 'Buenos Dias' when we enter a shop or when eyes meet walking down a street. It's so different from many places north of the border, where we hardly acknowledge anyone's presence, lost deep within our own world. Wherever we travel people want to engage with us, ask us where we're from, incredulous when we tell them we came from California on a sailboat. "Don't we have any fear?" they ask. They want to know how we are enjoying their country, and we always have a good word for them. Before long, we are sharing our feelings about everything from politics, and the sad state of the tourist economy, to their all-important families. We were often asked what we thought of our Presidents, Bush or Obama. Finding out that we were from California, they would laugh and say; "Oh, Arrr nold!"

On our numerous trips to the hardware store in Barra de Navidad, I became friends with the sweet daughter of the storekeeper. Liliana showed me her second grade workbook and gave me Spanish lessons while I taught her to say the same words in English.

Maria owned a small tienda (a store in the front room of her home) and helped provision the fleet with groceries, drinking water, and fresh produce. Her surprisingly well-stocked store carried all the basics, and she made a weekly run over the mountains to the Costco in Guadalajara for commonly asked for goodies and special requests. She brought back fresh lettuce, cheeses, peanut butter, nuts and occasionally, cranberry juice and fresh flowers. We not only purchased supplies from her, but over the years we became good friends. Every year we visit Maria and her family and practice our Spanish. Comparing notes with her about business and our children, we fill each other in on our lives. One Christmas season, she ushered us into a back room to show us the beautiful star shaped, papier-mâché piñatas that she and her daughters were making for the holiday season.

It's like a family reunion when we return to town and renew our friendships with Raul, the rotisserie chicken man, Edgar the hotel manager where we dock our dinghies, and another Maria, who runs our favorite laundry service.

In Ecuador, we hired Jorge to help with some boat projects and we soon met his sons. He was Mr. Mom to his four children allowing his wife to work at a coveted, higher paying, full-time office job. Because he was a hard worker, he was in high demand to do bright work and various boat chores. He was always on the dock waiting for us to dinghy him to our moored boat promptly at eight in the morning. Each day he worked for three hours before he had to go home to fix lunch for his children and pick them up from school. Among other jobs, Jorge helped us rebed all of our chain plates. We didn't mind paying him more than the going wage of $1.00 an hour, and gave him a few spare tools that we had on board. On a Saturday when school was out, he brought his eldest son who was also hard working. During their breaks and over lunch he would open up to us and tell us interesting tales about his family and how life was for him in Ecuador.

With the constant traveling of our peripatetic lifestyle, it is not always easy to say 'good-bye.' With our separate itineraries and time lines, some of us are off to distant lands. We might buddy boat for a while until plans diverge and then we say 'see you later' at the crossroads. The Internet has helped us stay in touch and following a cruiser tradition, we make sure to exchange boat cards, which include all of our pertinent information. In a world where we only know people by their first names and their boat name, it enables us to stay connected. The upside of saying good-bye is saying hello. In this small, intimate, but far-flung village on the water, there is an old or new friend sailing around the next point.

During the off-season, returning to our land based home, we visit with our cruising buddies, renewing the friendship where it left off. Our animated conversations with our fellow sailors feels like a breath of fresh sea air filling up our land locked lungs.

Cruising Options

~ On the Hook – The Relativity of Time ~

Early one morning at a perfect anchorage, I was struck with the startling realization that the cruising lifestyle has its own law of relativity relating to time. What kind of time are we on? I know it's something different when I've forgotten what day it is and we can't keep up with changing time zones when we arrive an hour late to a potluck after crossing the Sea of Cortez. In the art world we paint two-dimensional works on a canvas of a certain width and length. The tricks of perspective and shadows give the flat painting an illusion of three dimensions. 3-D glasses and now High Definition TV make a flat screen come to life giving shape and roundness to everything. A sculpture in three dimensions can inspire while we walk around an exquisite Venus, David, or The Kiss and see the form of the human body from all sides. Our everyday visual lives are lived in the three dimensions of width, length, and depth. Time, is often referred to as the fourth dimension and behaves differently depending on our orientation to the physical world. Einstein spent long hours capturing this concept and putting it down on paper with mathematical precision.

In our modern world the clock and calendar are measures of a certain kind of time that can unwittingly enslave us to their itineraries. Our ascent up the ladder of success depends on us keeping our lives organized and on time. We scurry here and there fitting in our three meals a day and hopefully enough hours of sleep to arrive at work at the specified hour, keep our appointments and take our breaks. Then we leave work to join the stampede at rush hour. Taking care of my family along with running my own business included making sure the children were on schedule, for school, appointments, homework, and activities. Many of us arrive home a bit frazzled from the daylong grind. The weekend is a slight variation, squeezing in an hour or two to do house projects, chores, and a few moments of entertainment penciled in before the time-fettered week starts all over again. I hope this isn't too cynical a portrait, but isn't this the stark reality of a certain percentage of our society? We tend to live a fast-paced life with a constant need to multi-task that leaves only a miniscule amount of time for quality of life and leisure. Looking at it from a pleasant anchorage, this life seems like a maddening, hectic pace.

When I step aboard *Harmony*, time and my attitude towards it are redefined. The cruising life is truly an alternative existence where we are free from the shackles of hours, days and weeks. On our journey at sea, time, as we know it, seems to be temporarily suspended and we lose our linearly structured bearings that are demanded of us on land. Life's decisions are made when the breeze picks up and we reef the sail, or the wind shuts down and we hitch up the snorting 'iron horse.' We live our lives, not by a strict sense of clock time, but unchained and free like the wind and waves. Salvador Dali's famous painting of the surrealistic, melting clocks [35] captures some of the flavor of our lives at sea. Behind the oozing timepieces the great outdoors serves as his backdrop. Rising with the sun, we breakfast with the birds and fish feeding at dawn. The special lighting exposes the fish and the opportunistic pelicans dive bomb the waters near shore. The gulls squawk to each other and announce the gossip of the day, while the sun peeps over the horizon. The bigger fish chase the smaller schools, creating fish boils, a frantic feeding frenzy. Thermal winds give their first offshore puffs. Our midday meal is taken when the blazing ball is near its zenith and we say goodnight when the red sphere creeps over the edge to the other side of the world, leaving behind sweet darkness. The flocks of egrets return to their island to roost. We start to feel in tune to nature's tempo, synchronized with the phases of the moon, intimately aware of its gravitational effects on the tides. The lighting fluctuates throughout the day dressing the water in a variety of blue, silver, and green hues.

When mariners make the shift to redefine time, we are also changing our western attitude towards success. Western society exerts pressures and expectations to climb the rungs of our career ladders where hopefully we receive better pay, more responsibility, and job satisfaction. With a bigger paycheck comes a bigger house in a pleasant neighborhood with manicured lawns, a new car, and the right schools for the children. A secluded, calm anchorage might seem boring to a Type A personality, who thrives on the frenetic activity of a productive life. Successful cruising, on the other hand, is determined by how much soul-satisfying fun we are having.

When we step out of our accustomed life to cruise the waters of the world, there is a continuing change of our inner settings, a readjustment of priorities, and an attempt at trying to understand what is important and relevant to our lives. When we sail along at 5 knots (on the average), we feel the intrinsic difference from driving at 70 miles an hour on the highway, or 600 miles an hour by jet plane. With this radical change of momentum comes a mellowing of our revved up, fast paced mindset, an opportunity to stop and take in the refreshing beauty all around. Plenty of time is available to hang out with friends so that relationships, even though brief, deepen quickly and lifelong connections stay strong.

Something happens to our body's clock when we set out to sea and the switching over to a separate reality in this mythical time zone is particularly challenging when we first leave the dock. To escape the magnetic pull of our old life, we first have to achieve lift-off velocity. There are so many things grabbing for our one last minute of attention, trying to suck us back into the vortex and keep us from escaping. Once we make our get-away the pace slows and nature's time begins to rule. The solar collectors have us powered up, the wind fills our sails, and it feels like we have arrived in Paradise.

When we sailors are slow to adapt to this shift in the relativity of time we inevitably find ourselves covered with boat bites. A toe snags on a cleat, or while clambering into the cockpit, a knee bumps the winch. When first back on board, I try to ease gracefully into this different flow, hoping to avoid a scraped shin or a head bump. Remembering to reduce my first world momentum, I purposely operate in slow motion, accepting the feel of this different dimension and the movement of the boat underfoot. Hopefully my heightened attention prevents me from making quick, dangerous moves.

In previous generations the clock or chronometer was one of the most important tools on a ship. It was the key to precise navigation in partnership with the sextant. These days our boat clocks remind us when the radio nets begin, when our turn on watch is over, or when the banana bread is done.

When we return Stateside, to the other world, it suddenly feels like we are running to hop on a spinning merry-go-round. While we acclimate, we hold on tight against the centrifugal forces of this alternate reality, a whirling, accelerated time zone. When we first ride in our car after being on board the boat for months, it feels like we are going so fast only to check the speedometer and it reads 35 mph! Then we crank it up to 55 mph, the scenery speeding by our windows, but it's not long before we have reached first world velocity, racing down the highway at 75 mph.

Cruising Options

~ On the Hook – A Shifting Reality ~

Cruising sailors tend to avoid the suffocating chains of convention. On Blue Mondays we become immersed in the blue skies and blue waters that kiss gently at the horizon. Snorkeling in their midst, we watch the iridescent, indigo colored fish darting in and out among the reefs. Hump day, Wednesdays is a good day to watch humpback whales breaching, slapping the surface, blowing their spumes. We pay our respects to the TGIF convention with our Friday night raft ups or dock parties, gatherings full of laughter, food, drink, and camaraderie. On the weekends, instead of parties until dawn, we take a break from the routine and go on a town run to load up with fresh vegetables and fruits, brought to the central market from the surrounding farms and villages. The voluptuous papaya, rich in zinc rejuvenates our vitality. The star fruit, guava, the royal pineapple, mandarin orange, mango, and the guayabana tempt the palette with a tropical blend. A stop in the helado shop for a refreshing ice cream cone is a special treat in the sweltering tropics. Fresh, in-season fruits and vegetables fill the small stores in the towns along our way. However, time travels on, and vine ripened produce does not keep in the heated tropics. We savor them while they last.

Taking the option to not listen to the news streaming in from the world beyond our corner of the anchorage leaves us undistracted. Relevant information comes to us over the nets and the rest of the day can be spent in the present, living here and now.

Unfortunately life can shift rapidly from elation to frustration when a boat malfunctions, or we are frightened by a stormy ride. Trouble sneaks into paradise and there is always something that needs attention on the boat. We can treat it as a glitch that can be fixed with knowledge gained, or does it seem like the end of the world? A bumper sticker said it well, 'Adventure or ordeal, it's all in the attitude.' When we can make the shift into a deep happiness and satisfaction, and become adept with the juggling act of life, then we are on the right track to a successful time on the water or anywhere.

Cruising Options

~ On the Hook – A Quest to Guatemala ~

In 2007 after leaving Mexico, we sailed down the Pacific coast of Central America and stopped in El Salvador. After completing our check-in with immigration, customs, and the port captain, we decided to take an inland trek with a mission, to sample some *ice bean* from the soy dairy in Solola. We had a personal connection to Guatemala that dated back to 1976, when an earthquake rattled the highlands near the small town of Sololá overlooking Lake Atitlan. This earthquake prone area located on the Pacific ring of fire has a major destructive tremor at least once every century. It is the principal reason why early settlers moved the colonial capital of the Kingdom of Guatemala from what is now called Antigua to Guatemala City. Seven volcanoes, one of which is still very active, surround the brilliant blue lake. *Plenty*[36], the relief agency of *The Farm*, together with the Canadian International Development Agency, CIDA [37], helped to rebuild a crumbled village near Solola with a population of approximately ten thousand people.

The Canadians supplied the materials, and *The Farm* sent forty of our best to aid in the reconstruction. The plumbers and engineers were called in when the natural spring that had supplied the village with water was now located a mile or so out of town. New piping was supplied by CIDA and an ingenious gravity fed water system was installed by the *Plenty* crew and local volunteers. At the time, Robert and I were managing the *Miami Plenty Center*, with our roofing and remodeling company which helped raise money to support our Guatemalan project. Young men from *The Farm* came to the center and learned a trade while helping to make enough money to wire $500 a week to Guatemala. Since we were totally vegan at the time, *Plenty* established a soy dairy in Sololá that is still thriving today called Productos de Soya. Thirty years later, and despite a prolonged civil war, a new generation is producing tofu (which they call queso de soya or soy cheese), tempeh, soy ice cream, and soymilk. Several area restaurants that cater to health conscious back packers and tourists, serve dishes of vegetables mixed with tofu and tempeh manufactured at the local soy dairy.

We left *Harmony* on the hook up the estuary at Bahia Del Sol, with our four solar panels keeping the refrigerator running and the batteries topped off while we went out on our quest. Catching the local bus for $1.75 (El Salvador and Ecuador use U.S. currency) to the capital, San Salvador, we rode for an hour through the rural countryside with crops growing, cattle grazing, fallow fields, and small houses dotting the landscape.

El Salvador was ravaged by a civil war that ended in 1994 and the terrible effects of war were palpable. Despite hardships, the El Salvadorian population has a positive attitude about rebuilding their nation and work hard to achieve a successful peacetime economy. We spent one night in San Salvador at a small hotel that cost only $12 and sampled the fare from a local cafe including papusas, a stuffed

Virginia and her daughter, Olivia, at the Soy Dairy store in Sololá.

corn tortilla with cheese, beans, or meat. It was a tasty adventure but unfortunately, as a result, our trek included a second mission to find a cure for Olivia's and my churning tummies. Was it from the ice in the lemonade? An herbal shop near our hotel made up a concoction that did surprisingly well until we could locate a pharmacy with a traditional western medicine cure.

A modern, air-conditioned bus carried us comfortably from San Salvador to Guatemala City easily transporting us across the border. Our regional visa included Guatemala, Nicaragua, and Honduras. For $25 per person, this four-hour bus ride resembled a first class seat on an airplane with a stewardess, snacks and plush, reclining chairs. From there we splurged for a $35 taxi to Antigua, a beautiful colonial town that has kept its historic flavor as a world heritage site. A fun afternoon and evening was spent, camera clicking away, exploring this enchanting town that was established in the 1500's and is filled with art galleries and beautiful architecture. Old cathedrals loomed as a backdrop of Antigua, some crumbling into ruins from the quakes of past centuries. Antigua is also known for its Spanish immersion schools where students spend a week or more living with a local family while exclusively speaking in Spanish.

After being thoroughly enchanted by Antigua, we climbed aboard a crowded van with fourteen fellow tourists who hailed from Japan, Europe, Australia, and the U.S. These shuttles make a daily run to Panajachel on the shores of Lake Atitlan located at 5000-feet above sea level. Long pants, socks, shoes, and warm shirts replaced our tropical weather gear. We situated ourselves in a cute little hotel off the main road, and explored the town where the cobblestone streets were lined with inviting restaurants. Persistent vendors sold their indigenous, brightly colored, woven materials and crafts.

Friday was market day in Sololá, a town located at the top of the hill overlooking the Lake. This quaint Guatemalan town was off the beaten path and tourist hotels and restaurants were scarce. We rode a taxi up the winding road with a driver who spoke perfect English, having spent years in the U.S. He knew exactly where we wanted to go when we asked him to take us to the soy dairy store. It was situated on one of the main streets of town near the busy, open-air market. Vendors' booths were lined up with a variety of goods including inexpensive plastic shoes and watches alongside the usual stalls of woven baskets filled high with nutritious fruits and vegetables brought in fresh from the farms. The array of colors, sweet smells, and the cacophony of the bustling scene transported me back to my shopping adventures as a child in the markets of Korea, including the sounds of a different language. We would have gladly loaded up on this great selection of produce if *Harmony*'s pantry hadn't been so far away. One of the amazing sights was a tribal woman dressed in her colorfully embroidered blouse and speaking in the clicking sounds of the Cakchiquel language of the Mayan people selling what looked like genuine snake oil. She was surrounded by a group of women dressed in their intricately woven tribal clothing and balancing bundles of goods on their heads while they stopped to listen to her spiel. Fascinating scenes unfolded around the plaza, with baskets filled with chickens and trucks piled high with bags of avocados. We wandered into a nearby auditorium where a program was in progress celebrating the local women who were responsible for innovative health, education, and business projects in the community. At one of their displays we purchased a few of their beautiful, woven wall hangings embellished with rainbow colored thread and intricate Mayan designs. Many of the women were well-dressed and sporting cell phones.

After a tour of the marketplace, we made our way to the Productos de Soya store for refreshing strawberry and pineapple ice

Guatemalan children enjoying soy bean cones.

bean cones. Several kids dropped by the dairy while we were there and we treated them to some cones and soon we had a regular party when more locals gathered for a treat following a busy morning of shopping. After a delicious break, we caught a tuk-tuk, (a three-wheeled taxi imported from India) to the soy dairy where the soy products were manufactured. The factory was a clean complex where a plaque from *Plenty* was displayed on the wall. What a satisfying feeling to see that something that we had been a part of so many years ago continued to thrive and produce valuable protein-filled food for the people in the area.

With Olivia along as our translator, we were able to have interesting conversations with people that we met along the way. Her fluency in the language enabled us to hear more about the culture, history, politics, and daily life than our limited Spanish usually allowed. With a feeling of accomplishment and an enjoyable vacation from our vacation, we had an uneventful trip back to *Harmony*, and as always it was great to be home again.

Cruising Options

~ On the Hook – Enchanting Ecuador ~

One might think that being on the Equator would equal hot, tropical, blue-sky weather, but to our surprise, the coastal areas of Ecuador were pleasantly warm but mostly overcast with an occasional few hours of sun during the afternoon. It was the first time since we had installed our four solar collectors that we had to think about running our Genset for power. Ecuadorian evenings were surprisingly cool and we needed to wear a light jacket and long pants. While visiting the Andes on an inland trip, we had to change over to full winter mode. The capital of Ecuador, Quito, is situated at the 10,000 foot level, and we bundled up in all the warm clothes we had packed. I purchased an alpaca sweater, and still we shivered in the cool, damp nights.

Our time in Ecuador was limited by family obligations, but we were able to squeeze in some fantastic trips to Quito and the indigenous craft market at Otavalo in the Andean highlands. We also spent a nice day with Olivia's exchange family in Quito with whom she lived while

A pilot aboard Harmony, *leading three boats over the bar into the Chone River, Bahia de Caraquez, Ecuador.*

studying abroad in high school. They toured us around to the special places in the city with an inside look from people who take pride in their hometown. Ancient Pre-Columbian sites nestled in the old part of town alongside the Incan walls and Spanish cathedrals. After several days in the city we boarded a $2 bus into the mountains for a week's stay in the quaint village of Peguche north of Otavalo, a town famous for its exquisite fabrics. Our suitcases filled up with beautiful and unique art pieces, tablecloths, rugs, alpaca scarves, and hats to take home to the family. A few of the villages in this area date back 13,000 years and we were invited to walk through an archeological site where an ancient ceremonial area was being excavated.

With a tip from a fellow traveler who happened to have lived in our hometown in California, we located a rustic hotel that included a delicious restaurant on the premises. Nearby there was a pleasant hike through fields and eucalyptus groves to a waterfall. The following day, we made a daylong trek to a Condor Ranch, high on a mountaintop, where raptors were exercised each afternoon and endangered species of birds were bred and protected. On the walk back we located a huge, carved megalithic stone in the middle of a field that looked as if it could have been used for ancient ceremonies. If only we could have stayed another week we would have sat in on an extraordinary gathering of shamans and holy men and women from many traditions of both North and South America who were attending a conference at our hotel. We comfortably meshed into the traditional life of the town, and attended a cultural and musical event in the central plaza. It was so safe there, young girls and women walked through the streets in the day or night without fear. It reminded us of our years on *The Farm* when the local villagers welcomed us, making us feel like a part of their large, extended family. In Peguche, believe it or not, there was a tie-dye operation where the owners gave us a tour. We marveled at the

Robert and Virginia overlooking Lake Atitlan in Guatemala. The lake is surrounded by seven volcanoes, with one currently active.

ancient, simplistic methods that managed to produce beautiful results. Vats of different colored dyes were cooking over fires. Young boys, squatting on their haunches, tied up the fabric, dunking the pieces in the vats and lifting them out with long wooden spatulas. Peguche is a weaving town, and everywhere that we walked we could hear the clatter of the modernized machinery. These mechanized operations combined strong and colorful threads into intricate patterns that harkened back to an ancient tradition. Days were spent exploring the surrounding villages, each known for their unique craft of leather, woodwork, furniture, or weaving. Taking a walk through a neighboring village, we passed by several homes of shamans with their hand-painted signs advertising their businesses. On a steep hillside a farmer struggled to coax his oxen to pull a plow. A family invited us into their small, cement block home where they operated an old style handloom in one corner of the main room. They made their living from weaving rugs of coarse wool in colorful geometric designs, reminiscent of Native American rugs from the Southwest United States. After purchasing a beautiful red, orange and black throw rug, we bid good-bye to the gracious family and their four children. Visiting these remote corners of Ecuador was like going back in time to a more peaceful and simple existence, in tune with the seasons and rhythms of the earth.

Most cruisers while in Ecuador visit the Galapagos Islands, travel the Incan trail to Machu Pichu, or take a boat trip to the reed islands in the middle of Lake Titicaca in Peru. Experiencing the majestic landscapes and varied terrain of this part of the world filled us with appreciation for its epic grandeur and beauty. But our family was calling, so cutting our journey short, we flew back to the U.S.

Cruising Options

~ On the Hook – Life's Juggling Act ~

With the children grown, finances somewhat in order, and parents still healthy, this large, post-World War II generation is ready to redirect into a new phase. Having dreamed about cruising for a long time, most of us didn't actually throw off the dock lines until later in life. Focused on education, family, and a career there hasn't been time for anything but an occasional vacation. Men have mid-life crises and woman have menopause. Our culture treats both of these events with foreboding, but it can be a signal for action, a time to switch into a different gear. Instead of a crisis, these events can signal a new beginning, a natural stage in life, a creative phase with a different focus. The time has come for new challenges that fulfill our inner most dreams, develop introspection, and pursue a spiritual awareness. In India, occasionally an older gentleman will leave his home for a while and pursue a spiritual life of simplicity and denial, searching for that soul satisfaction. For those of us in our culture who are trying to age gracefully, and accept the passing of the years as a boon rather than a curse, we look forward to travel, creative endeavors, philanthropy, hobbies and our family. Our 'Bucket List,' the things we want to do before we kick the bucket, is jotted down and we start checking them off.

Since there are many good years yet to live, our generation does not envision ourselves sitting in front of the TV, wasting away physically, and forgetting that we have years yet to enjoy a fulfilling life. While a few will talk of their impending death for the next thirty years, most of us have the attitude that we will accept this stage of life as a chance to dance into the shadows in style. There is too much to do each day, with no time to think morbid thoughts. The person in mid-life has the perspective of seeing forward and backward, knowing how important it is to make the most of each day. Many of us in the boomer generation are in the unique position of having elderly parents, some with failing health, children who are completing school and moving on into their adult lives, and now the grandchildren who are so special. They all need us from time to time, and to keep these relationships strong and healthy, while still escaping to the sea with our own dreams is the juggling act. For us the juggling balls consisted of time with our children, time with our parents, time making sure our rentals were doing well, and time on *Harmony*. To keep the balls all up in the air at the same time without dropping them was our challenge.

In mid-life, hormones are ebbing and flowing, signaling for a change, demanding that we pay attention. Our physical bodies want us to moderate, reach a comfortable balance, while we remain active, sharp-witted, agile, and flexible.

When our youngest left home to attend college, we jumped at the chance to sail the high seas. Ten years later, grandchildren are being born, and the trick is to balance cruising with spending quality and quantity time with our family.

Every October, having wrapped up our lives at home, we drive the three-day trip south to Mexico. Setting out before dawn to get an early start from home, we sail through Los Angeles at midday, avoiding the traffic snarls. On the edge of the extensive desert of Southern California and Arizona, we pull over to take a dip in the steamy, mineral pools of Desert Hot Springs. In the morning we travel on with our skin feeling refreshed, energized for the big push to Nogales on the U.S. side, to visit our cruising friends in their beautifully refurbished home. The next day we cross the border, pick up our visas, and continue another 250 miles to San Carlos, which is half of the way down the Sea of Cortez on the mainland side. In the work yard, we ready *Harmony* for another cruising season.

When in 2006 we decided to leave Mexico and check out Central America on our way to Ecuador, new plans needed to be formulated. We were going to be away from home for a longer period of time, but still wanted to be with the family for the Thanksgiving holiday and we could not miss our son's wedding in Hawaii at the end of the year. For six weeks we sailed that wonderful, downwind, island hopping, secluded anchorage cruise from San Carlos to La Paz, and left *Harmony* safely tucked away in Marina de la Paz. Our plan was to make our way back to San Carlos, pick up our car from the storage yard, and drive home since we would be ending up in South America and not returning to San Carlos. Then to add to the adventure, we would rent a car to San Francisco airport where we would catch a flight to Hawaii.

Arriving in La Paz, we assumed there would be no problems purchasing a ticket for the La Paz to Los Mochis ferry that would take us across the Sea to the mainland, and from there, a bus would return us to our van in San Carlos. Unfortunately we had forgotten that the

Christmas season is one of the most traveled months in Mexico. We always schedule plane flights months in advance to assure a spot on board, but didn't think about it when it came to ferries or buses. When we went to the ferry office, all the tickets for our dates were sold out! There was the option of taking a 22-hour bus ride north to Tijuana and catching another long bus ride to San Carlos. That didn't sound like much fun. Then one of our cruising friends came up with a workable solution. The plan was to take a nine-hour bus ride to Santa Rosalia on the Baja side, and take an inexpensive puddle jumper plane across the Sea of Cortez to Guaymas, where the local bus would drop us off in neighboring San Carlos. In La Paz, we had to deposit cash in the bank account of the airlines in Santa Rosalia to assure our seats on the plane. When we arrived in Santa Rosalia that evening, we found the little office and, sure enough, they had our names, and we were issued a ticket. After a good night's sleep in a little hotel, we gathered in the parking lot to load up the airport van with passengers and stacks of luggage were strapped on the roof. The van drove us to a runway 25 kilometers outside of town that stretched out amidst the cacti on the open desert. Military personal checked our baggage on a table set up in the open air. The waiting room was a shredded, windblown, blue tarp over a few wooden benches. The small, ten-seater plane arrived an hour late and arguments and hemming and hawing commenced, apparently concerning the number of passengers and the weight of the luggage. There were eleven people for the 10-seater plane. What to do? Soon we were all told to load up and they squeezed one of the children into a corner. The airplane rattled and shook, struggling to lift off, but finally, at the far edge of the runway, we were airborne. The view of the Sea falling away beneath us, sparkling in the sunshine, was spectacular. We flew over the Santa Rosalia to Guaymas ferry, which left early in the morning, another alternative for crossing the Sea. A huge cloudbank appeared in front of us and the pilot tried unsuccessfully to fly over it. We bounced around through the thunderhead until finally the captain nose-dived through the gray curtain, and we were beneath the clouds, flying close over two steep mountains on the approach to the landing strip in Guaymas. We had made it! And all this excitement including bus, van and plane came to the reasonable price of approximately $100 per person.

When we exited the bus in San Carlos, there to meet us was Will and Maggie who were serendipitously finishing up some business at an office adjacent to the bus stop. Our mouths dropped open in astonishment since we had recently e-mailed each other that we wanted to visit on our way home, but who was to know our time line on this open-ended journey. Part of the thrill of the adventure is savoring the coincidences that spice our travels. After lunch they graciously drove us to our van in the storage yard and, we were on our way north.

* * *

The juggling routine is always in flux and if we are lucky, our kids and now grandkids come to play aboard *Harmony* as planned. The second stateroom fills up with laughter and at night the salon foldout bed makes the third double bunk. While we are in Mexico, the trip for the kids is easy and relatively inexpensive. For two winters, Madison, our eldest granddaughter, and her family spent a week on *Harmony*. She practiced her swimming, played on the beach, went on a dinghy jungle ride through the mangroves, met new friends, and had a thoroughly enjoyable time aboard. Since that first visit, Onyx, Toby and Coral have all come down for a glorious time on the ocean. It is the perfect spot for family visits and these vacations are the best of times.

* * *

Three of our four parents passed on during the years that we have been cruising and during this time it was important for us to stay closer to home, making it easy for us to return stateside at a moment's notice. We visited our parents in the off-season and spent quality time with them, helping them with their to-do lists. At the beginning of our second cruising season, the autumn of 2001, we drove for three days to San Carlos and spent a week in the yard putting some bottom paint on *Harmony*. At last all the systems were set up and we were ready to sail on an overnight crossing to the Baja. In the late afternoon before we left, we downloaded our e-mail to find a letter from Robert's sister with the news that their father had passed away. Immediately we called for a slip in the marina and prepared for the trip to New York. Our buddy, Flint offered us a ride to our van's storage lot and we were off for the international frontier at Nogales. Arriving at the border before its 10 P.M. closing, we were soon back in phone range in the U.S. and contacted Southwest Airlines. They booked us a flight to New York City out of Phoenix, Arizona with a generous bereavement fare discount. The usually hectic airport was filled with even longer lines than usual with the increased security measures in place following 9/11. Since it had only been a few weeks since the horrific disaster at the Twin Towers, we showed our ID's four times, from one end of the airport to the other. When we finally boarded, I was sitting in the middle seat of a crowded plane, next to a businessman making his weekly flight to the Big Apple. When I asked him how he felt about flying he replied that his work had required him to board a plane as soon as he could after 9/11. He felt we were perfectly safe given all the new security in place. My concerns somewhat alleviated, we flew on an uneventful trip across our vast country. In the late afternoon, the plane gave a wide berth skirting Manhattan on our approach into JFK Airport, but in the distance we could still see the smoldering ruins of the World Trade Center. We could feel the shock and see the devastation this city had faced. Talk about culture shock. There we were flying into New York City, only twenty-two hours away from our calm, pristine anchorage, an inconceivable world away in Mexico.

The family gathered around to put Robert's father to rest and then after stopping in North Carolina to visit my parents, we traveled back to *Harmony*.

It was not long after our trip to New York and we were nestled in a quiet anchorage on the Baja, when we heard Robert's Aunt Kitty's had passed on. Relaxing in the evening's gentle light, we watched a large osprey land on our mast. She stayed the night, chirping her delicate whistle a couple of times before flying away in the early dawn. This osprey was so much like Aunt Kitty, considerate, warm, and sweet. The bird graciously left no fishy-smelling droppings on the deck. It sparked a long conversation of fond memories of her, and we fell asleep, feeling her gentle presence.

Several years later while crossing the border at Nogales at the end of another cruising season, we heard that my father was fading. Once again we set out on a speedy pilgrimage east, flying into Nashville, Tennessee. We rented a car and drove at NASCAR speeds (along with everyone else) into the mountains of North Carolina. Flipping through the radio channels we listened to a rousing gospel choir singing about how heaven's streets are paved with gold. While watching the sun's rays shine through a rainstorm in the mountains, creating magnificent rainbows, we received the call from my brother that my father had passed on. Exiting at the next off-ramp we watched nature's display form double rainbows, a celebration of his life, his love of the outdoors. With a heavy heart we proceeded up the twisting highway in a deluge of rain, the universe sharing our tears.

After six years in Mexico it was an easy decision to move further south into Latin America, with plans to leave our boat in Ecuador in the off season. Traveling down the Pacific Coast into fresh cruising grounds, we ended up anchoring in the tidal river at Bahia del Sol, El Salvador. We placed a call to Robert's mother, Anne, on Skype and heard the news that she had cancer. She said that she was feeling alright and wanted us to continue our trip south. We would put *Harmony* on a mooring ball in Ecuador, away from the lightning prone storms of Panama, El Salvador, and Costa Rica and head to New York City. The trip from El Salvador to Ecuador was on the fast track with only a transmission repair slowing us down for a few days in Costa Rica. Aside from that, we made good time and we were able to put *Harmony* safely away up the Chone River in Bahia de Caraquez, Ecuador and book a surprisingly inexpensive flight to New York City. In Ecuador we were closer to New York on the East Coast than to our home in California. A week of quality time was spent with Anne, helping her come to peace, before she passed on.

* * *

When our children were in their twenties, before some of them were married and had babies of their own, there were several precious years for us to venture out further from home on *Harmony*. On our way to Central America and Ecuador we heard the good news that more grandchildren were on the way. During this stage of life we decided to return to Mexico and be closer to California again, making it possible for us to continue cruising part time in between visits home. The juggling act continues and we have still been able to cruise for the winter season each year.

After Cruising

~ Swallowing the Anchor ~

An old cruiser's joke is that the natural progression for an aging sailor is to go from a sailboat to motorboat, motorboat to motor home, and finally motor home to rest home. As couples age, some cruisers sell their yachts and buy smaller boats closer to home. Flowerpots start springing up on deck and dock. They have lived the dream and have decided that the time has come to slow down. Wanderlust yearnings have been (at least temporarily) satisfied, and it may be time to call it quits. What does a cruiser do at this juncture in their lives? A huge world awaits them with more of life's adventures, but away from the wild, open seas.

Perhaps the time has come to move closer to family or find a place to settle down near friends. Having *swallowed the anchor*, often cruisers still want to stay in touch with their numerous cruising buddies and the community that shared their adventure. Active cruisers often e-mail their updates, and take retired sailors along on virtual trips to faraway places. When answering these letters, the former mariner knows how important it is for their friends to receive mail in a small anchorage far from civilization. When sailing friends come to visit, everyone falls back into old routines, sitting around sipping drinks and telling stories just like they used to in their cockpits. An invisible bond has been forged over the years where certain things are understood and a feeling of closeness pervades. Spirits are lifted, like a fresh ocean zephyr filling our sails, when we reminisce about the cruising days. To keep the ties strong, cruisers gather for small and large reunions on shore. Those who live in the same area congregate from time to time. One of the larger reunions in California was the Donner Lake Raft-Up near Lake Tahoe hosted by the former mayor and first lady of Tenacatita. Over one hundred people gathered by the shores of the blue alpine lake, bringing with them their favorite dish for a huge potluck reminiscent of the Friday night raft ups. Active cruisers home for the off-season joined in the festivities. Piloting a small airplane, a former cruising couple hopped down from Oregon. The ex-cruisers tell their tales and seem happy with their new jobs, which they proudly boast include health benefits! A similar large reunion is held in Washington State each summer and there are many gatherings wherever cruisers settle down.

Former employers are thrilled to welcome back sailors, who have finished their ocean-going adventure. A warm, welcome mat is laid out for their return. The challenge and camaraderie of their creative workplace is once again an integral part of their lives. This transition is eased with the knowledge that they have fulfilled their dreams of sailing and fit back into their shore life with undivided attention in their field of expertise. Cruising is like a smooth, feeling stone that they keep in their pocket and take out and rub from time to time. They relive the memories and weave an old tale or two for some dreamer who is eager to listen.

Ex-cruisers often choose their employment from the many jobs around the boating scene: marinas, chandleries, boat storage, and brokerages. They may be inspired with a great idea to start a new small business. The younger set, who were able to set sail for a year or few until their funds ran out, return to start a family and settle into a career. They buy land and build or fix up the house of their dreams, plant a garden, take up a hobby, and become involved in local activities. They continue to race boats on the weekends or cruise closer to home, staying active in the boating scene. Daniel created a wood shop in his garage in the Northwest and makes beautifully varnished wooden dinghies. His wife tends a lovely garden overlooking the water and weaves colorful shawls of exquisite design. Their sailboat is anchored in front of their home, and they take summer cruises to nearby islands. They have successfully incorporated their land and sea lives to include all of their loves.

An RV can take the place of a boat and the traveling adventure continues with campsites replacing anchorages and the highway a substitute for the ocean swell. Journeying to new places is still on the agenda, but with a less physically strenuous lifestyle. The weather is not the big issue as much as gas prices. Cruising guides for the road help lead to gorgeous campsites in isolated corners of the land. There are plenty of fellow land cruisers to meet and there is no shortage of nature moments. Having learned the secrets of how to live with each other in small spaces, the roaming lifestyle still beckons.

Cruisers, who have been gone for long periods of time, are usually happy to be home to spend holidays with the family. The next generations' lives become a priority and babysitting the grandchildren is not only a privilege and a pleasure, but also a welcomed gift to our children.

When we bought our boat and went south we fulfilled a dream and when we move on from cruising, our new purpose and path will reveal itself. Most of us, while we are out on the water, spend time dreaming up the next move, the next stage of our lives. What new exciting life experiences will pick up where our cruising life left off? The love of nature, keen awareness of living life on the edge, and the can-do and can-be spirit will remain with us while we cruise gracefully into another sunset.

In Acapulco we moored next to a boat that had spent ten years cruising on both sides of the Panama Canal. The mainsail was torn, the autopilot was on the fritz, and the boat looked beat up and weathered. They were on their way back to the U.S. in search of the mythical money tree, having scraped the bottom of their cruising kitty. They weren't looking forward to beating their way back north against the wind, swell, and currents or for that matter working again, but the Admiral longed for a house that wouldn't sink and a yard with a garden full of ripe tomatoes. When we're strung out, bad choices can enter the equation. Even though I brought them the latest weather report that called for particularly, strong, on the nose westerlies, they left the following day for Zihuantanejo. Unfortunately they got hammered and ended up returning to Acapulco with their tails between their legs having spent all day and precious diesel fuel going nowhere. Robert and I promised each other that we wanted to finish our cruise on a happy note with an enjoyable trip home.

We have proven that we can do whatever we put our minds to and this way of thinking carries over to our lives on land. As world ambassadors we learned that people everywhere love the same thing, to live in cooperative communities and raise their families in peace. When you make the most of life, the universe returns the favor in abundance.

When it is time to switch gears and find out what the next move is, you can be sure that a challenging and rewarding path is out there awaiting us. Since this next step has to incorporate at the very least the same level of passion and satisfaction as cruising, it promises to take us to ever more interesting places, within and without.

After Cruising

~ Looking for Real Estate in Exotic Places ~

Several of our friends sailed south or west until they found a place that caught their fancy and was easily affordable. Parking or selling their boat, these retiring cruisers bought or built a house, and settled down happily in a community far from their old home. Having applied for permanent residency in their new country, several of them started businesses to help boaters who visit their area. Ex-cruisers run marinas, sell and charter boats, manage diving operations, create haul out facilities, restaurants, Bed and Breakfast Inns, boat maintenance, and repair services. They might settle in a town close by the local marina where they keep their trusty steed in a slip. Taking day sails, joining in local races, and working on boat projects keeps them busy and satisfied. Several couples in their eighties that we have met in our travels are still happily dock-cruising. These couples do virtually no passage making, but they remain on their boat or in a house near the boating community, embracing their new country with its colorful culture.

Sailors invent a variety of original and unique places to put down roots. In the same adventurous spirit that they threw off the dock lines, they find their spot after cruising. Mariners like us who have children, grandchildren, or elderly parents usually like to stay closer to family. On the other hand, if you find an exotic place on the globe that feels like home, it could be the perfect place for your family to come for holiday visits.

Wherever ex-cruisers settle down in a distant, foreign port, they become beacons for the next generation of yachties coming their way. They share their experience and local knowledge with newcomers and understand what their needs are, having remained actively involved in the boating scene. Several couples offer services along the Pacific coast, and communities have grown up around these pioneers. Former cruisers in both El Salvador and Ecuador send out a guide or pilot to help yachts negotiate the shoal waters into their marinas, and make sure the check-in process goes smoothly. Other ex-cruisers have created successful marinas and dry storage facilities in Mexico. Several now have been passed down to the second generation. Taking a look ahead to contemplate future possibilities, plans, dreams, and expectations for the next stage of life is always an interesting, imaginative exercise.

You Can Never Go Back

Traveling back to California during the off-season, the realization comes to us that things are somehow different, we have been transformed by our cruising experience. Most people have difficulty imagining what we've encountered in our travels, but there is an occasional person who is hungry for our stories, listening intently while we weave a magical tale. Eventually we mesh into our life ashore and find ourselves in the swing of things.

When our daughter, Olivia, returned to high school after a year as an exchange student in Ecuador, she broadened her friendships to include Spanish-speaking and foreign exchange students, people who shared her new worldview. It was unsettling at first to realize how much she had changed, but when she accepted the reality, she was able to move on, incorporating her new planetary consciousness into her life at home. Cruisers go through a similar culture shock when they realize their experience has altered their course and irrevocably changed their perspective.

When we first return home we imagine ourselves as empty

vessels, rinsed clean by our experiences in nature and on the high seas. Taking in a taste of the latest news, we absorb the sensational headlines. What's going to become of our health care system? What about expensive wars, violent revolutions, sickness, and natural disasters? The daily pain that strangers are experiencing begins to fill up our containers. Consumerism blares noisily from billboards, TV, and parking lot-filled strip malls while at the same time many are out of work and struggling to make ends meet. We spend time with our adult children who shoulder some of society's burdens and we invite them to unload their troubles onto us. Our daughter, who is an ICU nurse, fills her shifts assisting acute care patients, amidst the constant struggle between being able to face death gracefully and not wanting to let go. Our son working in the educational system longs to help his students break out of their teenage anxieties, problems, and peer pressure to follow their dreams and find their life's passion and direction. Our adult children, raising their own children, want the next generation to experience nature in the middle of a hectic world. They make sacrifices to spend quality time with our blossoming grandchildren. The containers start to fill up with these stresses of life far away from our cruising tranquility.

After a season at home we return to *Harmony* and our beloved sea and we bring our filled to overflowing receptacles with us. Sloshing over the rails, we dump it all into the forgiving ocean that takes it in like our lungs take in the salt-flavored air. All of our cares are sucked out in a rip tide, not making the slightest dent in the persistent rhythm of the waves.

A Cruising Perspective

Before casting off our dock lines, we could never have imagined what dramatic changes would occur to transform the course of our lives. Cruising carried us into a new world, a new consciousness, and new cultures. Over the years, our contact with the sea, meeting friends from different nations, and travels through foreign countries altered our viewpoint. There were opportunities to encounter interesting people and see history up close while living an exceptional lifestyle. In the inevitable interconnectedness of life, we changed in the process and learned new values. The force fields blended and transformed us when we were exposed to new ways to observe our world. An adventurous lifestyle can blast narrow provincial perspectives into a planetary and universal awareness. All of us fly a courtesy flag in whichever nation we happen to be sailing in, not only to show our respect to our hosts, but also in an attempt to become in tune with the culture. Stereotypes are dispelled when we meet people one on one, proving that we are all human beings, similar in so many ways. Diversity draws out our imagination, imbuing each new place with a feeling of home. As itinerant ambassadors, it does not seem difficult to imagine peace reigning in the world. We often find ourselves in pleasant conversations with a taxi driver, a waiter, or someone behind a store counter. They appreciate hearing that we enjoy their country and think it is beautiful and friendly, with intriguing places to visit.

There is a recipe for long lasting peace in the world. We know how to travel lightly on the earth and sea, and have respect for another country's laws. The logic in their rules may be different from our own, but we see how it works in their culture. An exchange of our various customs, how we think and see the world enriches us both. We are aware of different belief systems, and we try to fit in while we are visiting. With these new attitudes, viewpoints, and coping skills we can't just return home and be the same people we were before we left. Sailors become renewed and reborn when challenged to venture

beyond their comfort zones. We carry home a valuable perspective, one that rises above the fear-driven background noise in our society. Ordinarily, the stress of the modern world clutters up our synapses with extemporaneous garbage, leaving us enclosed behind fearful imaginary walls. These unwarranted fears can block out those poignant moments of enlightenment, celebration, and synchronicity. When we are out on the open waters, an event like a whale sighting or a sunset will inspire the poetic muse within. The lightning bolt of creativity spurs people to pull out their long stored art supplies, writing paper, or musical instruments, and let the divine revelations work their magic. New thoughts, inventions, and philosophies clamor for expression. The cruising *zone* is where we commune with our higher self, nature, humanity, and a universal consciousness. We ride the wave, feel the sensations, spin the thoughts, and allow our spirits to soar. The wooden plaque over the cabin in our first sailboat, *Harmony* said it beautifully. "Come sail with me and worship nature."

Appendix A

Our Communication Toolbox

Researchers, Drs. Robert Levenson, John Gottman and Howard Markman[38] working at the University of California, Berkeley, and more recently at the University of Washington explored the ways that couples argue and fight. By observing how partners communicated, they were able to predict with amazing accuracy which relationships would survive and which looked like they might fall apart. In the cruising world it doesn't take all that much insight to see who is getting along and having fun and who isn't. A simple task like anchoring becomes an example of how the skipper and first mate treat each other. At one time or another, we all end up working it out with our partners, and these researchers developed simple ground rules for peaceful communication based on *Robert's Rules of Order*.[39] I incorporated some of their ideas in my book on relationships, *Love, Marriage and the Art of Raising Children* that *Includes the 101 Question Compatibility Test* and added a few of my own suggestions. When things have deteriorated to a contentious clash, this orderly format can restore reason and civility to a necessary discussion. These rules may seem rigid, stiff, or too formal at first, but if you customize them to your own taste and then use them on a regular basis, they can allow you and your partner an opportunity to pull yourselves out of the abyss.

1. Only one person speaks at a time.

2. The person speaking states the problem, the other listens.

3. The listener then acknowledges the problem in his/her own words.

4. The person who brought up the problem confirms that the listener has grasped the issue correctly.

5. The original speaker states how they would like the problem solved.

6. The listener makes concessions, compromises and agreements.

7. If there is another side to the issue, the same rules apply.

8. If anyone has felt offended, a heartfelt apology, a gentle touch, or show of tenderness can clear the air.

In addition, the following guidelines help create a willing attitude and loving mood for compassionate communication.

TIMING. Resentment starts to creep in and multiply when something is bothering me and I don't talk about it right away. Ideally, addressing the issue when it happens is the way to go, but if I have missed the opportunity to say something at the time it is happening, I still need satisfaction. When I question the validity of what's bothering me, it is an indication that I need to talk about it anyway. It is a bit like reefing the sails. When we start thinking about it, are we already too late? Timing is everything. There will be little chance of reaching a satisfying solution, if I bring up the problem when my partner has just come off of a stressful night watch, bleary eyed, hungry, and needing sleep. The situation has a better chance of working out successfully when I wait until he has eaten, showered, and had a nap. Knowing that there is a source of irritation that is itching to burst out and ruin the mood, I take a deep breath or ten and introduce issues gently and compassionately. Fortunately, on the boat we have all the time in the world.

SIGN THE CONTRACT. We begin these kinds of conversations by asking our partner if we can discuss something that is bothering us. If they agree, then we can continue. They may say, 'Uh,oh, what is it now?,' but when we make this process a habit, the trust builds and they still might say, 'Uh, oh,' but then 'Okay, what do you have for me?,' because they know it will be for the best. If your partner doesn't agree or gives a halfhearted response, then ask him/her when would be a more appropriate time. *If there is no appropriate time then there cannot be any more growth in the relationship.* By receiving their permission to participate in the discussion we are not in attack mode and the conversation can continue smoothly. By allowing our partner to choose a more opportune time, perhaps they will bring a receptive ear.

When our children were young there were times when we needed to tell them about unacceptable behavior. We insisted that they listen with respect and while they were at it, to make new habits for themselves. When the dust settled and we had time to reflect on what was happening, it was understood that the children are our mirrors, and their negative behaviors were usually a direct reflection of the way we acted, either mine or Robert's or a combination of both. Or were they perhaps testing us to understand the limits of their boundaries? More often than not, we found places within ourselves that also needed changing.

Then in a surprisingly short time, the children grew up into adults, and they requested that we please ask them permission before we gave our advice. It turned out to be a healthy step to change the parent/child relationship into an adult/adult friendship. After we became accustomed to the process, we realized that this was a reasonable request, and it proved to be an opening to a more trusting and respectful dialogue. Our adult children appreciated the change, and they became more receptive and respectful of what we had to say. Asking permission worked in our own relationship as well and we now use it before we deal with any touchy issues. It also prompted us to take it a step further. We wanted to define what this request for permission meant. We called it the *contract* and the following steps make up the guidelines.

a.   Can I talk to you about something?

b.   What I am about to tell you will be helpful to us both. It is necessary for our well-being. I will say it compassionately and truthfully.

c.   Please listen with respect and consider what I have to say. I would like a full agreement, but a 'maybe' is satisfactory. A 'no' is unacceptable. A 'no' response indicates that you do not respect my viewpoint enough to consider that what I am saying has any merit. It also might mean that you do not trust me enough to accept my information. A 'maybe, I will consider it,' is an adequate response.

d.   You can call off this discussion at any time, to be continued later.

With this agreement we were amazed at how responsive our partner was to what we had to say. When they were under no obligation to agree, since there was the 'maybe' option, my partner would be on the lookout for something that might help. It relieved the *stacked*, tense feeling from the equation and the atmosphere was more relaxed. Beware of someone giving permission reluctantly. Inevitably the situation deteriorates into an angry, frustrating quarrel, and rarely can any progress be made. *If there is reluctance, we ask if we can talk sometime when they will be more receptive. The message is not going to get through anyway. You cannot be attached to someone's enlightenment.*

MAYBE IS OKAY. When my husband brings up an issue, he states his concerns, uninterrupted. Hopefully I listen to the whole story and appreciate how courageous he is to talk about this difficult subject. Maybe he doesn't have all the correct facts, or is adding his own fears and subconscious attitudes to the situation. I take a deep breath and do not let my first response be 'No.' When your partner brings up an issue, is your first impulse to say, 'I don't do that!' Do you say, 'You don't know what you are talking about,' or 'You have it all wrong, I totally disagree?' Is there a tendency to put it back on your partner and say he is doing something wrong? In this case, 'no' becomes a defense and stops any change from happening. I try to anticipate the inclination to say '*no*,' pause for a moment and contemplate what my partner is saying and at least give him a '*maybe, I will consider it,*' or '*I will think about it.*' My partner would prefer a '*yes, you are right,*' but a '*maybe*' is so much better than a '*no, you are wrong. I didn't do that.*' Hopefully we evolve to gratifying statements like '*I don't want to have a habit that bothers you,*' or '*I don't want to be that way,*' or '*I understand what you are talking about and will change.*' Ideally I will realize that my partner has a valid point and needs me to understand what he is talking about.

When a couple does not keep current about what they are feeling, they allow garbage to collect in the relationship. The pile of unresolved issues can grow so high, that sooner or later, a couple will split up saying that there is too much refuse to deal with. The legal terminology for this mess is 'irreconcilable differences.' Dumping the trash of our relationship on a regular basis is a menial task, like boat maintenance, but essential to our long-term happiness and smooth sailing.

HUMOR. Occasionally while requesting a change that I have clearly formulated in my mind, I suggest the lines for a script hoping to show my partner what I am looking for. Creating the scenario that I would like to see or the words I would like to hear gives a new view on how things could be. There is usually a wide chasm between what we each have in mind. When we play act our lines it often comes out sounding funny and we both crack up. Humor is an art worth cultivating especially when you can chuckle at yourself in those humbling moments when you realize you've been an ass.

A light-hearted touch can ease the transition and challenges of change. Even if we shed tears as we grow and learn with our partner, a jovial comment or smile can make the solutions easier to stomach. When one of us has plowed through the muck, anger, and pain and made changes because we have listened to what our partner had to say, it becomes an occasion for laughter and celebration. Laughing at ourselves is a sign of maturity as well as making us more fun to be around. Humor makes light of the scary, ugly creatures that hide in the depths of our subconscious. When we do not take ourselves so seriously, it's easier to let go of grouchy and stubborn attitudes and the old monsters evaporate into thin air.

THE TALKING STICK. In some Native American meetings or ceremonies, a stick, pipe, feather, or some valued object is passed around a circle to anyone who has something to say. As long as that person is holding the stick, they may speak uninterrupted and be listened to with attention and respect. They then pass it to the next person wanting to speak, who receives the same courtesy. While the discussion proceeds, each person has a time and space to complete his thoughts. When we had family meetings we adopted this tradition and had a gnarled walking stick that we passed around the circle to whoever wanted to speak. If the relationship needs a talking stick find an object that holds special value to both of you. When we interrupt each other, communication disintegrates into an unpleasant shouting match. The person speaking should have the undivided, respectful attention of the listener.

TAKING TURNS.   Taking turns is one of those things we were supposed to have learned in kindergarten, but when it comes to communications in relationships, rather than taking turns with toys, we learn to take turns hearing each other's points of view. It takes nerve for my partner to bring up a topic that is bothering him, especially if it is something that he would like me to change. He worries that I will become angry or stubborn, will not hear him out, will disagree, and refuse to change, or come back with a barrage of excuses. There is a tendency when one person comes up with enough backbone to open up a discussion, that the other partner now sees it as open season to unload their pent-up issues. It is my partner's turn so I need to be sensitive to that. He should feel that I am genuinely listening. If there are other sides to the issue or other issues, eventually there will be time to have my say, but only after my partner feels that there has been a satisfactory resolution to what was bothering him. I may have to wait for another day to discuss my gripes, when I have to summon enough bravery to try *my* hand at it. If I can gracefully receive the information about myself, change, apologize, and notice positive results, maybe my example will be reciprocated when it is my partner's turn to listen to me.

LISTENING. Being defensive during discussions often squelches my understanding of my partner's perspectives, and I hear only what I want to hear. This can cause me to take things personally and become upset, feeling like I have been attacked, minimized and victimized. These misinterpretations color my initial response and inevitably, my reaction is one of resistance and denial. As a result, I fail to grasp or digest the crucial point that my partner is trying to make. Robert is trying to tell me something, and when I make closure with his content we get back on the right track. When I mellow out and drop my defenses, remembering that the love of my life is trying to break through my stale habits, I give him a break and listen when he says his '*peace.*'

APOLOGIES. In the heat of an argument, when one of us has made a valid point, responding with '*You are right about that,*' or '*I am sorry,*' has the power to alleviate the tension. We all know that it is difficult to admit that we are wrong or that there is something we need to change. **In order to keep a relationship flourishing it has to continually evolve.** When one person says, '*This is who I am, you can't ask me to be something different,*' (The Popeye Syndrome: 'I yam what I yam') the relationship becomes stagnant. At this juncture bringing a fair witness into the picture might help, but without doing some serious work the partnership will lose its vitality and slip into mediocrity. Is it worth being so stubborn as to jeopardize the relationship? Many separated couples can go back and remember exactly when one or both partners dug in their heels. Neither partner challenged the status quo to request that a transformation was needed, or one insisted on change and the other refused to budge. When we think about how much time, emotional energy, and work we have invested in our relationship, the decision to adapt is obvious. When we've done something that is unkind or crazy making, an apology helps return the love to the relationship.

It takes an extraordinary amount of courage to say 'I'm sorry' and break the cultural perception that an apology is a display of weakness and not necessary. Whenever I have said, 'I am sorry' for something that I have done to offend my partner, it was a step towards the acknowledgment that something needed to change. To continue on and make this metamorphosis is the real test, but a heartfelt apology can often kick start these transitions.

CHANGE. Issues that we need to change in ourselves will be there no matter whom we are with. These gremlins in our subconscious do not go away until we consciously usher them out of our lives. They are our personal baggage. It is part of the deck of cards that was dealt to us by generations of our ancestors, the society we were born into, and the accumulation of our own toxic habits over the years. The essence of who we are is not what is on the chopping block, not our style, our sense of humor, or our personality, but the part of us that makes it difficult to be in an intimate relationship. These annoying, divisive, unhealthy, and harmful habits include anger, unkindness, stubbornness, and defensive attitudes to name but a few. If we refuse to modify our actions we can end up in a lonely rut, whereas change carries us to a higher plane and a more gratifying experience.

When 'the grass is always greener on the other side' syndrome sets in, people separate, and decide to try their luck with a new partner. But if you are not in the habit of making changes, most likely your new partner will eventually dislike and confront your same issues. If you can make an agreement to work things out with each other, you can step up to the next level of personal evolution and 'love the one you're with.'

Discipline of the mind, body, and spirit is required to eliminate long-standing habits that continually sabotage our happiness. In each conversation there needs to be give and take. When two people are communicating and one is stingy or selfish with their energy, not wanting to hear it, being rude, etc., the other person feels cheated. Resentment and animosity lurk, and the love that has been created is whittled away interaction-by-interaction. We had to learn how to give and receive in our communications especially during a heated discussion. **Love reaches its full potential when feedback is given compassionately, received with generosity, and changes are made with grace.**

SURRENDER. It takes monumental courage to allow a transformation to happen. Loosening up enough to let go requires a surrender that in our cultural cosmology indicates signs of weakness or cowardliness. From time to time, I find that quiet place deep within and feel what it is like to totally surrender. Practicing with my partner is the true test. Even though giving up pride and stubbornness seems to threaten my very essence, it actually opens up the heart, and like a butterfly emerging from a cocoon, my unadulterated, lighthearted self blossoms.

Like a clogged artery that brings on a heart attack, stubbornness, pride, anger, and fear are the plaque that blocks joy, sweetness, and happiness from our lives. When our heart is opened, we are vulnerable. Take a step towards love and inevitably there is pain. Just like good cannot exist without evil, life cannot exist without suffering. A successful relationship requires 100% commitment from both partners, no holding back. It's not easy to give up everything, thaw out an iron-encased, cold heart, and let the walls come tumbling down. Only by giving it up, changing, surrendering, can we unblock the flow of love, and allow ourselves to be loved in return.

TIME-OUTS. Sometimes a discussion can become so heated that we need to disengage and take a break. We agree to a five-minute time-out or take the proverbial walk around the block (although admittedly this is hard to do on board). Both of us understand that the discussion is simply put on hold. We can take up the issue at hand at a later time when cooler heads prevail. There is a tendency to avoid getting *back into it,* but if we let things slide, they will come back to haunt us. Going to bed on a hassle is a no-no! This is different from '*bagging it*' because we are still able to work it out after the break.

BAG IT. Sometimes we come to the place where we agree to disagree. After everything is said and done, and there is still a disagreement, we '*bag it.*' Stating the problem clearly, we tie it up neatly and agree to bring it up again with a third party. We can then forget about it. It is no use ruining the cruise over one point. Outside help is available when we need it. Sometimes while mulling over what came down, a new perspective sheds light on the subject. A *big* person will acknowledge that their mate has a point. If this realization happens, we don't hesitate to admit that the other person was right. This may be what was missing in the bagged discussion and things work out easily. We then may not need that third opinion, and can realize how an acknowledgment can re-energize the situation and make way for a workable conclusion. *It takes two to tango* and after taking a moment to think about the issue at hand, often both partners gain insight and give apologies that opens up the way for new agreements.

THE FAIR WITNESS. Out in the cruising world, many of us are going through the same workouts, or have hassled our way through the same thing in the not too distant past. There might be professional counselors among the fleet, but often a good friend or a happy couple will fit the bill of a fair witness. If Robert and I cannot reach satisfaction on an issue, we bag it and the two of us can then bring it to a third party. The friendly referee can usually shed some light on the problem. Folks not actively involved in the argument almost always have a clearer insight into the issue, unencumbered by emotions. They bring a fresh perspective, and often a humorous approach to help us work things through to a successful conclusion. An impartial viewpoint is strictly a mirror held up for us to see what we need to look at. Then both of us have to then take the initiative and do the hard work required so love can flow and bonds grow stronger.

While on a long walk with my friend Adrian, on a beautiful beach, she asked if I could help her work through a few problems that she was having with her partner, who was habitually angry and stubborn. She mentioned how she often fell into the habit of snapping back with snide retorts that didn't make her feel good about herself. They had been together for many years and she was at the end of her rope, not wanting to live like this any longer. The loop was wearing her down and she was ready to call it quits. I said that she could start by changing the way she responded and see if that made any difference. Instead of nasty comments she could address the negative energy patterns and talk about the nature of the problem. It might require that she be stronger than she'd ever been before, state the truth, and remain calm and compassionate at the same time. I also said that she shouldn't be surprised if she knocked into an unyielding wall. It was going to take time and patience, persistence and decisiveness. Shortly after this encounter, Adrian and her partner began attending couples counseling. The dramatic shift in this couple's lives was an amazing example of how a mere suggestion could set off a string of positive changes. The awareness that a psychic overhaul was necessary electrified their relationship. It didn't mean that their struggles were over but instead of being stuck in an untenable situation, a *dynamic quality* had entered into the equation.

"NEGATIVE ENERGY HABITS." Arguing, complaining, spouting angry words, stubbornness, and waking up grumpy, are just a few negative energy habits that sap the strength and vitality from a relationship. Around and around the negative vibrations go, like a 'loop.' One partner does one thing and the other reacts in a certain predictable way. Every time this pattern comes up, the same scenario unfolds. The tendency is to want *the other person* to change what they are doing. **The secret to ending a 'loop' is changing what *you* do and refraining from your habitual retort when the loop *comes* 'round again.** As a result the loop collapses, the frustrations subside, healing takes place, and a door opens for a consensus to be made about the real issues that the loop represents. The recipe is simple enough, speak the truth, be original, humorous, hold the temper, and be nice.

BE NICE. Most of us indulge ourselves with rationalizations of why we can become angry, crabby, accusatory, blaming, shaming, or unkind. More often than not, the *good reason* is because of what someone else did, or some situation outside of our control. We might feel frustrated and feel that we have a right to take it out on someone else. This someone else becomes the closest target, our companion at sea. There is a certain comfort zone in this ugliness. These reactions have become normal, everyday behavior, which leave everybody drained by the end of the day. Approaching the situation with a positive attitude, humor, kindness, and a gentle hand is the catalyst that can banish anger and stubbornness. There is no reason to be nasty, despite any offense, the weather, or tyrannical officials. An angry attack, a tirade, sarcasm, and unkindness only creates resistance and resentment instead of the changes and positive results we are after. Amidst all the stormy astral weather, a dismount off of our high horse clears the air and we can move forward. Taking responsibility for our actions and treating everybody with decency is a basic premise.

Appendix B

Poetry Inspired by the Sea

The inspiration for this poem came on one of our passages across the Sea of Cortez from La Paz on the Baja side to Mazatlan on the Pacific mainland coast. We traveled for two days and two nights, a distance of approximately 200 miles. We were sailing in fifteen knots of wind with two to three foot swells, under clear blue skies, one hundred miles from either shore, mid-trip.

Heaven on Earth

The sea, a window to my soul.

Its depths,

The power,

The constant movement.

> *Tides*

> *Currents*

> *Waves*

> *Swell*

> *Wind*

Filled with life, hidden only from our eyes,

Vast to the endless horizon in full circle.

The rich colors - blues, greens, whites,

The gentle salt smell on the breeze.

Constantly changing.

The day sea, the lapping of the waves,

The night sea, the moon beams.

The disco colored phosphorescence mirroring

The points of starlight above.

Power and sheer terror in its union with the wind

Or subtle, rolling seas, sensual.

Depth reaching to my soul.

Harnessing only a minute amount of its

Infinite power to propel us across the surface.

Perched and balanced on the top of a wave,

Then let go to take a downward leap.

Vulcan – My Merlin

Emerging from the dark engine room below

Like Vulcan from his iron forge,

The salty sweat pours down his hot, red forehead,

His straining neck, and dripping from his nose,

As if he creates his own weather.

His hands and shirt stained

With the black lifeblood

Of the engine.

Doing what it takes

To mesh the knowledge

Of the inflexible steel

With the strength of his body.

Together with the grease, hardness,

And release of the metal.

Knowing which force and how much.

Being at one with the machine.

In tune, he can touch the disease

    And make it whole again.

Righty, Tighty, A Material Plane Dyslexic

Dyslexia in reading the physical universe,

Each instance is as if

I had seen it for the first time.

Sounding the letters out, each one,

Like I did the last time

I came up to this same place.

Righty tighty, Lefty loosy....

Right left, Left right.

Confusion in my mind.

The answer is not in the mind,

But in the feel of the metal.

This soul is attempting to become

At one with my

> *Iron, hard universe.*

Caught in the Storm

It was truly a dark and stormy night,

A moonless night with the friendly

Stars hidden by the squalls,

That raced across our radar screen.

Seas were all around, eighteen to twenty feet high.

Confused waves, nature's

Washing machine,

Were so high they showed up

As blips on the trusty radar.

The wind howled as the squalls passed over.

We struggled northward.

The weatherman had said there was a

Twenty-four hour window.

Our trip was to be twelve.

The storm had arrived early with

No place to hide along the rugged coast.

Off watch, I lay in my bed listening to

The boat's every creak and strain,

Every engine cough and grind,

Sinking deeper into fear.

Spiraling down deeper into the black hole.

Danger, Darkness, Despair.

Fear clutched my heart like a boa

Constrictor around a terrified mouse,

Squeezing my breath from my lungs,

Strangling me ever deeper into panic.

Imagination gone awry.

Fearing the worst-case scenario.

De-masted, swamped,

Boat sinking beneath us,

Out in a life raft tossed by the seas.

Cold, hungry, dehydrated, alone.

Washed ashore in crashing seas against the rocks.

My love of my life hurt or worse.

And me alone

To handle the boat.

The depth of the sea, the coldness, the darkness.

Until.....I hit the bottom of the downward spiral.

There was no place deeper to go.

I was warm in my bed.

The engine was humming along.

The sail was reefed and holding us steady.

My love was awake and on watch,

Strong, capable, fearless, trustworthy.

Harmony was holding us,

Like a mother rocking her baby

In her big, strong arms.

She kept us safe and secure,

Never hungry or tired.

Plowing through the waves,

Heaving into them,

Crashing down one wave's face,

Crawling up the next one.

Making steady progress around the point

Where the lighthouse beamed

Incessantly through the storm.

Here and now flashed before my eyes.

Here and now everything was okay,

If I could only stay balanced

In the fleeting here and now.

Not slipping into that downward spiral.

I could breathe. I had courage.

That gripping, chilling feeling faded.

I could put fear behind me.

I could even help out.

Here and Now.

I manned the radar.

I brought out some apples and water.

I kept a lookout for the squalls.

Here and Now.

Robert and the autopilot were in tandem,

Quartering to the waves,

Sliding down

Powering up.

Here and Now.

Dawn, the Prima Donna, procrastinating

Desiring to nestle in bed a bit longer.

It seemed as if she would never arrive,

But minute by minute,

As the earth turned.

The coastline mountains created a black silhouette

Against the clouded, gray morning.

Here and Now.

As light came we saw what we had been in.

Even bigger seas than we had imagined.

More confused, waves against the rocks,

Sending towering spumes of water
Skyward.

Here and Now.
We neared our destination.
Turning with the mighty seas behind us.
Riding the waves on a forty-foot surfboard.
Hundreds of feet forward.
Exhilarating, Hanging Ten.

Here and Now.
We approached the calm of the harbor buoy.
The seals nestled on the buoy,
Lounging in the rain.
Pushing each other off,
Cavorting in the water.
Jumping, leaping, spinning, playing.
The circus seals presenting
A private performance.
In the early morning, as another squall
Rakes over us in our protected bay,
We stop to enjoy the refreshingly, misty rain
On our faces, to laugh, celebrate.

Here and Now

We reach our slip.

Robert jumps off the boat and

Kisses the dock.

An old, gnarled fisherman greets us

With amazement.

"You have been out in that storm?"

Glad to help us with our lines.

Eating a hearty meal at a pier restaurant,

Our heightened awareness, our exhaustion

Exhilarates, psychedelic, hallucinating, joyful.

Sleep comes easily for hours.

When we awake the weather is clear,

Beautiful blue.

We mount our gallant steed

And sail off across the bay

Waters gentle, rolling seas,

Sails full.

Glossary

Some of the entries to this glossary have been collected from *Chapman Piloting* by Elbert S. Maloney, and *American Practical Navigator* by Nathaniel Bowditch. Bowditch abridged his definitions from *H. O. Pub. No. 220, Navigation Dictionary*, which can be consulted for more complete definitions. *Webster's New World Dictionary, 2ⁿᵈ Edition, Defender Marine Outfitter Catalog,* and *A Field Guide to Pacific Coast Fishes* were also consulted.

Aft cabin – A room with a bed, drawers and shelves for clothing, and often a head or bathroom in the rear or stern section of a boat. A larger (forty feet long or longer) sailboat will usually have two cabins, the front V berth cabin under the bow of the boat and an aft cabin.

Avon dinghy – A popular brand of dinghy has been manufactured for nearly 50 years. An inflatable raft with large diameter tubes to provide buoyancy. It is propelled by an outboard motor anywhere from 2 hp to 15 hp and always carries a set of oars in case the engine fails. A dinghy is a cruiser's 'car' providing transportation to shore from an anchorage or to visit neighboring boats. They have been used as the power source for the yacht when an engine fails, and as an emergency life raft.

Bimini top – A heavy canvas or sunbrella (sun resistant cloth) shade cover stretched over a frame above the cockpit to shield the sailor from the intense sun's rays and salty spray

Bonita – A type of tuna with silver and black coloring and horizontal stripes

Booby – A brown and white bird with distinct blue webbed feet. The feet coloring can vary from a light blue, (the blue-footed booby), light green, yellow, or a bright orange. They nest on the ground often on secluded islands in warm climates and feed on salt-water fish

Boom Vang – removable block and tackle that serves to hold the boom down and flatten the mainsail.

Bosun's Chair – Seated in this canvas chair a crewman is hoisted up the mast to check for cracks or failures in the rigging, to retrieve a lost halyard or to make repairs. There are pockets on the outside of the chair to hold tools and parts. A mast halyard and an alternate line are secured to the chair to assure the safety of the crewman. One person will man the lines cranking the crewman up the mast using a winch. A sailor can hoist himself up in his bosun's chair with the right gear

Bruce anchor – A modern lightweight style anchor, the Bruce originated in the United Kingdom, developed for offshore oil and gas well drilling rigs and scaled down for small crafts. This is a burying type anchor designed to right itself no matter how it lands on the bottom and is shaped so direction of pull can change through 360 degrees, once it is set, without breaking out, yet intentional breakout is easy on short scope. The anchor works well in mud, sand, and rocks

Bushing – An insulated lining inserted into a machine part for reducing the effect of friction on moving parts or for decreasing the diameter of a hole

Clogged Head – Because mineral deposits collect in the pipes of the boat toilet (head) from the interaction of salt water, minerals, and urine, the pipes can become clogged and need to be taken apart and banged to dislodge and break up the crusty calcium deposits. An unpleasant job, it has to be done from time to time.

Confused Seas – When the wind comes from one direction and the swell from another, around a point or promontory or during a squall, the seas and wind can come from different directions and create a washing machine type chop

Cosmic Joke – The universal paradoxes of life. Here are a few examples: everything in the universe is perfect despite what we would consider imperfections. It is a perfect whatever it is. When some misfortune occurs, the silver lining or deeper meaning reveals an actual blessing in disguise. The unusual coincidences and incongruous happening that spontaneously occur blow your mind and make you laugh.

CQR anchor – A brand of anchor invented in England by Professor G. I. Taylor of Cambridge University and named "secure." The plow-like head digs into the soft bottom, is buried in the sand and holds. There is a tendency for this anchor to plow through slick muddy, mucky bottoms such as found in the lagoon at Barra de Navidad, Mexico when the strong afternoon winds blow

Danforth anchor – A brand of anchor developed by R. S. Danforth and is excellent in mud and sand. It often does not hold well in grassy bottoms and can be used on rocky bottoms with caution. Pivoting flukes are long and sharp so that heavy strains bury the anchor completely. It works down through softer bottoms to firmer holding ground below, burying part of the line as well.

Davits – Mechanical or stationary pair of curved upright metal arms extending over the side or stern of a boat. They are equipped with pulleys and lines whereby the dinghy can be lowered, suspended, or hoisted up and stored attached to the davits

Dinghy – 'Dink' for short is the cruiser's car. This can be a small inflatable, a collapsible and easily stored dinghy or a hard (wood or fiber glass) open boat. They can be rowed or sailed, but more commonly has an outboard motor to propel it to shore, to snorkeling grounds or to visit other boats. If there is an engine failure and no wind to propel the Mother Ship a dinghy has been tied up to the main boat and pushed it along slowly to a dock or a place where it can be anchored. While underway the dinghy is stowed on deck, or on davits, or occasionally if going for a short distance, towed behind the larger boat

Displacement Boat – A boat that achieves its buoyancy (flotation capability) by displacing a volume of water equal in weight to the hull and its load, whether underway or at rest. It cruises through the water rather than planing on top of the water's surface

Dodger – A covering over the cockpit to keep the weather or ocean spray out, somewhat like an extended windshield. It can be made of a canvas or sunbrella (a sun resistant material) or a hard dodger made of wood, steel or fiberglass.

Dorado – A pelagic fish also called a dolphin fish of beautiful iridescent colors. It is a large, swift marine game fish and excellent eating (called Mahi-Mahi in U. S. restaurants). The male has a distinct, large square head.

Electro San Waste Treatment System – A macerator that is attached to the head (boat toilet) and grinds the waste before it is flushed. Coated electrodes use salt water to kill bacteria and viruses without the addition of harmful chemicals. It discharges with treatment levels that are safe for environmentally sensitive areas

EPIRB – An Emergency Position Indicating Radio Beacon that is battery powered and when activated sends out a continuous signal that helps rescuers locate a boat in an emergency situation. An EPIRB is activated when a situation becomes so dangerous that the boat may be abandoned or there is a serious medical emergency. It identifies by satellite signal the location of the boat in trouble. The beacon is registered with the Coast Guard so it can be identified and then located and rescued by the closest boat in the area or by a Coast Guard boat or helicopter

Fathometer – A trademark name for a depth sounder, an electronic devise for determining the depth under the keel of the boat. Depth is determined by measuring the round-trip time for a pulse of ultrasonic energy to travel from the boat to the bottom of the water and reflected back to the boat. The depth sounder provides valuable information when anchoring or passing through narrow channels

Foulies – A nickname for foul weather gear, rain and spray resistant clothing worn during cold and rough weather to keep the sailor warm and dry

Freeboard – The height of a boat's topsides from the waterline to the deck

Going Aground – When a boat runs or is driven by winds and swell on shore, on a sandbar, or reef

Grounding Out – Another way of saying Going Aground. When a boat hits the sea bottom or becomes stuck on the bottom or reef

Ham Radio – A single side band radio set up with marine frequencies capable of communications over thousands of miles. Used when going off shore and out of range of the VHF radio. A license from the FCC is required to operate on the designated radio frequencies

Hanging locker – A closet tall enough for hanging clothes. On a boat, closets, chests and storage areas are called lockers.

Head – A toilet on a boat or the small room where the toilet is located with a sink and possibly a shower

Heave To – Positioning the sails and rudder so that the boat ideally lies 45 degrees from the wind while making very slow headway. The helm is lashed downwind, to keep the boat headed up. A small, strong storm jib is sheeted to windward to hold the bow just off the wind.

Heeling – Leaning significantly to leeward. This happens most dramatically when a sailboat is beating or sailing as close into the wind as possible while still maintaining its speed

Hobby Horsing – The action of a boat when it is pitching into waves and swell and sets up a vertical motion as the bow rises and falls. Depending on the wave size, hoppy horsing can be very uncomfortable. This can happen at anchor and under way

Iron Genny – A nickname for the engine on a boat that can be gas or diesel. Word origins: When sailors did not have enough wind to fill the Genny (Genoa sail– a large sail for lighter winds), it was time to turn on the engine

Islander Freeport – A brand and model of sailboat built in Costa Mesa, CA. There are 36', 38', 40' and 41' Islander Freeport models

J Boat – A brand of sailboat known for its lightness and speed built to win races. They are built with carbon fiber material and often use Mylar sails

Jib sail – A sail before the mast, also called a head sail

Jury-rig – The ingenious way a sailor fixes a broken part to allow the boat to arrive safely into a port or anchorage

Kedge anchor – An anchor of any type that is used to get a boat free when it has run aground. The anchor is carried in the dinghy or thrown into deeper water to work a boat off the shore

Kedge off – Using a kedge anchor to get ungrounded. Carrying an anchor out in a dinghy as far out as possible and setting it firmly. When the tide rises or the wind comes up, pulling against the anchor can loosen the hold and the boat floats free

Ketch – A sailboat with 2 masts, a main mast and an aft mizzen mast. The shorter mizzen mast is stepped forward of the rudder post.

Knot – A unit of speed equal to one nautical mile per hour. On salt water, distances are measured in nautical miles, slightly more than 6,076 feet, a unit about 1/7th longer than the statute mile used on land, 5280 feet

Lofrans windlass – A brand of windlass, a winch that electronically hoists and deploys the anchor

Lowboy – A lowered, flatbed trailer on wheels. There are special designs that have hydraulic arms with pads on the ends that lift up and secure a boat that is being hauled. A semi-truck or a tractor pulls the lowboy and the boat can be hauled in or out of the water or trucked down a highway to another destination

Lying Ahull – In heavy storm conditions all sails are dropped and secured, the helm lashed to prevent damage to the rudder, and the vessel left to find her own way

Mal de Mer – The French phrase for seasickness

Mizzen sail – The sail hoisted up the mizzen mast, the smaller mast on a ketch stepped forward of the rudder post toward the rear or stern of the boat

Mooring balls or buoys – A semi-permanent anchorage installation. A large floating buoy attached to a chain that is attached to a heavy weight or mushroom anchor on the bottom. A boat can use a shackle to attach a line to a loop on the ball or there is a pennant or rope on the buoy to grab a hold of and attach to a cleat on the boat. This holds a boat securely and is used instead of an anchor, often in crowded anchorages

Motor sailor – A subcategory of sailboat that is built with a larger engine and is designed to sail when there is sufficient wind and motor if there are light airs. It carries enough fuel to motor for longer distances and is a compromise between a sailboat and a motorboat. As a result, a motor sailor is less efficient under sail than a sailboat and slower under power than a motorboat

On the hard – Storing a boat on stands or cradles on land. Accessible for long-term storage as well as during rainy or stormy seasons

Outboard – A portable, gasoline engine which is mounted on a boat to propel it. An outboard motor is also the propulsion for a dinghy. When the yacht is underway the outboard for the dinghy is usually removed from the raft and stored in a safe spot on deck. By contrast, an inboard motor is built into the boat and is a permanent fixture

Pactor Modem – A brand of modem that is designed to hook up to a Ham/SSB Radio to receive e-mails and weather information aboard the boat.

Power windlass – An electronic winch used for deploying or retrieving an anchor with the touch of a button. It has a cradle for the anchor chain called an anchor gypsy or rope drum.

Propeller – Thrust for the movement of a boat through water using a motor is achieved by the rotation of a propeller, which draws in water from ahead and pushes it out astern.

Quartering to the Waves – Steering a boat with a quarter of the deck facing the direction of the wave set to aid in the speed and also to create a more comfortable ride.

Radar – An excellent aid to marine navigation especially at night or in foggy conditions. The radar sends out brief pulses of super-high frequency radio waves that are reflected by objects at a distance. The time that it takes for the pulse to go out and the echo to return is a measure of the distance to the reflecting object.

Refrigeration – Although newer boats have made big improvements, the standard sailboat refrigerators are a storage unit with insulated sides, and tops that double as a counter. They tend to be deep and can store food for long passages. Because of their shape, we find ourselves emptying food on the counter looking for a cold drink at the bottom of the refrigerator. It's different from the spacious frig that we have at home, but we are grateful to be able to keep our food for longer periods of time especially in the hot temperatures of the tropics. A boat refrigerator is run by a compressor and is generally the largest user of energy on a boat

Reefing the Sails – When the winds reach a certain velocity and the boat is overpowered, reefing the sails or making the sail area smaller reduces the force received. The sails come with reef points and ties so that reefing can be managed during a blow. A prudent sailor reefs the sails at the first inclination of heavy weather while it is still manageable on deck. Modern main sails can often be furled into the main mast and can be reefed by furling the sail to the size best suited for the conditions. Sailors often reef at night as a precaution if the weather is changeable to avoid having to reef in the middle of a dark night

Roller furling Jib – The jib sail is the sail on the bow of the boat. It is either hanked on or furled. A hanked on sail has hardware that is hooked onto the forestay and hoisted with a halyard. A roller furling jib, a more recent innovation, has a sail that is wrapped around its luff (leading edge). It can be played out to the size best suited for the wind conditions

Roseate Spoonbill – A large, long legged wading bird up to 31 inches tall with a 47-51 inch wing-span. This bird has a long neck, a spatulate bill, and is often confused with a flamingo because of its pink coloring. The bright red on its wings and spoon shaped bill distinguishes it from a flamingo. The Roseate Spoonbill flies with its neck outstretched and nests in the mangroves

Scope and How to Calculate It – The ratio of the length of the anchor rode to the height of the bow of the boat above the bottom of the body of water. The amount of scope determines how secure your boat is attached to the ground if wind or swell were to come up. A suggested amount of scope is for every one foot of depth, allow six to seven feet of scope. The depth on the Fathometer should be added to the amount of freeboard of the hull to determine what the scope should be. Tides need to be considered when calculating the scope

Shaft alley – In a large ship the shaft which is a huge metal pipe connecting the engine to the propeller is near the bottom of the ship in a long alley. There is a cat-walk that the machinists use to service the shaft

Single Handed Sailor – A sailor traveling alone, without crew

Single-Side Band Radio – A radio aboard ship used as an enhancement for the VHF (Very High Frequency) band for ship-to-ship communications. Used by merchant vessels and yachts to receive weather data, e-mails, Coast Guard, and other authority communications. Single Side Band (SSB) radios also function when cell phones do not, due to cell tower availability or signal strength

Skip Jack tuna – Another name for a Bonita tuna. A common fish caught in Mexican waters. It has dark meat with a strong flavor. If the lighter parts of the fish are chilled for four hours or more, a delicious, tender, non-fishy tasting sashimi is the result

Spars – The term "spars" is used broadly to cover masts, booms, gaffs, etc. Masts are the principal vertical spars from which the sails are set. The horizontal spar along the lower edge of a fore-and-aft sail is a boom. When a four-sided sail has its upper edge laced to a fore-and-aft spar, that spar is a gaff. Aluminum has replaced wooden spars for the most part in modern sailing yachts. On our ketch, the main mast is 45 feet high

Thru Hull – A shortened form of 'through the hull.' A through hull fastening is a hollow bolt that goes all the way through the hull, secured with a washer and nut on the inside and a backing block is generally used to distribute the stress and gain additional strength. With an on/off valve these holes can connect the drainage from a sink, toilet, or shower, incoming water for the engine heat exchanger, or cockpit drainage. They are usually made of bronze or brass, metals that are not easily corroded in salt water

Trimaran – A sailboat with a principal central hull flanked by two smaller outboard hulls. A catamaran has two hulls of equal size held apart by rigid structural members often holding the main living area

V berth – The bed or cabin in the front or bow of the boat with a V shaped bed that follows the contours of the boat

Winch – A mechanical devise either hand or power operated, for exerting an increased pull on a line or chain, such as a jib sheet

Windlass – A particular type of winch, usually an anchor winch, with its drum on which the line is wrapped turning on a horizontal axis. A power windlass is an electrical mechanism that powers the anchor chain to be hoisted and deployed. Situated on the bow of the boat, it has easy access to the anchor

Zinc – A sacrificial anode that is pressure die-cast. It prevents electrolysis in the sea-water from destroying important boat parts like the propeller, shaft and thru hulls. Zinc is used in sea-water, aluminum in salt and brackish water and magnesium in fresh water.

Bibliography

Andreas, Connirae and Tamara Andreas, *Core Transformation*. Moab, Utah: Real People Press, 1994.

Bowditch, Nathaniel, *American Practical Navigator*. Washington D.C.: U.S. Navy Hydrographic Office, 1962.

Bradshaw, John, *Homecoming*. New York: Bantam Books,1990.

Bradshaw, John, *Healing the Shame that Binds You*. Deerfield Beach, Fla.: Health Connections, Inc. 1988.

Cantrell, Debra Ann, *Changing Course: A Woman's Guide to Choosing the Cruising   Lifestyle*. Camden, Maine: International Marine Publishing, 2001.

Casey, Don, *Dragged Aboard*. New York: W.W. Norton and Co. 1998.

Casey, Don, and Lew Hackler, *Sensible Cruising, The Thoreau Approach*. Camden, Maine: International Marine Publishing, 1986.

Castenada, Carlos, *The Teachings of Don Juan, A Yaqui Way of*

Knowledge. Berkeley and Los Angeles, CA: University of California Press, 1972.

Copeland, Liza and Andy Copeland, *Cruising for Cowards*. Vancouver, British Columbia: Romany Publishing 1997.

Crane, Paul S., *Memoirs*, Volume 1, Self-published, Black Mountain, NC.1989.

Defender Marine Outfitter, 2010 Marine Buyers' Guide, Waterford, CT.: Defender Industries, Inc. 2010.

Doane, Charles, J., "Sail", *The Purity of Motion*. November 2007, 28-30.

Edelman, Hope, *Motherless Daughters, The Legacy of Loss*. New York: Dell Publishing 1994.

Esarey, Cawrse, *The Motion of the Ocean*. New York: Touchstone, Division of Simon & Schuster, Inc., 2009.

Eschmeyer, William N., Herald, Earl S., Hammann, Howard, *A Field Guide to Pacific Coast Fishes*. New York: Houghton Mifflin Company. 1983

Fike, Rupert, Editor, *Voices from The Farm*. Summertown, TN: The Book Publishing Co. 1998

Gaskin, Stephen, *The Caravan*. Summertown, TN: The Book Publishing Co. 1972, 2007.

(Gaskin,) Stephen, *Monday Night Class*. Santa Rosa, CA.: Book Farm. 1970. Reprinted: Summertown, TN: The Book Publishing Company 2005

Gaskin, Stephen, *This Season's People*. Summertown, TN: The Book Publishing Company 1976.

Giesemann, Suzanne, *It's Your Boat Too: A Woman's Guide to Greater Enjoyment on the Water*. Arcata, CA: Paradise Gay Publications, Inc. 2006.

Gleser, Virginia, *Tie Dye! The How-To Book*. Summertown, TN.: The Book Publishing Co., 1999.

Gleser, Virginia, *Love, Marriage and the Art of Raising Children*. Buenos Aires, Argentina: Harmony Enterprises Book Publishing, 2005.

Guralnik, David B., Editor in Chief, *Webster's New World Dictionary*. 2nd College Edition. New York: William Collins +World Publishing Co., Inc. 1980.

Hay, Louise L., *Heal Your Body*. Carson, CA: Hay House, Inc. 1982.

Hay, Louise L., *The Power is Within You*. Carson, CA: Hay House, Inc., 1991.

Hay, Louise L., *You Can Heal Your Life*, Carson, CA.: Hay House, Inc. 1984.

Hendrix, Harville, *Getting the Love You Want*. New York: Henry Holt Company LLC. 1988.

His Holiness the Dalai Lama and Howard C. Cutler. *The Art of Happiness*. New York: Riverhead Books, 1998.

Jeffers, Susan. *Feel the Fear and Do It Anyway*. New York: Fawcett Columbine, 1987

Jessie, Diana, *The Cruising Woman's Advisor*. Blacklick, Ohio: International Marine/Ragged Mountain Press 1997.

Jones, Tristan, *The Incredible Voyage*. Dobbs Ferry, NY: Sheridan House, Inc. 1977.

Kornfield, Jack, *After the Ecstasy, the Laundry: How the Heart Grows Wise on the Spiritual Path*. New York: Bantam Books, 2000.

L'Amour, Louis, *Education of a Wandering Man*. New York: Bantam Books, 1989.

Lawler, Michael, "Doing Marriage Preparation Right," *America*, December 1995-January 1996,12-14.

Lee, Rae Ellen, *If the Shoe Fits, The Adventures of a Reluctant Boatfrau*, Dobbs Ferry, NY: Sheridan House, Inc. 2001.

Lerner, Harriet Goldhor, *The Dance of Anger,* New York: Harper and Row Publishers, 1985.

Lewis, Leland R., *Sea Guide Volume II*, Newport Beach, CA: Baja Sea Publications, Inc, 1974.

Maloney, Elbert S., *Chapman Piloting, 57th Edition.* New York: Hearst Marine Books, 1985.

Morgan, Lael, *The Woman's Guide to Boating and Cooking*, Toronto: Abeland-Schuman Canada Ltd., 1968.

Moore, Robert and Gillette, Douglas, *King, Warrior, Magician, Lover.* New York: Harper Collins Publishers, 1990

Northrup, Christine, *The Wisdom of Menopause,* New York: Bantam Books, 2001.

Orman, Suze, *The Nine Steps to Financial Freedom,* New York: Crown Publishers, 1997.

Pardey, Lin, *Cruising in Seraffyn,* Camden, Maine: International Marine Publishing, 1989.

Pardey, Lin and Larry Pardey, *Storm Tactics Handbook, Modern Methods of Heaving-to for Survival in Extreme Conditions.* Arcata, CA: Pardey Books, 1996.

Parsons, Kathy, *Spanish for Cruisers: Boat Repairs and Maintenance Phrase Book*, Hallettsville, TX: Adventuras Publishing Co., 2000.

Pirsig, Robert M., *Zen and the Art of Motorcycle Maintenance,* New York: William Morrow and Co, Inc., 1974.

Real, Terrence, *I Don't Want to Talk About It,* New York: Fireside,. 1997.

Rey, H.A., *The Stars*, New York: Houghton Mifflin Co., 1980.

Roberts, John, Susan, *Why Didn't I Think of That?*, Camden, ME: International Marine/Ragged Mountain Press, 1997.

Ridihalgh, Lindam ed. *Escape from Someday Isle, Living Aboard*, Austin,TX.: Living Aboard, 2003

Robbins, Tom, *Fierce Invalids Home from Hot Climates*, New York: Bantam Books, 2000.

Romano-Lax, Andromeda, *Searching for Steinbeck's Sea of Cortez*, Seattle, WA: Sasquatch Books. 2002.

Rosin, Hanna, "Separation Anxiety," *The New Republic.*, May 1996, 14-18.

Scherer, Migael, *Sailing to Simplicity*. Camden, ME: International Marine, 2000.

Scmitz, Anthony, "The Secret to a Good Marriage," *Health*, March/April 1995, 50-56.

Siegel, M.D., Bernie S., *Love, Medicine and Miracles*, New York: Harper and Row Publishers, 1986.

Steinbeck, John, *The Log from the Sea of Cortez*, New York: Viking Press, 1977.

Sullivan, Amy and Donnelly, Kevin, *Cruising 101*, San Diego, Ca.: Free Fall Press, 1997.

Warren, Neil Clark, *Finding the Love of Your Life*, Wheaton, Ill: Tyndale House Publishers, 1992.

Wolf, Sharyn, *How to Stay Lovers for Life*, New York: Penguin Books, USA, Inc., 1997.

Wood, Charles E., *Charlie's Charts of the Western Coast of Mexico*, Surrey, BC, Canada: Charlie's Charts, 2001.

Notes

1   Carlos, Castanada's *Teachings of Don Juan, the Yaqui Indian Spiritual Guide* gives insights into how a vision quest might be experienced. Castenada, Carlos, *The Teachings of Don Juan, A Yaqui Way of Knowledge*. (Berkeley and Los Angeles, Ca: University of California Press, 1972.)

2   *Timeless Myths* www.timelessmyths.co.uk/women-board-ship-bad-luck.html

3   A detailed story of Admiral Yi's naval exploits can be found at http://en wikipedia.org/wiki/naval-history-of-Korea-myeong-nyang-strait.

4   A detailed story of MacArthur's famous Inchon landing can be found at www.Kmike.com/inchon.htm

5   Timothy Leary captured the attention of a generation with this famous quote among others. You can read more of his quotes at http://thinkexist.com

6   Selected transcripts of Monday Night classes held in San Fran-

cisco in the late 60's and early 70's can be read in *Monday Night Class*. (Gaskin,) Stephen, *Monday Night Class*. (Santa Rosa, Ca.: Book Farm. 1970. Reprinted: Summertown, Tn: The Book Publishing Company 2005.)

[7] Read of the adventures of the Caravan and selected transcripts of some of the meetings held along the way in *The Caravan*. Gaskin, Stephen, *The Caravan*. Summertown, Tn. (The Book Publishing Co. 1972, 2007.)

[8] For more interesting and entertaining tales from The Farm written by those who lived there including a story, "The Yellow Canary" by Robert and Virginia Gleser, read *Voices of the Farm*. Fike, Rupert, Editor, *Voices from The Farm*. (Summertown, TN.: The Book Publishing Co. 1998.)

[9] Gleser, Virginia, *Tie Dye! The How-to Book*, (Summertown, TN.: The Book Publishing Co., 1999.) pgs. 7-12,

[10] Robert Pirsig, *Zen and the Art of Motorcycle Maintenance: An Inquiry into Values*, (New York: William Morrow, 1974). Pirsig wrote this book about his journey with his son Chris (who later died in 1979) that became a classic tale of a father and son searching for personal meaning in the modern world. Pirsig was highly influenced by eastern philosophies that he studied at the university.

[11] Larry and Lin Pardey, the well-known, long-time sailors, have chronicled their cruising adventures in several critically acclaimed books. See Pardey, Lin, *Cruising in Seraffyn*, (Camden, Maine: International Marine Publishing, 1989. (Pardey, Lin and Larry Pardey, *Storm Tactics Handbook, Modern Methods of Heaving-to for Survival in Extreme Conditions*. (Arcata, CA: Pardey Books, 1996.) and http://www.landlpardey.com

[12] Here's a short rundown of what part a sacrificial zinc plays in

protecting the propeller shaft and other underwater metal parts from the corrosion of electrolysis. Just having a large piece of metal dangling in a salt-water solution will cause electrolysis. A molded piece of zinc is screwed onto the propeller or shaft and sacrifices itself for the sake of the shaft. Not to get too complicated and academic, zinc is low in the order of things on the periodic table and has a higher propensity to absorb the electric discharge and attract the elements found in salt water. Bronze, brass and aluminum are a more noble medal than zinc, so the zinc will corrode before the propeller or shaft. Electrolysis is also caused by our insistence on having electricity aboard our boats. Well, no getting away from that. Unfortunately most of us have that electricity bleeding off into the salt water through our ground plane, propeller, and thru-hulls. It's as if wherever we go we are in a great big low voltage wet cell battery just like a giant car battery, and there is constant corrosion from the electrolysis that we are creating. Electrolysis can get extremely high in marinas

[13] The 105' trimaran, *Groupama 3* set the new Jules Verne round the world speed record, circumnavigating in just over 48 days in March of 2010. Reported in the article, "Great Deal on a Used Boat", *Latitude 38*, Vol. 395, May 2010, pg. 80.

[14] From Tony Bennett's song, "I Left My Heart in San Francisco". The song was written in 1954. Tony Bennett popularized it in 1962 and it became his signature song. It was recorded in 1962 on his album of the same name. It is now San Francisco's city song. Http://en wikipedia.org

[15] Permission was granted to tell this story by Lee Risler, *Kiwi Sandals*, Victorville, Ca.

[16] *Charlie's Charts* are a popular series of cruising guides that

describe the best anchorages along our routes. Wood, Charles E., *Charlie's Charts of the Western Coast of Mexico*, Surrey, BC, Canada: Charlie's Charts, 2001.

[17] *The Baja Sea Guide, Volume II* is an excellent resource for navigation, history and interesting notes about the passage down the Baja. Not that much has changed over the years. Lewis, Leland R., *Sea Guide Volume II*, (Newport Beach, CA: Baja Sea Publications, Inc, 1974.) Scammons Lagoon and the California Gray Whale, pgs. 67-79. La Palmita, a stop over for water for the Manila Galleons, pgs. 85-86

[18] Parsons, Kathy, S*panish for Cruisers: Boat Repairs and Maintenance Phrase Book*, Aventuras Publishing Co., Distributed by Paradise Cay Publications, Arcata, Ca. 2000.

[19] More on culture shock: When our daughters each spent time as exchange students in Spanish speaking countries during high school and college we became better acquainted with the phenomenon of culture shock. They all returned fluent in Spanish which among other things gave them a leg up in the bi-lingual job market of California. The American Field Service organization, which sponsored them in high school, was founded after World War II with the premise that peace and understanding would prevail if German and American students could live in each other's homes and attend schools together. Since those early days they have expanded their program and sponsored thousands of teenagers from many countries around the world. Their fifty years of experience has made them aware of how unnerving culture shock can be. AFS sent a pamphlet home to the parents that explained what to expect in the coming year including a chapter on culture shock. As parents we were encouraged to write letters to our children that before the days of the Internet could take weeks to arrive. Upset, homesick emotions in a letter from our

daughter would be long forgotten by the time we received her letters. The organizers beseeched us worried parents not to call or visit, which would have disrupted the student's life and could open the door for the culture shock roller coaster ride to begin all over again. Later when e-mail was available, we were able to keep in closer touch. When we were talking long distance with Olivia about plans for her scheduled return from Ecuador, one of the things she said was, "I'm not ready for Raleys!" Raleys is a large, grocery store located around the corner from our home with bright lights, the rain on the vegetables with an accompaniment of thunder recordings, and choices galore. How could she compare that to the small, dark, sparsely stocked tiendas (stores) where she had bought her groceries for the last year? A friendship had developed between her and the storekeepers who greeted her each time she came in, and asked her about the goings on in her life. She was not ready for the impersonal, hectic pace of California. Her time was up, however, and it was time to make the switch.

20 *The MacMillan Dictionary* defines cosmic joke as often humorous, very big, important, or difficult to understand. Leslie Fieger gives a good example in her essay "Cosmic Joke". "The good news is that you can have everything you idealize and desire. The bad news is that you already do." www.slideshare.net/cashilmktg/cosmic-joke. An interesting article about a cosmic joke is "The Human Genome Project: A Cosmic Joke that has the Scientists Rolling in the Aisle" by Bruce H. Lipton Ph.D. Www.hofmann.org/papers/HumanGenome-cosmic-joke.html

21 Stephen Gaskin was the spiritual teacher on The Farm. See Bibliography for books of his teachings: *Monday Night Class, The Caravan* and *This Season's People.*

22   Edelman, Hope, *Motherless Daughter: the Legacy of Loss*, (New York: Dell Publishing, 1994.)

23   Jeffers, Susan. *Feel the Fear and Do It Anyway*. (New York: Fawcett Columbine, 1987)

24   His Holiness the Dalai Lama and Howard C. Cutler. *The Art of Happiness*. (New York: Riverhead Books, 1998.)

25   Jones, Tristan, *The Incredible Voyage*. (Dobbs Ferry, NY: Sheridan House, Inc. 1977.)

26   Siegel, M.D., Bernie S., *Love, Medicine and Miracles*, (New York: Harper and Row Publishers, 1986.)

27   Permission granted.

28   Slocum, Joshua, *Sailing Alone Around the World*, Biblio Bazaar LLC Reproduction Series, pg. 37-39. For more stories see www. bibliobazzaar.com/copensource

29   *Love, Marriage and the Art of Raising Children* was written for my teenage children when they began to date in high school. I hoped that the difficult lessons Robert and I had learned during our forty years of marriage and the changes we went through, could help them make intelligent choices in their relationships. The *101 Question Compatibility Test* and subsequent answers help sort out a new relationship and determine whether it has strong enough legs to stand on. When our children said it was a help to them, it motivated me to share it with other teenagers and adults. I especially wanted to include anyone who has been through tough times in their past relationships and is still looking for happiness and love. It was a book I wish I had read when I was nineteen. Gleser, Virginia, *Love, Marriage and the Art of Raising Children*. Buenos Aires, Argentina: Harmony Enterprises Book Publishing, 2005.

[30] L'Amour, Louis, *Education of a Wandering Man*. New York: Bantam Books, 1989. pg. 37

[31] To read more about *Starship's* adventures go to blindsailing. blogspot.com

[32] Permission granted.

[33] Doane, Charles, *Sail Magazine*, "The Purity of Motion", November 2007, pg. 28-30.

[34] Rey, H.A., *The Stars*, (New York: Houghton Mifflin Co., 1980.)

[35] *The Persistence of Memory* by Salvador Dali, 1931, MOMA, New York.
Disintegration of the Persistence of Memory by Salvador Dali, 1952-54, Dali Museum, St. Petersburg. Fla.
http://en.wikipedia.org/wiki/the-persistencepersistence-of-memory

[36] In partnership with CIDA, Plenty helped rebuild San Andreas Itzapa near Solola, Guatemala in 1976. They rebuilt 1200 homes, 12 Schools, and clinics. See: www.Plenty.org

[37] Canadian International Development Agency. See: www.acdi-cida.gc.ca/home

[38] Art and Science Perspectives, *Newsletter of the University of Washington College of Arts and Sciences*, Autumn 2000. www.timeforfamilies.org

[39] For more on Robert's Rules of Order see www.robertsrules.com

About the Author

An ocean child from her earliest memories, Virginia Gleser grew up sailing on the Yellow Sea off of the coast of South Korea In 1970 she moved to San Francisco, the center of the counter-culture revolution, complete with its beautiful bay filled with alluring, graceful sailboats. Thirty years later after a life filled with love and adventure with her husband, Robert, they left San Francisco Bay in October of 2000 aboard their 40' ketch Harmony and sailed down the Pacific coast of California and Mexico to begin their cruising odyssey. In 2007 they explored Central America and further south across the equator to Ecuador and the intriguing continent of South America. Returning to Mexico, they continue to divide their time between cruising and enjoying their large family in California.